THE SKIPPER'S WAR

DRAGON SCHOOL, OXFORD
&
THE GREAT WAR

THE SKIPPER'S WAR

DRAGON SCHOOL, OXFORD
&
THE GREAT WAR

DESMOND DEVITT

London and New York
27 Old Gloucester Street
London WC1N 3AX
www.scalapublishers.com

ISBN: 978-1-78551-303-9

Editor: Catherine Bradley
Cover and endpapers design: The Old Chapel Graphic Design, Ivinghoe
Typesetters: Ace Software Exports Ltd, Gujarat, India
Printed and bound in Turkey

Contents

Foreword

Rory Stewart

My father always returned from Malaysia or Hong Kong to join me at the Dragon on Remembrance Sunday. I remember how straight he stood to attention, how cold the wind was and how bleak his face. His only brother, George, had been wounded at Alamein and killed in Sicily. I remember the Celtic cross on the memorial. But I do not think I ever focused on the names below. Nor would I then have thought it possible to learn very much about the names recorded on the cross – almost a hundred years since their deaths.

Desmond Devitt, however, by drawing upon a remarkable range of letters and obituaries, sermons and poems, has brought them to full and remarkable life. Some of those names were very well known and perhaps still should be today – William Leefe Robinson, for example, awarded the Victoria Cross for becoming the first pilot to shoot down a German airship over London. Ronald Poulton was the popular, record try-scoring captain of the English rugby team, who led them through the 1914 Grand Slam. Others were quieter boys who made less impact on their schools, colleges and regiments. Almost every type of boy is represented on that cross because almost 20 per cent of the Dragons who served were killed (almost 40 per cent were wounded).

Few, however, were untouched by the character of their headmaster, 'Skipper' Lynam. All the early writing from the front is shaped by the Skipper's Dragon School. One former pupil under an artillery barrage reflects that its 'flashes were even more brilliant and alarming than Skipper's lighting in *Macbeth*'; another consoles himself with a fragment of ancient Greek and then cheerfully asks for the accents to be corrected by 'someone in VIa'. All the letters home mirror the Skipper's insistence – rare in a Victorian schoolmaster – that children should be openly affectionate to their parents. Both Skipper's love of adventure (displayed in his cruise through the uncharted waters of the far North) and his endearing scruffiness are reflected in his young protégé Jack Haldane – described by General Haig as 'the dirtiest and bravest' soldier in the army.

Devitt tells us that Skipper once purchased a parrot on the advertiser's promise that it could 'speak three languages, recite Kipling, sing comic songs and make friends at once' – and one senses that this was his ideal for boys as well as talking birds. Hence, in part, his deep affection for George Fletcher (killed in 1915), who combined literary flair (describing a German attack as a combination of 'rustling in the turnips' and 'Sennacherib'), a love of pranks (he liked to creep across no man's land to pin flags to the German trenches) and a deep and serious knowledge of German language and culture. The writing of these young men – irreverent, improbably learned, tough, decent and occasionally a little donnish – is Skipper's Dragon School to the core.

The boys were far from clones, however. Skipper insisted that the job of his school was to allow the full development of original characters. He was thus as deeply fond of the astonishing intelligence and learning of Hugh Sidgwick (in the habit of improving his civil service memoranda by translating them in and out of ancient Greek) as of the tougher, less scholarly Jack Smyth. And Skipper's willingness to publish Smyth's poem – in his school magazine – shows how honest he was prepared to be with himself and with eight-year-old boys about the bleak and random horror that lay beneath the haunting nursery rhyme:

Modern Warfare
(Or how to get knocked out without seeing a German).
Ten British Officers sitting in a line:
One stopped a 'pip-squeak', and then there were nine.
Nine British Officers – What's to be their fate?
One dropped a live bomb, and then there were eight.
Eight British Officers looking up to Heaven:
Down came a German bomb and then there were seven.
Seven British Officers leaning on their sticks:
A sniper drew a bead on one, and then there were six.

The story of these hundreds of lives and deaths connected by five years in a north Oxford prep school is almost an encyclopaedia of the war. The Dragons evacuate from the beaches of Gallipoli, are killed at the third Battle of Ypres, meet Lawrence of Arabia and Marie Curie, grapple with the German High Seas Fleet in the Battle of Jutland, save the wounded at the Easter Rising and are shot out of the sky by Baron von Richthofen. Desmond Devitt catches their very varied responses to these theatres without judgement or preference. He reveals the strong character of Roderick Haigh – oarsman, marksman and holder of scholarships to Winchester and Oxford – and carefully records both his view that 'We are all inspired with the justice of our cause, and by the fact that we are fighting for the cause of honour and liberty throughout the world' and his belief that 'it is the highest honour to which a man can attain – to die for one's country'. But he gives equal space to the Old Dragon who wrote bleakly of Gallipoli that 'it is sickening to think that we have been under fire for six months and that the total result of our fighting is that we have got to go and leave our material and everything, especially some 100,000 dead, in the hands of the Turks'. He describes the intellectual who revelled in killing, alongside the decorated hero who killed himself in depression after the war. The men are portrayed not as victims but as original human beings whose charms and character persist as they struggle – in their own, individual way – with exhaustion, absurdity, mud, cacophony, gas and death.

So many lives lost: yet this book is equally a portrait of how those who survived mourned the dead. Ronald Poulton was shot by a German sniper while standing still on a trench parapet at night – like a British officer in Jack Smyth's nursery rhyme of modern war. But it is the full and beautiful heroism of his life and rugby that was commemorated by his peers:

Ronald is dead; and we shall watch no more
His swerving swallow-flight adown the field
Amid eluded enemies, who yield
Room for this easy passage, to the roar

Of multitudes enraptured, who acclaim
Their country's captain slipping towards his goal
Instant of foot, deliberate of soul –
'All's well with England; Poulton's on his game.'

And so Devitt records the single sorties across the shellfire of no man's land to rescue or bring ammunition to others, and the charges towards a hidden trench – entirely admiring their heroism. He is deeply respectful of everything that an Edwardian gentleman would wish to be. But he is equally at home with a much more modern sensibility: war's moments of dark humour (Jack Haldane experimenting on himself with mustard gas, accompanied by his father the Professor) and its bleak absurdities (the young pilot who struggles through his flying exams and then, on one of his first flights, stalls his aircraft at 200 feet and plummets to his death).

The Skipper's War powerfully juxtaposes the horrors of battle with the courageous endurance of wartime school life. For a headmaster who had shaped so many young lives, the desolation of loss was acute; it shattered families too. Devitt acknowledges this, giving space not only to Skipper's memory of George Fletcher's brother as a Norse hero and an Achilles, but also to the more private reflections of Paddy Burton's father:

You were, of all these dear familiar things,
Part of our daily life that still drags on
And still around small, trivial objects clings
The sweet and subtle fragrance that is you,
Half balm, half torture to the stricken heart.

There is nothing patronising in this book. We see these boys and men in the force of their individual personalities. We understand their hardiness, kindness, chivalry, humour and moments of despair. Devitt's ability (and that of the Skipper before him) – to see the boys so clearly, to love so warmly both warriors and more awkward souls, and to be so comfortable with their varied values – is not simply a testimony to the heart of a great schoolmaster, but also a sign of how much the character of Skipper's school still continues in the Dragon a century later.

This is a way of remembering that would have seemed truthful and generous to the Old Dragons themselves. This is how they should be remembered. This is, I suspect, how they would have wanted to be remembered.

Preface

Before the hymn the Skipper would announce
The latest names of those who'd lost their lives
For King and Country and the Dragon School.
Sometimes his gruff old voice was full of tears
When a particular favourite had been killed.
Then we would hear the nickname of the boy,
'Pongo' or 'Podge', and how he'd played 3Q
For Oxford and, if only he had lived,
He might have played for England – which he did,
But in a grimmer game against the Hun.
And then we'd all look solemn, knowing well
There'd be no extra holiday today.
And we were told we each must do our bit,
And so we knitted shapeless gloves from string
For men in mine-sweepers, and on the map
We stuck the Allied flags along the Somme;
Visited wounded soldiers; learned by heart
Those patriotic lines of Oxenham
What can a little chap do
For his country and for you –
'He can boil his head in the stew',
We added, for the trenches and the guns
Meant less to us than bicycles and gangs
And marzipan and what there was for prep.

John Betjeman
Summoned By Bells[1]

The future Poet Laureate John Betjeman attended the Oxford Preparatory School (as the Dragon School was then known) from 1917 to 1920.

Founded by Oxford University graduates in 1877, it was a small school, only reaching 100 pupils in 1905. With the exception of two girls, two Brazilian boys (at the school for a single year) and two boys who died in 1906, 84 per cent of the 1905 year group joined the Armed Forces in the First World War: 24 of them (25 per cent) were killed. Skipper Lynam, headmaster from 1886 until 1920, had kept in touch with many of his former pupils and some had indeed become 'particular favourites'.

The school's magazine, *The Draconian*, tells the story of the war years at length. It features some 700 pages of articles, letters, poems, pictures and drawings from those who fought, together with many insights into the life of the wartime school attended by Betjeman and his contemporaries.

Much of this has been published as a blog (www.skipperswar.com) throughout 2014–20, told as through the eyes of Skipper Lynam at the time. However, this form did not allow any context to be provided nor could it address many leading questions, such as what lay behind this extraordinary relationship between a preparatory school, its headmaster and its Old Boys? Much has been made of the influence of public schools on the officer class of this generation. However, for these men the earlier influences of Skipper Lynam and the O.P.S. may have been even more significant.

It was not a school steeped in tradition, but one moulded around the character and beliefs of Skipper Lynam. One Old Boy, Frank Daniel, noted this in a reminiscence written many years later.

> *The Skipper's personality was reflected in the whole atmosphere of the school, which was characterised by a healthy buccaneering spirit of independence, surely unique amongst Prep Schools of the day, and remembered with affection by all who were privileged to share it.*[2]

Unlike today's schools, where laws and regulations may seem to dictate their every move, Skipper was at liberty to adopt a curriculum of his choice, create his own rules (if he wished) and act as a truly independent headmaster, not answerable even to a Governing Board. It was *his* school, to do with what he would. His school was not typical, but was peculiar to its time and place. It is therefore necessary to understand the nature of this Dragon education in order to make sense of the feelings that the Old Boys had for Skipper and all that they encountered in their adult lives.

Does this mean that Old Dragons were very different to all those others who took up arms in 1914–18? Ultimately maybe not: but they felt different. Perhaps this had something to do with their social backgrounds – often the pupils were sons of Oxford dons, clergy, doctors, schoolmasters and the military. As the school's War Memorial Committee noted, in reflecting upon the scale of a possible memorial, 'Our boys are not drawn from the wealthy classes'.

The story does not end with the war in 1918. The Commonwealth Graves Commission records the deaths of those who died serving in the Forces (usually from wartime wounds) up until 31 August 1921. For many of those who fought, serious injuries (both mental and physical) were to remain with them well beyond the Armistice.

> *Possibly a collection of the admirable letters and articles sent us by Old Boys during those terrible years may come later. They would form a splendid volume.*
>
> *Skipper Lynam, 1921*

These words, which appear in the specially prepared 100th edition of *The Draconian*, have inspired this book. The archive of material on which it has drawn has lain largely forgotten until now, but it – and indeed Skipper himself – are more than worthy of what I hope might be considered 'a splendid volume'.

Desmond Devitt
Oxford, September 2020

Chapter 1
Summer Term 1917

Prizegiving Day

One day in late July 1917 the chairs were all set out in the Victorian-style school hall and on the balcony overlooking it, in serried ranks facing the stage. On them were seated the assembled company of parents, staff and 153 children of the Oxford Preparatory School (O.P.S.). There were many guests too – notably a number of wounded officers recovering in Oxford from injuries sustained in the First World War. They had been regular visitors to the school during that term.

The hall itself, built in 1895, was typical of many schools of that era. Six classrooms led into it, and the space would be classified as 'multi-purpose' today. Ropes hung from the beams to allow for P.E., while a stage could easily be erected at one end for school plays and concerts. Most importantly for the children, it was play space. The hall was the centre of life at the school, but it was also used for more formal occasions such as on that summer day: Prizegiving Day.

On to the stage came those invited to give away the prizes and make speeches. Presiding over the occasion was the headmaster, Charles Lynam, known to all as the 'Skipper'. Not noted for his sartorial elegance, he had clearly made an effort; he looked almost smart in his dark suit when he stood up to address his audience.

Among them were the ten-year-old John Betjeman and his parents. This was the end of John's first term at the school. It had been a term in which war shortages were biting. The effects of the German decision to undertake unrestricted submarine warfare, sinking any shipping approaching the British coastline, were becoming serious. The country relied on imported food; at one point it was estimated that there was only six weeks' supply of corn in the country. Feeding nearly 80 hungry boarders was a major concern for the school. Mindful of this, Skipper reassured attentive parents that their children were being well fed:

> *We have had potatoes regularly, no meatless days and plenty of bread – the only rationing has been in sugar and each boy has had first his eight and latterly his six ounces per week besides cooking sugar, also golden syrup and always jam.*

Despite the exigencies of war, John Betjeman's first term had not been one of dull routine but stimulating variety: picnics, bike expeditions, collecting eggs and

Left: The Oxford Preparatory School Hall (built 1895)

photography were all mentioned by Skipper. Indeed, he had succeeded in keeping the conflict at least at arm's length for the boys in his care. As Betjeman later observed:

> *... for the trenches and the guns*
> *Meant less to us than bicycles and gangs*
> *And marzipan and what there was for prep.*[1]

John won no prizes that day. However, the Betjemans would no doubt have approached the Skipper's brother Alfred Lynam (nicknamed at an early age and known thereafter as 'Hum') to express their thanks for looking after their son so well (John later claimed Hum was like a father to him). It was indeed thanks to Hum that John had been admitted to the school in the first place.

John Betjeman at Cliff Bank, c.1914/15

The Betjemans had been regular visitors to Trebetherick in Cornwall, where Hum and May Lynam went on holiday with their children, Joc and Audrey, since before the war. John was an only child and he needed companionship – or perhaps an audience. On holiday he was able to roam with other children. A shy child, he still knew how to make other children laugh and they enjoyed his company. There were many pleasant distractions, such as treasure hunts and cricket matches, but these adult-organised events were less to John's liking.

On one occasion when his parents had to be away, John had stayed with the Lynams at Cliff Bank, their summer home in Trebetherick. 'There was a wonderful bond of jokes in the Lynam family, and I was able to share in it,' he recalled. He described himself as being a distinctly difficult boy at that time; Hum had to speak to him about not teasing his son Joc so much. He did nonetheless learn the joy of laughter. 'I think

'Hum', Mrs 'Hum' and their children (Audrey and Joc), 1910

it was from those days that I can date my desire to make jokes, possibly rather too many of them,' he wrote.

When John became unhappy at Highgate Junior School, which he attended from 1915 to 1917, discussions between Hum and John's parents no doubt followed. John had been bullied – his Germanic name did not help in this regard – and he had had to endure chants of 'Betjeman's a German spy'.[2] Hum persuaded the Betjemans that boarding might be good for John, who would, of course, then be with some of the boys he had befriended in Trebetherick. John was duly enrolled for the Oxford Preparatory School in May 1917.

The Skipper and his School

When the future Poet Laureate arrived at the O.P.S. it was in its 40th year. The school distinguished itself from other preparatory schools in a variety of ways – in addition to an excellent classical education it boasted shorter hours, longer holidays (plus many extra half-holidays on the whim) and more independence. As headmaster, Lynam made it clear to adults and children alike that he preferred a more informal form of address than was customary for headmasters of that time. 'I confess to not attaching much importance to outward politeness,' he said. 'I hate to be called "Sir" every half-minute; I prefer to be called "Skipper".'[3]

Nor did he dress formally. Seven-year-old Per Mallalieu, a future Labour politician and father of Baroness Mallalieu Q.C., remembered seeing the headmaster for the first time as a new boy the previous term. He was struck by Lynam's appearance, which reminded him of

> *a retired pirate because he looked relaxed and jolly, and because a parrot was nibbling his ear. He was wearing a faded boater, a flannel shirt open at the neck, a woollen tie knotted near the top of his breastbone, a blue suit and carpet slippers.*[4]

A traditional Victorian schoolmaster the Skipper was not. Now aged 59, he had been headmaster for 30 years. John Betjeman, like many young boarders, initially experienced extreme homesickness – something many schools of that time would have regarded as a weakness to be scorned. However, Skipper believed in keeping the home ties strong, encouraging parents to visit the school whenever they could, and was therefore very sympathetic. Certainly his kindness struck a chord with John, who many years later still remembered how the Skipper had walked up the road with him, an arm around his shoulder, with words of comfort to match.

At the O.P.S. Skipper hoped his boys would learn self-reliance and enjoy some freedom. In the absence of meaningless, often stultifying convention, he offered pupils the chance to develop their own characters.

An O.P.S. education was a classical one. Nearly half the periods would have been spent learning Greek and Latin, but it was less than in similar schools. A boy in the top form at the O.P.S. was spending some 13 of the 28 hours of lessons and prep (homework) on Latin and Greek, 6 hours each on maths and English (which included some history and geography) and 3 hours on French. One lesson a week was used for art. However, there were a number of optional extras such as carpentry, fencing, music (piano), boxing, riding, dancing and a photography club. There were organised games at least twice a week. Rugby and hockey were the main sports in the winter and cricket in the summer, but there was also swimming (in the River Cherwell) and some athletics.

Not all their time was organised, however, as the Skipper firmly believed that 'a boy will never learn to use time properly unless he is allowed to waste it; and he will never learn self-control unless he has the opportunity of getting into mischief'.[5]

Such a philosophy ensured there was plenty of free time, in which boys could choose their own activities. Some went to the University Parks or into town; the more adventurous roamed the River Cherwell or took off on their bicycles. The young John Betjeman, already with a keen eye for architecture, liked to visit local churches:

> *Bicycling off to churches in the town;*
> *St. Andrew's first, with neo-Norman apse*
> *St. Old's – distinctly Evangelical –*
> *And, Lower still, St. Ebbe's, which smelt of gas.*[6]

The fact that the children were given such freedom to roam meant that they were more aware of life outside school in general and the war in particular. They may well have seen the 'Dad's Army' of the day, the Oxford Volunteer Training Corps, which included various elderly learned professors – and even on occasion the Poet Laureate, Robert Bridges – marching by. The Third Southern General Hospital was set up in Oxford, so ambulances coming up from the railway station and 'walking wounded' on the streets of Oxford would have been common sights. Per Mallalieu later recalled this evidence of war.

> *There were the wounded officers at Somerville, officer cadets with white bands on their caps learning semaphore in the Parks, pilots learning to fly on Port Meadow, Australian soldiers kissing girls in punts on the Cher.*[7]

As inter-school matches had fallen victim to wartime restrictions, including petrol rationing and quarantine, the boys were delighted to have any opposition. The Fathers' Match was no doubt one of the highlights of John's first term. '*Veni, non vidi, victus sum*,' summarised one cricketing father, lamenting that 'I came to the match. I did not see any of the three balls delivered to me; and I was beaten by the first straight one'. In his defence, it has to be said that the playing field was not entirely level. The fathers had a choice of a cricket bat, in which case they had to retire at 15, or a broomstick, in which case 25 was the maximum score they were allowed. *The Draconian* recorded that many proved overconfident and suffered the result: 'The broomstick tempted them and they fell'.

Strangely perhaps, it was on the cricket field that the war came closest to these boys. At this time Somerville College, a neighbour of the Radcliffe Infirmary, had been converted into a hospital for wounded officers at various stages of recovery. Both Siegfried Sassoon and Robert Graves spent time there, although never together. Sassoon spent his final week gaining strength by canoeing up the Cherwell; however, as it was mid-August 1916, the school would have been deserted, with everyone on their summer holidays. Robert Graves enjoyed not only roaming the gardens of Somerville in his pyjamas and dressing-gown, but also walking down the main road, St Giles, into the centre of Oxford similarly attired.

Each week the wounded officers provided one, or even two, teams to play against the Skipper's boys, something they evidently all enjoyed. Along with those fit enough to play came others who clearly were not. These soldiers, some in bath chairs, watched the matches and took what exercise they could around the boundary.

Visits from Old Boys, either recovering from wounds or on leave, were always welcomed by the boys – not least because these heroes would ask the Skipper to grant an extra half-holiday, requests that he seldom turned down. Lieutenant Colonel 'Fluff' Taylor, a veteran of the Boer War, for example, requested two 'extra halves' and two evenings of 'no preps'. Another visitor was 18-year-old Nevil Norway, replete with exciting stories of his family's time in Dublin the previous year. His father had been in charge of the Post Office that was attacked by Irish Nationalists on Easter Sunday.

The term also saw injuries to a few O.P.S. pupils, as recorded in the school magazine for the Summer Term 1917.

> *Little Laurie Salkeld, whilst winding up the caravan engine, got a backfire and broke his wrist. Francis Wylie, too, got run over by the roller when rolling the* [cricket] *pitch, but most fortunately escaped severe injury.*

Their parents would no doubt have sympathised with the children, but there was no question of attributing blame to the school. Such accidents were accepted as the fortunes of school life and the consequences had to be stoically endured.

* * * * * *

Despite the school's best efforts, the boys could not be entirely shielded from the realities of war. Most daily assemblies would have consisted of the usual mixture of religious and administrative matters, but there were three assemblies that term in which the death on an Old Boy was announced. Individual names, such as that of Humphrey Arden, would have meant nothing to John Betjeman and his fellow new boys. The idea of death probably meant little too, but they soon learned how to react to such news.

And then we'd all look solemn, knowing well
There'd be no extra holiday today.[8]

Humphrey Arden (2nd Lieutenant, Royal Garrison Artillery)

The son of a vicar, Humphrey Arden would have followed in his father's footsteps but for the war. Although he had only spent two years at the O.P.S., he had won a scholarship to Radley and was one of the many Old Boys who kept in touch with his old prep school headmaster, contributing regularly to the pages of the school magazine, *The Draconian*. Skipper must have felt his loss acutely. He later wrote of Humphrey as

one of those whose lives gave promise of a brilliant future. A Cambridge honours man, a great athlete, a musician of no mean promise, one who exercised extraordinary influence on his fellow men, a lover of all the arts and of everything beautiful.

Humphrey's battery was under fire when he was hit and he died of his wounds shortly afterwards, on 6 June. Only a week before his death his fellow officers had unanimously decided to recommend Humphrey for the M.C. which had been offered to his battery. His grave is in Bailleul Communal Cemetery Nord in France, now run by the Commonwealth and War Graves Commission. It is the only war grave on which an affiliation to the O.P.S. is recorded.

For the Skipper these were painful times. By August 1917 he would have mourned the loss of 49 Old Dragons, all of whom were known to him as children and many of whom had kept in contact with him ever since. By this stage some were not just Old Boys: they had become close personal friends.

* * * * * *

The affiliations of Humphrey Arden inscribed on his tombstone: B.A., O.D. (Old Dragon), O.R. (Old Radleian)

The boys soon learnt to recognise these 'special' Old Boys when their names were read out, as they could see their headmaster was visibly upset. This made a strong impression on them, John Betjeman in particular:

Before the hymn the Skipper would announce
The latest names of those who'd lost their lives
For King and Country and the Dragon School.
Sometimes his gruff old voice was full of tears
When a particular favourite had been killed.[9]

'Particular Favourites'

The war coincided with a large number of 'his boys' reaching their prime of life; some were deemed to be among the brightest and most talented of their generation. There were four Old Dragons, 'particular favourites' perhaps, whose stars shone especially brightly in the O.P.S. firmament.

Like many, Hugh Sidgwick came from an academic background; his father was a Fellow and Tutor of Corpus Christi College. He arrived at the O.P.S. in 1891 and left four years later, approaching his 13th birthday and in possession of the top scholarship to Winchester College. Skipper pronounced him to be 'the ablest boy that ever came to the Dragon School, and withal one of the most lovable'.

Walter Moberly, a contemporary of Hugh's, remembered being taught with him in the top form.

Hugh Sidgwick, aged c.12

> *With Hum* [Lynam] *to teach us and Sidgwick to set us a standard we had a most stimulating time; and I remember nothing to compare with it until I reached Senior Sixth Book at Winchester under Dr Fearon … In general his pre-eminence was unchallenged and unchallengeable … I have never known any other case of a boy's being so completely on a pinnacle by himself.*

In addition to winning virtually every academic prize going, Hugh played the violin and sang in school concerts. He acted in Shakespeare plays, won the quarter mile in 1895, got his 1st XV rugby and 1st XI cricket colours.

Hugh was also a boy of considerable character, as Walter Moberly affectionately recalled:

> *He took part with the same zest and enjoyment in what I may call the social politics of school life ... He was the best of good company. He was always witty; and his descriptions of persons and events were a genuine joy to his listeners; but I cannot remember that his wit was ever salted with malice.*

* * * * * *

In September 1897 Professor Poulton, living in adjoining Banbury Road, sent his younger son along to the O.P.S. as a day boy; he was aged just eight. Ronnie was small for his age and did not make significant impact during much of his time at the school. He was a late developer; only in 1901 did he begin to catch the eye as an athlete, and as a rugby player in particular. That same year he was picked for the 1st XV and was finding his way through opposition defences with a 'regular rugby swerve', as one member of staff told his father.

The following year, his final one at the school, Ronnie scored a record-breaking 15 tries against the St Edward's Juniors. The following summer he captained the 1st XI, a task for which one of Skipper's staff, G.C. Vassall, felt he was admirably suited.

> *He always got the best out of his side and they would have followed him anywhere ... He was always the life and soul of the party when we went by train or in a brake to play cricket matches. So much so that we used to offer him 6d if he could last for five minutes without speaking! Sometimes the rest of us would go on talking; sometimes we would all sit silent, watch in hand – but he never won the 6d.*[10]

Ronnie also had much to offer on the stage. Skipper chose him for the part of Mark Antony in *Julius Caesar* and the reviewer of the play was most impressed.

> *I never remember to have seen, even at the O.P.S., anything to equal his splendid conception of this, one of Shakespeare's greatest characters: the perfect taste of his elocution, his command of pathos and of irony and his beautiful self-restraint were indeed amazing in a boy of his age.*

However, it was on the sports field that his greatest talents lay. G.C. Vassall, himself an expert long-jumper, helped Ronnie to improve what was then referred to as the 'broad jump'.

> *I remember his surprise and delight when I showed him that he must jump high if he wanted to jump far. He was sceptical to begin with and finally made me change into running shorts and spikes. 'I can see better what your feet and legs and knees are doing like that,' he said. Next day he came running up with: 'It's quite true, I can do nearly two feet more'.*[11]

On his final Sports Day in July 1903 Ronnie jumped 16 ft 11 in (5.15 m), a new school record. He swept the board that day, coming first in the 100 yards, quarter mile

Ronald Poulton as Mark Antony, aged c.13

and high jump – and was also awarded the Athletics Cup. Skipper proclaimed him to be 'the best all-round athlete who we have ever had at the school'.

Ronnie's time at the O.P.S. was now coming to an end, a situation that he acknowledged with regret.

The next day we had the Speech Day, my last day as a schoolboy at the O.P.S., but 'the old order changeth, yielding place to new' and I had to go to a Public School some time. But I was very sorry to leave.[12]

Meanwhile Skipper's report that 'His presence is like a gleam of sunshine' indicated he was equally sorry.

* * * * * *

The Haldanes represented the intellectual aristocracy of north Oxford. Jack's father was Professor John Scott Haldane, brother of Lord Haldane, Secretary of State for War (1905–12). An eminent scientist, his father was inclined to use himself or his family for his experiments, rather than animals. Jack helped his father in scientific endeavours from an early age. At the age of three he was required to give blood samples to aid his father's investigations, while his sister Naomi (later to be Naomi Mitchison) – one of the very few girls to attend the O.P.S. at that time – used to invite friends home from school not so much to play as to provide more blood samples. It was perhaps appropriate that the family motto was 'Suffer '.

Jack was a precocious boy, to say the least. He was able to read by the age of three, his mother having taught him 'partly in self-defence, for when he became absorbed in a book he ceased to ask questions'.[13] As he grew up, Jack continued to be involved in his father's work. At an early age he was taken down a mine and asked by his father to demonstrate the effect of breathing 'firedamp' (methane).

> *My father told me to stand up and recite Mark Antony's speech from Shakespeare's* Julius Caesar ... *I soon began to pant, and somewhere about 'the noble Brutus' my legs gave way and I collapsed on to the floor where, of course, the air was all right. In this way I learnt that firedamp is lighter than air and not dangerous to breathe.*[14]

Jack arrived at the O.P.S. in 1898, aged six. A shy boy, he could be quite aggressive towards those who invaded his personal space. He became an obvious target for baiting, as his ensuing loss of temper provided great entertainment for his

Jack Haldane, aged 14

contemporaries. *The Draconian* described one dramatic example.

> *The small and agile Grundy so vexed with his water-pistol the unarmed Haldane, vast but clumsy, that Haldane lifted a whole tree from the Mound and chased – but kept missing – his tormentor with wild swipes of trunk and roots; and when the bell rang, reeled into Maths mouthing 'I wish I could kill. I wish I could kill!'*

By February 1900 Jack was already making his mark at O.P.S. The school sent numerous exhibits to an English Educational Exhibition at the Imperial Institute, among them Jack's illustrated diary for his summer holiday the previous year. *The Draconian* reported the results.

> *J. Haldane's diary was much read, and great wonder expressed at such a production by a boy of six. One visitor was overheard exclaiming, 'I don't believe any boy of six knows all about an anemometer!' but he didn't know our scientific Jack.*

Jack started in the bottom form with Miss Bagguley. Here he learned by heart *The Battle of Lake Regillus* by Thomas Macaulay and was invited to recite some of it at a school concert. His mother recalled Jack's performance.

> *Skipper gave him a 'leg-up' on to the platform, and started him off with '"Ho, trumpets, sound a war note!" – Now you go on'. So Jack did, and took the hand that Skipper presently raised to check the flow as an encouragement to continue. The Skipper tried again, saying that it was very nice, but that was enough for this time. 'Don't you really like it?' Jack asked. 'I can tell you lots more if you'd like me to.' This, of course, raised a roar of laughter, but the Skipper made it all right by explaining that it was getting late, and that some of the others wanted a turn!*[15]

In February 1905 Jack played Pistol in *Henry V*. The boys of O.P.S. were expected to be able to take criticism, both privately and publicly, and *The Draconian* reviewers were expected to give negative as well as positive comment.

> *Pistol is an exceedingly difficult part, and as to Haldane's acting of it, painstaking and conscientious to the last degree as it was, it is difficult to say whether it were a qualified success or a partial failure; we incline, however, to the latter view, mainly because of his bad elocution and because he would roll about.*

Jack prospered academically, in 1904 winning the top scholarship at Eton – the first time that a boy from the O.P.S. had achieved this. But Skipper was pleased with him for another reason too. He had placed a bet with Dr Williams, the headmaster of rival Summer Fields School, that Jack would beat their candidate in the examination. When Jack's mother met Dr Williams at a college dinner party, she gathered that her son had made the last term an extremely expensive one for him!

* * * * * *

Jack Smyth arrived at the O.P.S. in September 1901 very independently, but in a rather undignified fashion – with the help of a lamp post. As he recalled:

Jack Smyth, aged 13

It was just before my eighth birthday that I set off on my new bicycle from 24 St Giles for my first day at the Dragon School ... My departure was not very dignified as I was unable to get on to the machine in the orthodox way but had to make use of the nearest lamp post, by the aid of which I somehow clambered into the saddle. At the end of Bardwell Road there was another friendly lamp post against which I came to rest.[16]

As Jack Haldane had done, he started in the lowest form. He remembered the Skipper as being 'unorthodox, unpunctual and untidy to a degree ... His sense of humour was a thing that bubbled out of him in a deep chuckle and [he] was always kindly'.[17] With Jack's own father an army officer in far off Burma for his entire school career, the Skipper seems to have become a surrogate father to the boy.

Having made his way to the top of Miss Bagguley's form, he finished his first year in style by winning the 100 yards race for the under-nines. Then, out of the blue, he fell ill with what he later described as a combination of dropsy and Bright's disease 'with several other complications'.[18] Two years went by when he was unable to attend school, during which time he swelled up like a balloon and grew weaker and weaker 'until I couldn't even read a book'.[19] Yet Jack's recovery from the disease was almost as sudden as its onset. His nurse, thinking Jack was dying, decided to offer him whatever he would like to eat and for some reason he chose a steak. Although this cannot have been the only reason, it did prove a turning point. By the Easter Term of 1905 he was able to return to school.

It was some time before Jack caught up, both academically and physically. He was, however, a very determined boy.

> *I started to train and harden my very flabby body in every possible way. My unfortunate younger brothers were pressed into service and made to run, box and skip in addition to all the games they had to play at school. Every morning before breakfast they had to run with me to Wolvercote cemetery. I had established myself* in loco parentis; *I heard their prep, made them recite poetry and was a general thorn in their flesh. But somehow they seemed to like it and to thrive upon my very Spartan treatment.*[20]

Jack played Juliet in the 1906 production of *Romeo and Juliet*, receiving good reviews. If this did not necessarily suggest a military future for him, the following year was more promising in this regard. He played a very youthful Macduff in *Macbeth*, resembling 'a sort of Sir Galahad in his armour'. On this occasion, as the *Draconian* reviewer noted, 'he showed plenty of fire when his opportunity came in the final scenes'.

Sport at O.P.S. gave plenty of opportunity for Jack to excel. In his final year he was in the 1st XV, captain of the 1st XI soccer, vice-captain of the 1st XI hockey and captain of the 1st XI cricket team. In 1908 Jack left, thanking 'the Skipper, Hum, Cheese, Pug and the others of that grand crowd at the Dragon School who really did make schooldays for myself and my brothers the happiest days of our lives'.[21]

All of these four boys could have been expected by the Skipper and their families to have gone on to glittering careers. The fortunes of war intervened, however; by July 1917 one was already dead and another would not see out the year.

End of Term

Even in the midst of grief and loss, life at the school had to go on; the Skipper made sure that the Summer Term of 1917 ended on a lighter note for the children with a fancy dress dance. John Betjeman seems to have been absent, but Hugh Gaitskell (future Chancellor of the Exchequer and leader of the Labour Party) appeared as an Indian rajah. The Skipper himself came as a scarecrow – he probably did not need much make-up.

With Prizegiving over, the term came to an end. The boys went off for the holidays, encouraged both to write a holiday diary and to collect conkers, which should in due course be taken to their nearest railway station. 'Horse chestnuts will set free grain for food, as they can be used for a process in which grain has now to be employed,' the public was told. If this seems rather vague, it was because the Government wanted it to be so.

The Government may have been keen to keep the reasons secret, but the children worked it out for themselves. Per Mallalieu recalled in his autobiography how 'for no reason that I ever heard – we pretended to ourselves they were needed to make explosives – we delivered bags of horse chestnuts to the Great Western Railway station'.[22] He did not know how near the truth he had been. Conkers, scientists had discovered, could be used in the making of cordite. Normally cordite was made using imported timber, but grain and maize had become substitutes during the war. In order to fight the shell shortage, the need for cordite was great – but by 1917 the activity of German U-boats in the Atlantic meant that there was a growing food shortage as well. So John Betjeman and his friends were set to the task of gathering conkers – one small way in which these young Dragons could 'do their bit'.

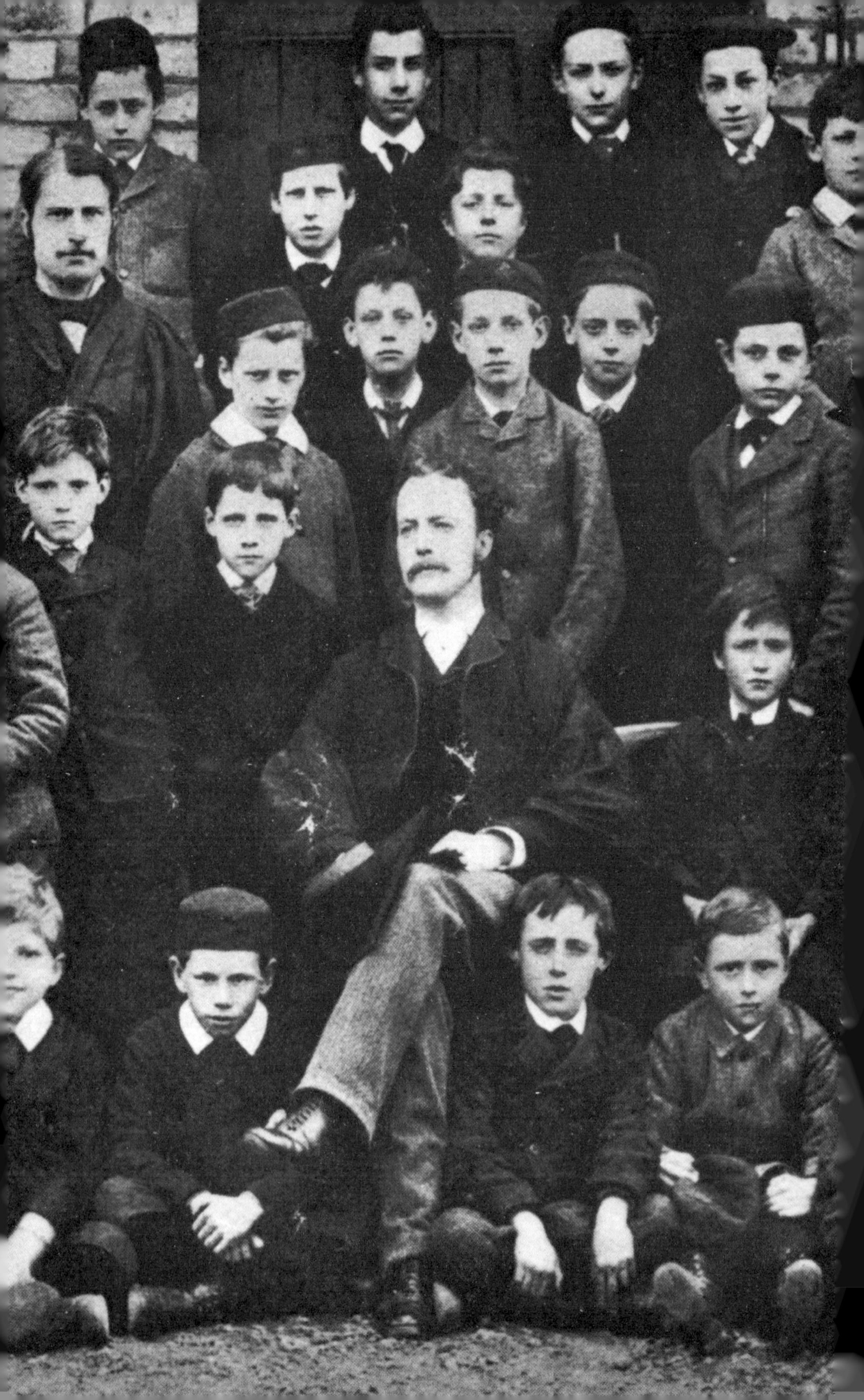

Chapter 2

The Oxford Preparatory School

That his Old Boys should still in their adult years have such close ties to their preparatory school in general, and to the headmaster, the Skipper, in particular, was extraordinary. Why was this so? The fact that the O.P.S. was a comparatively young and small school, principally serving the Oxford community, was certainly part of the answer. More importantly, the Skipper, who was just as interested in the children as he was in his school, forged this friendship, which was to make him one of the most loved schoolmasters of his generation.

The story of this remarkable school starts in the world of *Alice in Wonderland*.

'The Oxford Little Boys' School'

In 1877 the Fellows of the Oxford Colleges were released from the celibate life by the recommendation of a Government Commission on the Universities. Prior to this only the Heads of Colleges were permitted to be married, although more and more College Fellows were in clear contravention of the rules as they then stood.

As a result, in the same year, a school was founded by a 30-strong group of Oxford University people, including four Heads of College and seven professors. Among this body was the Dean of Christ Church, who duly sent his tenth and youngest child to be schooled at what was at first called 'The Oxford Little Boys' School'. He was Dr Henry Liddell, whose daughter Alice had been befriended as a child by a maths don at the college, Charles Dodgson. The stories that Dodgson told Alice, published in 1865, had become famous as *Alice's Adventures in Wonderland*, Dodgson having adopted the pen name of Lewis Carroll. Alice herself was a young woman in her twenties when the school opened in 1877, but her youngest brother Lionel was one of those 14 children who became the first 'Dragons'.

It was one of Lionel's contemporaries, Clement Rogers, who claimed responsibility for the Dragon name. He described how it came about, after a game of football.

> *The first game was not a success. There was no-one to coach us and we had only the vaguest ideas about the rules, so the game consisted of argument and soon petered out. So we foregathered under a tree to discuss things …*
>
> *Someone suggested our forming ourselves into a club. We all agreed …*

Left: Detail of the first school photograph with its headmaster Mr A.E. Clarke, 1881

> *The first question was, of course, what we should call ourselves. With a badge in mind I made a suggestion … I had heard that there was a 'Governing Body' of the School, and one of them was a Mr. George of New College. I thought of the gold sovereign then in currency with the figure of St. George and the Dragon on the back. So I suggested, 'There's a Mr. George who is one of the governors or something. Let's be the Dragons'.*[1]

Brook Kitchin's Dragon badge, 1877

The boys then decided that a badge was needed, and various sisters and mothers were approached. One of these original badges still survives; it was the work of the mother of Brook Kitchen, another of the first Dragons.

Charles Dodgson's photograph of the Kitchin children portraying the story of Saint George and the Dragon, 1875

Charles Dodgson was also known for his great interest in photography. He took some 3,000 photographs, some portraying members of 'Dragon' families. By co-incidence, one of Dodgson's pictures (taken in 1875) features Brook Kitchen as Saint George killing the Dragon, as he came to the rescue of his sister Xia.

The governors appointed Mr A.E. Clarke, late of Magdalen College, as the headmaster, and he and his 14 charges were soon ensconced in rooms at 26 St Giles. By 1879, however, numbers had grown to 30 and the school moved to a house in nearby Crick Road. This was to remain their home for the next 25 years and in 1886 Clarke changed its name to the Oxford Preparatory School, or O.P.S.

The first school photograph with its headmaster Mr A.E. Clarke, 1881. Among the pupils are Brook Kitchin, Arthur Percival and Reggie Tyrwhitt

The Clarke era is described by an O.P.S. boy of the time, Lawrence Stubbs, writing in April 1908. He reckoned there was too much learning by heart and over-coaching in order to win scholarships (23 of which were won between 1877 and 1886). Nor did he feel prepared for public school lessons, lamenting that 'much drudgery and many tears might [have been] saved were things explained a little better in the beginning'. Clarke was also a strict disciplinarian, as the Skipper's much younger brother and erstwhile pupil of Clarke's, Hum Lynam, recalled.

> [We] *learnt our Greek grammar so that we never forgot it, and the weekly 'review' which he* [Clarke] *held of each form was a dreaded period, which seldom passed without at least one 'whacking' for unsatisfactory performance.*[2]

Stuart Taylor, known throughout his life as 'Fluff', had 'reddish hair ... [an] honest freckled face and bright dancing eyes [and was] dressed in a sailor suit'. He also had painful memories of those times (he was at the school from 1882 until 1886), later describing an incident involving 'a boy called Hall', his neighbour in Miss Macey's class. One day Hall decided to amuse himself by forcibly sticking a pin into Fluff's leg. His victim stifled a very natural yelp and vowed to exact revenge.

Unfortunately Hall turned out to be neither so brave nor as honourable a schoolboy as Fluff. When the latter struck, 'Nothing could have drowned the hideous yell which Hall emitted'. The classroom happened to be above the headmaster's study and immediately Fluff heard the door open and bang shut below, followed by hurried footsteps up the stairs. 'One moment for explanations, none for tears or expostulations, and I found myself in the strong grip of Mr. Clarke being borne hurriedly downwards,' he recalled. What happened next can be guessed, 'Fluff' confining himself to the comment that 'the rest of the story is painful telling'.

Charles Cotterill Lynam

As the school increased in size a new teacher was needed, and in 1882 Clarke appointed Charles Lynam, a young undergraduate keen to augment the meagre allowance he received from his father. The two men were to become friends, and Lynam later described Clarke as 'a good and wise friend and headmaster'; he gratefully acknowledged that 'he was most forbearing with the many mistakes made by a young and untrained teacher'.[3] In these early years Lynam was described by one Old Boy as 'hot-tempered' and 'too swift in punishment'[4], but clearly these faults disappeared with time.

Clarke allowed Lynam to run the sport and out-of-school activities. As with many a young schoolmaster, he probably got a bit carried away with his charges. On at least one occasion Lynam admitted that he should probably have been given the sack.

> *After taking the Cricket XI in a brake to Cothill, on our return we found a police sergeant awaiting us at the boarding house, and with him a rubicund gentleman with a bandaged eye, who complained that we had all shot at him with pea-shooters when crossing Folly Bridge.*[5]

Whether they were all guilty as charged is not clear. One version of events records that Lynam himself, having confiscated the pea-shooter on the outward journey, was the offending crack-shot.

Lawrence Stubbs remembered rambles with Lynam affectionately.

> *Sunday afternoon walks with the Skipper speedily became a great institution, while the fact that the Skipper's horribly radical ideas as to the rights of property involved us in thrilling adventures, probably did not make them any less attractive.*

One such adventure took place on an expedition up the River Cherwell. A bailiff armed with a stick and a dog tried to turn them off a field where they had landed for tea and a game of rounders. After Lynam's threat to 'set the boys on him' if he did not go away, the bailiff departed, much to the boys' delight.

In 1884 Charles Lynam's younger brother Hum came to live with him so that he could attend the O.P.S. as a pupil, and in 1885 Charles was married to Catherine Hall, who was to help him look after Dragon boarders for many years. The following year the Clarke regime came to an abrupt end: after a short illness he died of pneumonia. Aided by a loan of some £2,000 from his father-in-law, Lynam managed to buy the school from Mrs Clarke in January 1887. Although he was as yet to be known as such, the Skipper was now in charge.

Coincidentally Charles Lynam was one of 14 children – the size of the first intake to the Oxford Little Boys' School in 1877. Charlie, as he was then known, was the son of Charles Lynam, an architect living in Stoke. His father was often absent from home and his mother's influence was the stronger. His younger brother Hum saw that, even as a child, Charlie was developing skills that would serve him throughout his career as a schoolmaster.

> *To us younger brothers Charlie was the 'big brother' in the best sense. He assumed the paternal role when a spanking was necessary and kept the peace amongst us, not by exhortation but by starting some game or occupation in which all could be employed with interest.*[6]

In January 1873, at the age of 14, Charlie was sent off to be a boarder at King William's College on the Isle of Man. His father was not a wealthy man, but four more of his sons were able to follow in Charlie's footsteps.

King William's was not a traditional Victorian public school. Indeed there were aspects in common with the O.P.S. in that the regime allowed Charlie much freedom, as he happily acknowledged.

The Skipper (Charles Cotterill Lynam)

> *My love of the sea was first developed at that most delightfully unconventional school King William's College, Isle of Man. Games were not then compulsory. Occasional roll calls were things of scorn; and from noon until 6 p.m. it was possible to sail the sea in a 'loaned' harbour-master's boat or a friendly fisherman's larger craft, to climb mountains, to fish the streams, and even to make first efforts at sketching or geology.*[7]

Charlie met with much success: he won the theological prize twice, was in the 1st XV rugby team, became a prefect and finally, in 1879, won an Open Scholarship to Hertford College, Oxford, to read maths. However, this did not prove to be to his liking and he later switched to history. Even then, Charlie was clearly intent on studying more widely. Hum recalled that his brother 'could not do with the limitations and exigencies of syllabuses, but ranged widely on the literary and biographical sides of the subject'.[8]

Hum also believed that at this stage Charlie was 'a pronounced radical, and something of an agnostic'.[9] Although he continued to attend church to please his mother, he was very critical of the nature of the services.

There was time at Oxford for some sailing and of course some rugby, which one can imagine he played with a lot of enthusiasm or 'dash'. The University team was a strong one, and for three years Charlie featured in the three-quarter line. It was a pity that he did not have a 'Blue' at the end of it, but he did not make himself available for away matches – probably for financial reasons.

The *Blue Dragon* and its Skipper

That Charlie should have become universally addressed as the Skipper emanated from his lifelong interest in sailing. His character and spirit of adventure are made very apparent in '*Nimium ne Crede Experto*', a poem written by 17-year-old Hugh Sidgwick in 1899.

'This narrow strait,' (the Sailing Directions said)
'Is full of rocks and difficult to enter;
Whirlpools are common here at every tide
There are uncharted reefs on every side
And currents (twenty knots) along the centre.'

'Come,' said the Skipper, 'We will go in here.'
(We went in there.)

'There is no sand,' (the Sailing Directions said),
'The anchorage is thoroughly unsafe.
There is no shelter from the frequent squalls
Boats should go on to Lock MacInchmaquaif.'
'Come,' said the Skipper, 'We will anchor here.'

(We anchored here.)

The Skipper points the way

Frank Sidgwick (Hugh's older brother) knew the Skipper better than anyone when it came to his love of the sea. As with his schoolmastering, Skipper's approach to matters nautical smacked of the gifted amateur. Although he had these natural gifts, he did learn a lot by dint of experience – and in both of these loves of his life he was a natural leader.

The Skipper and his favourite pipe, 1910

[He] *had no respect for unthinking convention or over-careful professionalism, 'one mustn't' and 'one can't' ... Amid the escapades of his most unseamanlike crew, nothing could perturb him but the loss of his tobacco pouch. But his easy good-humour did not mean that he failed to recognise or shirked his responsibilities as skipper. When making a difficult harbour, Skipper would take the helm himself: 'Thank you: I always run my own ship aground.'*

Apart from the adventure to be had on a cruise with the Skipper, there was the camaraderie among friends and the enjoyment of his little eccentricities.

Any cruise might have a new bye-law or a new anathema, and coming aboard, old hand and novice alike had to look out for signs of an innovation, and walk warily lest they stumble against it. Which was the orthodox site for the 'oof-pail' this cruise? Could one set sail without first hauling the bathing-ladder on deck, or not? Might a volunteer cook use the new 'deep-frying' pan, or was it taboo, for the Skipper's use only? Where were the gramophone records kept this cruise? That lump of wet fabric that you have just swabbed the decks with, is one of the Skipper's knitted waistcoats ... In the depths of that enchanting marine Jungle, the cruising Blue Dragon, *there was a Law; and sometimes it sprang out at you, growling – till it grinned.*[10]

His first yacht was christened the *Yellow Dragon*. Following its demise on the Happisburgh Sands in 1891 Skipper commissioned a new boat; this was built on nearby Port Meadow in Oxford. Launched the following year, it suffices to say that he sailed her 'down the Thames and kept turning to the right until she made Cape Wrath'.[11] Thus started a series of holiday adventures with family and friends, all recorded in the *The Logs of the Blue Dragon*.

These logs were published thanks to Frank Sidgwick. Less academic than either his father or his younger brother Hugh, he was sent to Rugby rather than Winchester, and subsequently confessed that he was the only member of his family not to achieve a first-class degree. Nonetheless, he did win the Chancellor's Medal for English Verse at Cambridge and then decided on a career in publishing.

On leaving Cambridge he became a junior partner with the publisher A.H. Bullen, with whom he served an apprenticeship. This put him in a good position to ensure the publication of Skipper's first volume. In 1907 he set up his own firm of Sidgwick & Jackson and all future logs were published under this banner. As would be expected of the Skipper, these logs were designed to entertain as much as to inform; clearly as much pleasure was derived from the writing of them as from the reading.

In my Blue Dragon *logs, I have always tried to make the reader intimately acquainted with the little party on board; to make him realize to some extent the characters and idiosyncrasies, the amusements, and – if you like – fads of each of us. I am afraid that it will have been gathered from much internal evidence that we are not a very 'yachty' company. The language is not nautically correct; the burgee has been known to flutter all night – nay, sometimes all week, or all month – and that not only when, north of the Arctic Circle, we had the midnight sun ... It is true that I have occasionally had amongst my crew one who has distinctly 'yachty' instincts, and coils ropes and puts things ship-shape at every opportunity; but I fear he has found it impossible to reform an incorrigible Skipper: and even he – the young reformer – has been known to leave fish-hooks and fishy fragments of bait about the decks!*[12]

Adventurous Skipper may have been, but he was never reckless. Risks were there to be taken, but only when they had been weighed up. Clearly, he did not always get it right, as he himself was happy to admit.

In telling the stories of my voyages in the Blue Dragon I *and* II, *I have never minimalized or concealed misadventures – however much to my discredit as Skipper they may have been. Probably as the years go on and one gains in experience, and possibly in caution, these misadventures become less frequent and less reprehensible. One would like the reader to realize that what is left out is the anxiety and responsibility one constantly feels. There are precious young souls on board; the sea and the wind are strange and unknown forces: they sometimes seem to be imbued with the characteristics of human beings in an exaggerated form…*[13]

Jack on the bowsprit of the *Blue Dragon*, 1910

In addition to his own family, Skipper would take along other members of the Dragon staff and Old Dragons such as the Sidgwicks, as well as current Dragons.

Jack Smyth was one such young Dragon. He went on three cruises with the Skipper, the first up the east coast of Ireland, the second up the west coast of Scotland and the third to Orkney and Shetland, describing with relish how the boys 'ran wild like small savages without a care in the world'.[14] Although conceding that the *Blue Dragon* crew 'were often very amateur indeed',[15] and that it was fortunate his mother was unaware of some of the adventures they had, he had high praise for the Skipper.

Jack cited one memorable occasion when his headmaster's quick thinking saved the day:

We were somewhere up in Shetland when the time came for me to catch a steamer for the south to be returned to the bosom of my family. As usual on the B.D. *no one quite knew what the time was and the Skipper and I were just halfway over to the pier when the steamer left. Fortunately she had to pass quite close so we waved and shouted, not thinking for a minute that she would stop. However, the monster did stop, towering high above us, and let down a rope ladder. With my boots slung round my neck – my feet had expanded so much from going barefoot for a month that I couldn't get them on – and my small suitcase, I swarmed up the ladder. As I reached the deck, surrounded by curious passengers, the Skipper cupped his hands and bellowed, 'Have you got any money, Jack?'*

I felt hastily for my purse and shouted back, 'No'.

'Have you got your ticket?'

And again the answer was 'No'.

The ship's siren hooted and the Skipper grinned back quite happy in the certainty that some good Samaritan would look after me.[16]

The undoubted highlight of Skipper's sailing career came in 1912, when he took leave for a term to sail his boat over to Norway and up the coast as far as the North Cape. Nevil Norway, a pupil at the O.P.S. at the time, was very impressed. Many years later he recalled the Skipper's character and exploits.

> [He was] *a man accustomed to hardships and to risking his life in a mild way, unlike many schoolmasters. If I have learned one thing in my fifty-four years, it is that it is very good for the character to engage in sports which put your life in danger from time to time. It breeds a saneness in dealing with day-to-day trivialities which probably cannot be got in any other way, and a habit of quick decisions.*[17]

That year the Skipper won the Royal Cruising Club Challenge Cup for what was – in the eyes of the judges – the most meritorious cruise of the year.

The Skipper and crew of *Blue Dragon II* and the Royal Cruising Club Challenge Cup, 1912. From left to right: Hugh White, Blair Watson, Leslie Eastwood. Seated: the Skipper

> *To have rounded the North Cape in a 15-ton sailing yacht is a considerable feat, although, as it happened fine weather was met with in the portion of Mr. Lynam's cruise which was in the open sea. Part of this cruise was undertaken very early in the season when the cold was very severe, and the long and very intricate navigation amongst the islands on the Norwegian coast, and in the sounds and fiords between Trondhjem and Hammerfest was, notwithstanding difficulties from imperfect charts, successfully undertaken both in the spring and summer cruises, without pilots or local assistance. The fact that this cruise was considerably the longest, extending well into the Arctic Circle, and that considerable part of it was through channels unexplored by British yachtsmen, has led me to give it the preference.*[18]

The *Logs of the Blue Dragon* were further promoted by way of the journals of the Royal Cruising Club. Their readership included the author and journalist Arthur Ransome, who concluded:

> *The Royal Cruises have not lost the art of telling what happens. I envy them. I think I had better buy a boat.*[19]

Blue Dragon II in Vaila Sound, the Shetlands, 1909, a watercolour by the Skipper

A Dragon Education

The Skipper was to remain at the helm of the O.P.S. until 1920 and the course he took was decidedly his own. Yet was there anything really different about the O.P.S. and the education (in the broadest sense) that Skipper's Dragons received? What did his Old Dragons think? Hugh Sidgwick noted that the school 'evokes a loyalty similar in kind to those of the best public schools'. At one Old Dragon dinner (c.1908), he spoke about the distinctive character of the school and its training.

> [Hugh] *found it in the Skipper's refusal to force his boys into one or other of two or three conventional moulds, in his positive encouragement of originality, in the opportunity given to boys to discover their own peculiar interests and gifts; so that, if you were to collect a number of Old Boys in after-life and to ask what was the common stamp that the School had set on them, you would be able to point to no single machine-made quality, but you might observe that everyone was very much himself.*

Skipper himself spoke and wrote extensively of his views on the education of the young. In 1908 he addressed the headmasters of the Association of Preparatory Schools, outlining aspects of his personal credo.

We have failed in proportion to our apparent success, unless we have helped a boy to develop his mind and his capacities in his own way, unless we have given him full scope for all of imagination and originality that is in him, unless we have let him know the causes of the sin and suffering in the world, unless we have made his heart beat with the heart of mankind, unless we have made him scorn to do what others do because they do it, unless we have shown him the falseness of all the gods of society: gold, sham religion, conventionality, the sham patriotism which assumes that one's country must be in the right and that one Briton is worth two foreigners merely because he happens to be a Briton. Unless we have done or tried to do these things we have failed.[20]

Nor was Skipper happy to see emotions stifled.

We have failed if our boys are ashamed to kiss their parents in public; and if they take refuge in that cowardly subterfuge of 'schoolboy honour' when they see bullying or cheating or vice, without protest; if they fall in line with the miserable rules of school etiquette, which, among other silly things, try to prevent two old friends from speaking to one another, because they are not in the same house.[21]

Unusually for the time, he was also a believer in co-education, declaring that 'the presence of girls in one's school is quite as good for the masters as for the boys and for the girls themselves'.[22] For him, education should be considered 'a means of making us more human'[23] – a process in which he believed co-education could play a significant role.

I have sometimes been, shall I say, criticised for admitting a few very select girls to the School. Personally I have no doubt whatever of the good effects it has on the boys, nor of the benefit that the girls themselves obtain. It is absurd to say that it makes the boys girlish or the girls boyish … The prejudice against the presence of girls at a preparatory school is merely a silly conventional attitude …

*By the bye, I have never heard any objections to co-educat*ing*!*[24]

In his speech to parents in July 1901, Skipper noted some differences between the O.P.S. and other schools.

1. *We do not have such long hours, and we have more holidays. Many masters never give extra halves: I give a good many – perhaps too many …*
2. *Our boys have more independence, and less supervision: thus certain headmasters have expressed horror at the way I let my boys go into Oxford, if they ask me; go on the river; go and see their parents in term-time … I hate the entire severance of the family ties by keeping a little boy three months from his home.*

It has been objected that the masters allow the boys to treat them with too little respect. A respect which means subservience and politeness, with disdain and sneering behind their backs, is to my mind most rotten. What I believe to be the true attitude of masters

> *to boys in a Preparatory School is – be an elder brother* out *of school, and a master with the power of at once claiming and getting the closest attention* in *school.*[25]

Nonetheless, O.P.S. was an academic school, and the winning of scholarships mattered – and not just for their own sake or for the honour of the school. In August 1907 Skipper, looking back on the 44 Dragons who had won scholarships to Winchester in his time, stated that 'in not more than three cases could the parent have reasonably afforded to send his son to the Public School without a scholarship'. This provision of opportunities to those otherwise denied them was a powerful motivator for a headmaster whose own background was not overwhelmingly wealthy.

Despite this, Skipper also believed that the requirement for winning scholarships should not override the need for a broader education. Less Latin and Greek were taught at the O.P.S. than at other preparatory schools, meaning that Skipper's boys were less well drilled in grammar and syntax than their competitors. Yet there were compensations.

> *We do more mathematics, and considerably more English history and literature. Our top 30 boys all get up very thoroughly a whole play by Shakespeare every year, besides learning a great deal of Tennyson, Milton and miscellaneous poetry. Also every boy in the School is taught drawing.*

Nor did the Skipper countenance adding extra lessons, as some schools did, as he had an aversion to 'cramming'.

> *Of one thing I am convinced, viz., that boys have quite long enough hours of work – no boy under 14 can really profit by more than 30 hours per week including preparation.*

Skipper's Dragons consequently arrived at their public schools having experienced a rather richer educational diet than was usual for that time – something that C.S. Lewis was quick to observe on his arrival at Malvern College in 1913.

> *Among other New Bugs of my year, too, I met a pair of boys who came from the Dragon School at Oxford (where Naomi Mitchison in her teens had just produced her first play) and from them I got the dim impression that there was a world I had never dreamed of, a world in which poetry, say, was a thing public and accepted, just as Games and Gallantry were accepted at* [Malvern]*; nay, a world in which a taste for such things was almost meritorious.*[26]

This eclecticism, fostered by the Skipper, was maintained by using his Old Boys to provide a form of external appraisal.

> *The work of the school has been in various departments examined and criticised. The examiners' reports will appear in* The Draconian. *Though the examiners are, as usual, Old Boys, their reports are on that account none the less critical, impartial and useful. They remember the standard as it was in their day and would be the first to note any falling off.*

The enthusiasm and commitment of former Dragons was a valuable tool for pupils and teachers alike – as well as for the parents, who could read it all in *The Draconian*. For example, when Hugh Sidgwick examined the VIth form in 1906, he was critical of the lack of detail and accuracy, adding that the children would have to catch up in this area at their public schools. Of a poetry recital in December 1913, *The Draconian* recorded, 'Of 35 boys, half got practically full marks, and there was only one failure, L. Dobbs.' (This label, if that is what it was, clearly did not deter young Leonard unduly. Within ten years, in 1921, he was to become the winner of the first ever British Skiing Championships.)

Nor were the staff immune from criticism, as Skipper was also happy publicly to acknowledge any shortcomings.

> *In French the top and bottom of the school are good, the middle divisions are weak. There is a lack of organisation in this subject and next term the French teachers must meet and arrange the work properly – Division III was doing a more advanced French reader than Division I, which is absurd.*

The necessary changes were made and the next term Skipper declared that there had been a 'distinct improvement'.

> *We have abandoned the rather empiric and confused methods that were in vogue last year, and have contented ourselves with regular grammar, exercises and translation. In the lowest forms the little ones are merely taught orally and from pictures.*

* * * * * *

It was the Skipper's belief that an acting knowledge of at least one of Shakespeare's plays should form part of an O.P.S. education. His productions were by no means highly polished, as he characteristically preferred 'the haphazard to ordered method'. Thus, in November each year, the two top forms would read though the play in their lessons. There would be a certain amount of acting, the parts would be split up among the children and they would have all been asked to learn passages for prep. Some of the more difficult passages were explained by the Skipper.

> *The boys soon get the drift of the thing, and gradually grasp the various scenes for themselves. I always prefer that they should form their own ideas, even if not quite accurate ones, than I should give them mine … 'Clarendon Press' notes, all philological and critical comments are rigidly avoided.*
>
> *By the Christmas holidays the whole form has learnt a good many speeches and scenes, and then comes the selection of performers for the various parts … In the holidays the parts are learnt, and when the boys come back we have Wednesday, Thursday and Friday for rehearsals.*[27]

The performances were much lauded, and the Skipper carried this tradition on through the war years.

During his time as headmaster, the Skipper was responsible for 31 productions of 12 different Shakespeare plays – *Macbeth* and *Merchant of Venice* seemingly his favourites (with five productions each). This tradition was to have a 75-year run, from 1888 to 1963.

* * * * * *

Out of the classroom, Skipper's children were to be both seen and heard. Sixty years later Naomi Haldane remembered being in the school hall, 'in the middle of the tumultuous screaming, shouting, bouncing, tearing break'. In this melée they were unsupervised by adults, who concerned themselves with other more pressing matters.

Naomi also remembered the games they played outside.

> *Our war games were in a sense plays.* [We] *had 'forts' in the thorn hedges on both sides of the field. The gangs used to be quite tough with one another and I suppose a spot of sado-masochism does one no harm so long as one grows out of it. We always hoped for a bit of treachery in order to punish the offender – or be punished.*

Francis Wylie (who arrived at the school in 1912) also remembered the 'gangs' that children used to form, and take very seriously. He particularly recalled wild games of bicycle polo on fields and roads around the school, as well as wonderful 'spy games' on bikes all round Park Town and the allotments. Such freedoms were clearly an outlet for youthful energy and a tonic for growing minds.

* * * * * *

The Skipper – not surprisingly for a lover of sailing – was a 'fresh air' man. Following a visit to Switzerland in 1909 (where his brother Hum had to retreat from time to time to recover from tuberculosis), he wrote with enthusiasm of the climate and country.

The Lynams on holiday in Montana, Switzerland

> *Oh that all our boys could spend their Christmas holidays in the grand invigorating air and surroundings of Montana, Villars or Chateau d'Oex! Cold dry air and sunshine, and out all day tobogganing, skiing, skating; up with the sun and to bed soon after it sets, dog-tired – instead of the raw damp slush of our winter climate; the late hours, the 'stodging' feeds, the pantomimes, the 'fugging' over fires, lolling in arm-chairs and general demoralisation.*

When designing the new boarding house (School House) with his architect father, Skipper had a plunge bath (10 × 10 ft (3 × 3 m) long and 4 ft (1.22 m) deep) included on the first floor. It was intended to be used by the boys every morning – and indeed by the Skipper himself.

> *A narrow ledge enabled the shivering plunger to make his way, crab-wise, round to the far side whence a good standing jump would get him back with enough bounce to get him out again with the period of total immersion reduced to the possible minimum. The extra loud splash just two minutes before the final gong would be the Skipper, about to make good his daily boast that he could be last into the Plunge and still ready for breakfast, subject to his own interpretation of 'ready', as not including, for instance, the doing up of any buttons, a refinement that could be added during Prayers.*[28]

The procedure left a strong impression on O.P.S. pupils. John Wilmers, who left the school in 1915, remembered it in a *Draconian* article.

> *If you did not get to the dining room fully dressed before Skipper arrived and the prayer preceding the meal had already started, you risked having to pay a penny fine or, if you so preferred, to receive one with the cane.*

7 a.m. bathers, summer 1917

Alternatively, there was the River Cherwell. A fair number of pupils bathed every morning in the river before breakfast. In the Christmas Term of 1916 the temperature ranged from 58 degrees Fahrenheit (20 September) to 34 degrees (16 December). The plunge and morning swims do not seem to have been compulsory, certainly for those with colds, etc., but there was often a monetary reward for those who completed a term without missing a day.

Even on board the *Blue Dragon* the Skipper regularly took a morning dip. On his award-winning cruise to the Northern Cape in 1912, for instance, he swam each morning. The habit could be perilous, as on Easter Day, 7 April.

> *There were six inches of snow on deck, and I had to grope about bare-footed in the snow to find the bathing ladder. The consequence was seven of my toes got partially frostbitten, and I had no feeling in them for the rest of the cruise ... My doctor told me that it was only owing to an exceptionally good circulation that I had not lost the toes.*[29]

* * * * * *

In an age before antibiotics, the children's heath was a continual concern. In *The Draconian* of 1911 G.C. Vassall, the editor – clearly with the agreement of Skipper – provided a précis of Dr Almond of Loretto's *The Making of Healthy Men*. He included Dr Almond's views on Physical Education, which saw a close connection between health and character.

Dr Almond also believed in corporal punishment ('two or three strokes on the back with a light cane'), deeming that the alternatives would take up time better used for other things. However, he often gave the boys the alternative of doing an imposition, only to find that in fact the boys preferred the caning. Why was this so? Almond offered an explanation.

> *A boy likes to feel that he has made a ready atonement for his fault, and has done with it; the sudden pain is followed by a great sense of relief. A right-minded boy also takes a pride in enduring pain bravely.*

This was certainly true of John Betjeman.

> *'Who's talking here?' The dormitory quailed.*
> *'Who's talking?' Then, though innocent myself,*
> *A schoolboy hero to the dorm at last,*
> *Bravely I answered, 'Please sir, it was me.'*[30]

Three with a gym shoe was bravely borne and his assailant – and mentor – 'Tortoise' Haynes complimented him on the way he had 'owned up' and taken the punishment, commenting:

> *'Reckon yourself henceforth a gentleman.'*[31]

Skipper also believed in 'the efficacy of the cane'. However, corporal punishment did not meet with universal approval among parents, and Skipper entered into a correspondence with a number of them in 1905. Skipper maintained that 'for faults of forgetfulness, carelessness, and a repeated neglect of work … it seems the simplest, least hurtful, and most efficient corrective'. He also maintained that boys preferred it to impositions (copying out lines and other repetitive tasks) or other alternatives. Nonetheless, he did concede to a degree:

> *I am perfectly willing to substitute the plan of sending home any boy who is sent in to me, with a note saying that the boy in the ordinary way would be punished, a note which must be delivered directly by the boy, who must immediately bring back an acknowledgement of its receipt.*

One can imagine that very few Dragons of that time were likely to have taken this option, whatever their parents' feelings on the matter.

* * * * * *

Skipper was clearly more approachable than many a headmaster of his era. As with his views on corporal punishment, he was prepared not only to listen to but also to accommodate parental views. The children were not to 'grouse' and neither were the parents, who were instead encouraged to 'come and have it out' with the Skipper. He assured them that if problems were based on fact, he would do his best to correct things, but also warned them not to rely on 'afternoon tea gossip' for information.

Clearly there were a number of issues that did concern the parents – and on certain matters they were prepared to 'have it out' with the Skipper. One such issue was handwriting.

One particular boy's handwriting had been very neat until he came to the O.P.S. It then became untidy and the parent suggested more time should be devoted to improving the standard of handwriting in the school. Skipper accepted the first point, but believed 'this is a necessary stage which most boys go through, whilst forming a style'. The parent was not convinced: if his handwriting had been good when he came, why could it not continue to be good? Skipper explained that 'at the very earliest stages writing is an end in itself, and the achievement is to write beautifully'. As the boy grows older, however, 'writing is recognised as a means of expressing what is known, and the boy thinks that so long as he knows a thing, it doesn't much matter how he puts it down'. He assured the parent that once the pupil discovered that it did matter, which he would in due course, he would 'reform' of his own accord. When the parent questioned the need to wait for this process of self-correction, Skipper responded with vigour.

> *I hope it is reasonable not to lay an exaggerated stress on neat writing in the middle of the school. Excellent hand-writing often goes with very moderate ability and slackness of thought. It is, after all, more promising to write sense execrably than nonsense beautifully.*

Despite his belief in allowing a pupil to develop over time, the headmaster did accept the essential point being made, as he made plain.

> *Before a boy leaves, we expect him to write sense at all events legibly and neatly.*

Nor was the matter of the school uniform dictated by the headmaster. A notice posted in *The Draconian* informed readers that in the interests of 'health and neatness' (among other things) Eton collars would give way to 'white flannel shirts with collars attached'. Parents were invited to give their views.

The next term a letter was sent from Skipper to the parents stating that, as he had received no objections, the changes would go ahead. In fact, the Skipper had received one letter, stating that if he proposed 'to put the boys into paint and feathers, the particular parent would be satisfied that it was best for them'.

Agreement was not unanimous, however. When letters from a couple of parents 'expressing disappointment' did emerge, Skipper replied that 'it is not a law of the Medes and Persians' and that he hoped the parents would try it. However, he assured them, 'it is not compulsory in the sense that a boy will be turned away from school if he does not conform.'

* * * * * *

Another aspect of the O.P.S. that many boys appreciated was its love of pets, which had long been a part of school life there. The Skipper credited a young Dragon by the name of Alan Haig-Brown, who attended the school from 1888 to 1890, as the person responsible for this.

> *His love of animals showed itself at a very early age; he was the originator of 'pets' at the Dragon School, and the goat which trotted about with him was the forerunner of many and various kinds of two, four and even no-legged successors; ducks, hens, kittens, snakes, tortoises, rats, mice, parrots, macaws, cardinals, cut-throats, budgerigars,* et hoc genus omne, *may all claim to owe their appearance among us to Alan. Some of us may remember his introduction of a huge snake into the drawing room of 28 Norham Road, and the hysterics of a parent.*

Skipper's study, as G.C. Vassall, the editor of *The Draconian*, described in the December 1912 edition, resembled a zoo; it was difficult to imagine serious business being conducted there.

> *Two parrots, 27 small birds and 5 canaries enliven the atmosphere of the Skipper's study. A few small birds live loose, whilst Joey and Polly fly about the room, and occasionally devour or otherwise destroy papers of value, such as the boys' poems or exam papers; they also nibble bits with great discrimination out of the best books.*

Certainly Polly was more welcome than Joey, being noted for his 'fluent and melodious conversation'. On the other hand Joey, a little ring-necked Indian parrot, could certainly disrupt proceedings with his usual refrain:

> *Wake up Polly, I feel sick ,*
> *Send for the doctor quick, quick, quick … QUICK*
> *You scamp Polly, fetch the policeman.*

Chris Jaques, a wartime Dragon (1914–17), remembered that Joey 'would sometimes sit on the Skipper's shoulder during a meal in the Dining Room. It did not pay to arrive late or be spotted misbehaving at the table, as Joey would be transferred to the offender's shoulder 'to administer a sharp nip to the nearest available ear'.

Not all Skipper's birds were successes, however. One that he purchased could, according to its advertisement, 'speak three languages, recite Kipling, sing comic songs and make friends at once'. None of this turned out to be true and the bird was quickly dismissed.

* * * * * *

All these elements were constituent parts of an O.P.S. education as experienced by those who went off to fight in the First World War. As with their contemporaries in other schools of the time, they had learned to fight their own battles at school with little parental involvement, to accept discipline and to develop a considerable amount of resilience. Yet O.P.S. pupils had also been allowed greater freedom, as Skipper believed 'that the boys [should] learn to look after themselves and use their own common sense and independence, instead of always waiting to be told, and expecting to be looked after'.

This greater independence was much envied by the boys of nearby Summer Fields School. They could not ride about on their bikes, as Dragon boys did, nor roam the River Cherwell unsupervised, 'ragging about in four-oared boats or canoes'. The Skipper's more adventurous approach to life was summarised in the quotation made famous by *Swallows and Amazons*: 'Better drowned than duffers, if not duffers, won't drown'. Arthur Ransome would have thoroughly approved.

Dragons loose on the Cherwell

Chapter 3
Growth and Development

Throughout the 1880s and early 1890s the school continued to grow, such that another move became necessary. A site was leased from St John's College in nearby Bardwell Road, and money was raised for a purpose-built hall and surrounding classrooms.

This move into the new premises in 1895 coincided with the Royal Commission on Secondary Education recommending co-education in day schools. Skipper took note and floated the idea of including girls in the lower forms. No doubt he was partly influenced by the fact that his own daughter Kit was approaching school age.

Kit duly entered the school in September 1896, to be joined in 1901 by Deta Sergent, following in the footsteps of her brothers Victor, Dick and Noel. A steady trickle of girls joined the school in the years that followed, but not more than one new girl a term, by all accounts. They were usually daughters of members of staff or sisters of current Dragons.

Kit, according to one of her fellow Dragons, was once 'sent in' to Skipper. When a master felt that a pupil's work or behaviour merited it, he would send the offender to the headmaster, where a 'whacking' would be the almost inevitable outcome. In this case, whether before or after such an event took place is not clear, Kit apparently 'got hold of the cane and chased the Skipper out'.

The Staff

Skipper needed and indeed found talented staff to join him – many of whom would have been more likely to be found teaching older boys at a public school. In 1900 G.C. Vassall joined the staff. As with many Dragon teachers he acquired a nickname, in this case 'Cheese' – a play on his initials. He taught both Classics and English, and was to become one of Skipper's greatest supporters.

Vassall was also a talented sportsman. At Oxford he had been President of the Athletic Club and he distinguished himself by winning the University Long Jump three times, as well as coming second in the Amateur Championship of 1899. Captain of the University Association Football Club, he played for the Corinthian XI in 1904 that defeated Bury, the F.A. Cup holders, 3–1. He was good enough to be selected to play for England, but turned this opportunity down to play in the Varsity Match, with which the game clashed.

Left (front row): Naomi Haldane, Kit Lynam and Jack Smyth in *Romeo and Juliet*, 1906

In 1901 Lindsay Wallace, a pupil at the school when the Skipper took over from Mr Clarke, returned to O.P.S. as a member of staff. Known to one and all as 'Pug', he was an all-rounder. A soccer 'Blue' and more than useful at any sport, he could also deal with both the very able and the more academically challenged. In his free time Pug made sure he found time for physical exercise too.

Hum, Pug and Cheese, 1907

He acquired the weather-beaten complexion that goes with a liking for the outdoors and the open air in all weathers. He started each day, summer and winter, with a bathe in the Cher[well], *whose ice had to be several inches thick before he would admit defeat, and he liked it to end, whenever possible, by rowing up the river, even on the darkest night, to Marston Ferry, where for many years the Victoria Arms dispensed a mulled ale that could be relied on to put all schoolmasterly problems into perspective.*[1]

Pug's teaching methods could be imaginative. In demonstrating latitude and longitude, for instance, he tied strings 'up and down and around his head'. A piece of chalk, balanced on the top of his head, represented the North Pole.

Between them, Cheese and Pug would clock up a total of 77 years' service.

By 1905–10 Skipper's earliest pupils of the 1880s were in their thirties and wedding bells were ringing for some. Few marriages can have given Skipper more pleasure than that between Pug Wallace and Deta Sergent. Both had attended the O.P.S. as pupils and they met again during the Skipper's 1906 cruise on the *Blue Dragon*. This took them from Oban, via Barra, up the coast of the Outer Hebrides and by the time they reached their final destination, Stornoway, they had announced their engagement.

The wedding took place in April 1908, in the South of France where the Sergents lived, with Kit Lynam one of the bridesmaids.

A later addition to the staff was Gerald Haynes, known as 'Tortoise'. He was an inspiration to many boys, particularly those of the non-sporting variety, such as John Betjeman:

Much do I owe this formidable man
(Harrow and Keble): from his shambling height
Over his spectacles he nodded down.
We called him 'Tortoise'. From his lower lip
Invariably hung a cigarette.[2]

Deta Sergent and Pug Wallace: an Anglo-French alliance

Tortoise Haynes hard at work marking, aided by a cigarette

Young Per Mallalieu remembered both the cigarette and the fact that Tortoise had the habit of 'applying board compasses to the bottom of any boy who failed to prepare his Mansfield Latin exercises. Once, during a prolonged fit of coughing, he swallowed a still smouldering Gold Flake and lost his voice for a fortnight, but he continued to teach effectively by board compasses alone'.[3]

What was it about Tortoise that inspired Betjeman?

> *... rather his kindness and his power to share*
> *Joys of his own, churches and botany,*
> *With those of us whose tastes he could inform.*
> *He motor-bicycled his life away,*
> *Looking for orchids in the Wytham Woods,*
> *And Early English in Northamptonshire.*
> *He was the giver: ours it was to take.*[4]

To these characterful men can be added Hum Lynam, 'Daddy' May, Pilky (who taught the Greek alphabet thus: 'Alpha Beat her Gramma and Dealt her a terrific blow which made her Sigh long'), Miss 'Billy' Pinhey, Miss 'Baggs' Bagguley, Cosmo Lang and J.B. Martin.

On arrival at the school in 1901, Giles Dixey found himself being allocated J.B Martin's maths set, following a typically Skipperesque 'assessment' of his mathematical ability. Skipper asked his new recruit how many half-crowns there were in a pound. While he might have hoped for an answer of eight, Giles suggested five. 'In here!' Skipper exclaimed, as he opened the door to Mr Martin's room. It was a good choice as far as Giles was concerned.

> *There from the beginning I scored a regular 50%, owing to* [Mr. Martin's] *gruff but heartening system of marks: 'Two if it's right, one if it's wrong'.*

The Draconian

The development of the school from this period is well documented, thanks to *The Draconian*, its unique magazine. At a time when most school magazines were designed to record the year's highlights, listing the scholarships and sports results, *The Draconian* was very different. It was originally the work of three young Old Dragons, Robert Johnson, Robert Holland and Henry Spurling, all then at Winchester College and wanting to keep in touch with fellow Old Dragons. The stated object of this magazine was clearly set out.

> *To tighten the bond of union between friendships that would otherwise be severed … to hold constantly before the minds of all old Dragons the duty they owe to their old School, and to remind them that it is their after successes that are conclusively to establish the real worth of the teaching at that School.*

The first edition came out in 1889, and Skipper was happy to encourage such a venture. When the boys got into financial difficulties with it in 1893, he agreed to take it over. Thereafter *The Draconian* became the networking success of its time, firstly under the editorship of Skipper and then, from 1896 until 1907, under Hum.

Old Dragons were encouraged to come back and visit the school and to contribute letters and articles to the magazine. The Old Dragon rugby, hockey and cricket matches were all written up and their life achievements and publications recorded, along with births, marriages and deaths.

Old Dragons were thus accustomed to reporting their experiences back to Skipper and Hum well before the First World War. The magazine featured poetry too, and numerous letters. Hum was even happy to include the occasional humorous send-up. This letter appeared in the August 1906 edition of the magazine.

> *My Dear Hum,*
>
> *I know you always like to hear what O.D.s are doing in the great world outside; so, as the only O.D. now in prison, I think I have a claim to be heard. I write this in the customary manner, with an old toothpick, on a scrap of paper hidden carefully from any gaoler, and with my own blood …*
>
> *After breakfast we go out and dig drains in the country. It is a healthy and pleasant occupation, and brings back the old, old days when I was* proxime accesit *for the Gardening Prize (Under 10). I took a walk the other day – at least it was more like a run:*

but a warder came up and made a race of it. I held him well at first, but he kept a little in reserve, and just caught me in the straight. So I am still here ...

I like the fellows I work with very much. They have all led interesting lives, and are singularly free from social prejudice and from merely conventional morality ...

I hope to be out next year, unless they send me to Broadmoor. That is a very nice place, and in charming country, but they say its intellectual level is lower. When I come out, I shall, of course, be delighted to come and lecture to the School on my experiences.

Yours ever,

342

Dartmoor Prison

In 1908, after 12 years as editor of *The Draconian*, Hum Lynam handed the baton to G.C. Vassall, who was to continue in this role until his death in 1941. In so doing, Hum remarked on how *The Draconian* differed from the normal school magazine whose '*raison d'être* is to enable Johnny to see his name in print, and Johnny's mother to point it out to less fortunate mothers'. In its magazine, as in so many aspects of school life, the O.P.S. trod its own path.

* * * * * *

The First World War was not the first conflict to feature in its pages. The start of the new century was marred by the news of losses in the Boer War: over 30 Old Dragons served, of whom four died. With *The Draconian* now established as a conduit for communication, Captain Stuart Taylor, still known from his Dragon days by his nickname 'Fluff', wrote back extensively. Alfred Spurling, besieged in Mafeking with Baden-Powell, even managed to get a letter through by way of a native runner, who made it through the enemy lines – if not all the way back to Oxford!

Maurice Church was one of Skipper's closest sailing friends, and another master who had himself been an early pupil at the O.P.S. before returning to join the staff. In 1900 he enlisted as a Trooper in the Oxfordshire Yeomanry, only to be killed in a skirmish at Hartbeestfontein, in what is now the North West Province of South Africa, in February 1901. 'His loss leaves a blank and a void, which cannot be filled up,' wrote Skipper – hoping, no doubt, that he would never again have to experience the loss of friends and Old Dragons in war.

* * * * * *

Yet tragedy and loss could also occur within the school itself. In January 1906 the term started with the usual Shakespearian production – *Romeo and Juliet* this time. Despite an outbreak of illness striking only days before the first night, requiring six parts to be reallocated, the play was described as 'a veritable triumph' by the *Draconian* reviewer Jack Gamlen (O.D.).

Jack Smyth won acclaim for a remarkable performance as Juliet.

Denis O'Sullivan

His striking dignity did not leave him for a moment. He was never tomboyish, never giggled, never thought that he was looking ridiculous. In consequence he made a thoroughly human and feminine Juliet.

The part of Mercutio was played by Denis O'Sullivan, who also won much praise.

[He was] *as good as good can be … His moment of triumph came at his encounter with the Nurse* [Kit Lynam], *but his death was finest of all. We missed him dreadfully afterwards.*

The Easter Term was a notoriously bad time for illness, and in 1906 earache, chickenpox and whooping cough had all struck. By a most terrible quirk of fate, days later Denis was himself taken ill with pneumonia. He died a week later.

Skipper wrote to all the boys to break the news.

My dear boys,

It is very sad to think that we have lost our dear chum Denis, the brightest, kindest, merriest and bravest of us all. Whilst ill he was so patient and plucky, never complaining, 'so sorry' when his weak hands spilled the medicine, so grateful for all that was done for him.

I think he first knew of his dangerous condition on Wednesday night. He said to me 'I always tried to please you Skipper, I don't know if I did'; and then he told me of things he wished he had not done and said he was awfully sorry; then after a time he murmured 'For Jesus Christ's sake, Amen'. So I asked him if he would like to say 'Our Father', and he said 'Yes, awfully', so we said it together and then he said his favourite hymn was 'Lead kindly Light'; and when we had said it through he sang the last verse most sweetly.

He constantly mentioned his special friends Jack, Geoffrey and Naomi and several others. He always recognised me with a smile and even asked for a Blue Dragon story! He sent his love to you all and passed away from us quite peacefully. Now he is happy and at rest.

Yours affectionately,

C.C. Lynam

Denis O'Sullivan's grave in Wolvercote Cemetery, Oxford

The Dragon boys and staff were all present at Denis's funeral and his burial in the Wolvercote Cemetery. He had been one of 13 boys in the top form. Of the other 12, four would not survive the war.

* * * * * *

In happier times, bicycle expeditions were a regular highlight of Dragon life. The summer of 1909 saw trips out to Shotover, Marcham, Tubney, Abingdon, Stonesfield and Stanton Harcourt (all between 5 and 10 miles distant). The one to North Cerney in the summer of 1910 was written up for *The Draconian* by one of the boys. Having gone by train to Fairford, they bicycled to North Cerney – clearly with little idea of the way, as they had to ask for directions at every village.

On arrival, there followed a cricket match against a local team of boy scouts. The match was conveniently tied, but then the real fun began.

> *Someone bagged one of the Boy Scouts' caps, and this led to a battle; after about ten minutes ragging they collected their troops and sounded the charge. They were much older than we were for the most part, and they outnumbered us, but we were not going to be beaten. Keyworth had a tremendous fight with the 'Samsonian Beefer' (aged 19) and everyone did his best to sit on the scout he had got hold of. Buck held down a writhing mass of three scouts, and Flea and Way wrought frightful havoc.*

At this point the boys were told to stop. The Rectory lawn was 'covered with Dragons sitting on scouts' who, in the Dragons' eyes at least, were comprehensively beaten. The battle ended with the O.P.S. boys raising a cheer for their defeated antagonists before trooping off to bed. This was an opportunity for further fun and games, as our young Dragon correspondent revealed.

> *We ragged about and had swimming races and diving, and then we sang songs... At about half-past eleven we made an effort to go to sleep.*

The next morning the boys started for home, stopping en route for lunch in Burford. Clearly it was a good one, as Billy Smyth recorded in the hotel's visitors' book.

> *Four cyclists arrived at the Inn of the Bull;*
> *They came very empty and went away full;*
> *Their names were the Skipper and Billy and Flea,*
> *And Geoffrey;*[5] *a hungrier four ne'er did you see.*
> *The fare was roast beef with potatoes and peas,*
> *And raspberry tart, and some excellent cheese;*
> *A fair maiden served us with all of the best;*
> *But who wrote this poem will never be guessed.*

* * * * * *

Moving on to Public Schools

Dragon Eton scholars, 1906: Bob Bourne, Robin Laffan, George Fletcher, Jack Haldane and Regie Fletcher

The underlying purpose of a preparatory school such as the O.P.S. was to prepare its pupils for senior independent schools, known then as the public schools. Although Winchester had been the preferred destination of many of the academic parents of early Dragons, Eton was gaining in popularity. A particularly talented group of the Skipper's Dragons was making its mark in College (the house at Eton made up exclusively of those winning the scholarships).

Bob Bourne (top left) was developing into a talented rower. Robin Laffan (centre) was Captain of the Wall Game (played only at Eton and incomprehensible to the outside world!) and also was responsible for introducing rugby at Eton. George Fletcher (top right) was Head of School, while Jack Haldane (bottom left) was still settling in as the top scholar of his year, together with Regie Fletcher (bottom right), who had won the 11th scholarship that year.

Jack Haldane was finding life at Eton tough. He was bullied, and his intellectual arrogance did not go down well.

> *During one term he was beaten every night for a week, at least once on the soles of his feet. When Lord Haldane officially visited the school his nephew was forcibly prevented from meeting him by the drastic process of being pinned down under an up-turned table loaded with bags of sand.*[6]

Jack's mother was perfectly aware that he did not enjoy life at Eton and even suggested that, with his father's permission, he might leave the school. Although Jack's response was that he did not want that 'exactly', he cried and confessed that he 'couldn't bear the place'.[7] Even a man-to-man discussion with his father revealed little more.

One criticism of the O.P.S., with its less formal atmosphere, was that it did not necessarily prepare pupils for what was in store for them at the public schools. The transition from the O.P.S. to Clifton College was not easy, for example, for Tankred Behrens. Skipper wrote to his parents to warn them, in a roundabout way, that Tankred could be 'spirited'.

> *A boy of his strength of character and keen sense of justice was a difficult study for a young headmaster … and I fear that in many cases my treatment of him may not have been judicious ... We had many a row! Some his fault and some no doubt mine, but I hope and believe that we shall always be friends.*[8]

If the accommodating Skipper had found him difficult, then there was going to be trouble ahead.

In due course Mr and Mrs Behrens sent Tankred's first term's report, about which they had concerns, to the Skipper. He replied in reassuring terms.

> *It is, I assure you, better than most boys (especially scholars) get during first term – the idea is that scholars are likely to be cocky and think themselves great swells and so they must go down a peg!*[9]

As Tankred progressed up the school at Clifton, he found it more difficult to accept the authority of older boys over him. He was beaten for 'systematic insubordination', but, unusually for boys of that era, recounted the episode to his parents in a letter home.

> *The sixth as a body called me up and gave me a licking. I suppose they thought they were going to reduce me to tears. However, I just calmly contemplated the despicable idiots (that is three out of the total of six) while they licked in and when they had finished, put on my coat and laughed at them.*[10]

Of course, not all O.P.S. boys would have experienced this treatment, nor would all those who did have responded to it in this way. There were many schools – and, more importantly, housemasters – who came to see the worth of the Skipper's Dragons. Many, such as Jack Smyth, went to Priory House at Repton. Here the housemaster was Harry Vassall, brother of G.C. Vassall and a rugby legend. Harry had been Skipper's captain when he was up at Oxford; he subsequently became a close friend who often sailed with the Skipper on the *Blue Dragon*.

Jack Smyth was in fact fortunate to attend Repton at all. The Skipper's 50th birthday had occurred in 1908, and on the annual summer Prizegiving Day he had stipulated the present he would like. With typical altruism, he requested subscriptions to a Leavers' Fund to enable him 'to give leaving exhibitions to help boys whose parents are not very well off to go to a good public school'.

With his usual confidence that this would come about, Skipper immediately awarded the first such exhibition to Jack Smyth. His mother must have been delighted, although in a short speech she admitted she sometimes felt 'quite jealous of [Dragons'] devotion to their school – they never want to be at home!'

Meanwhile another Old Dragon, Ronnie Poulton, was having a much smoother ride at Rugby. By his third year he had established himself in the 1st XV, winning his colours when still aged only 16. The poet Rupert Brooke, then in his final year, played alongside Ronnie in the centre.

Some six years later, Frank Sidgwick's publishing firm was in its fourth year and, in June 1911, he was approached by a young Old Rugbeian keen to publish a volume of poems. 'If you thought it worth doing,' wrote Rupert Brooke, 'could you see me any time?'[11] Frank agreed to see him. Exactly two months later an agreement for Sidgwick & Jackson to publish 500 copies of *Poems of 1911* was signed by Brooke at his home, the Old Vicarage at Grantchester. The contract was witnessed by a guest, Virginia Stephen, later to be famous as Virginia Woolf.

Two other Old Dragons were in School House at Rugby with Ronnie, and all three were creating a good reputation for the O.P.S. The Skipper was delighted, as he wrote to Ronnie:

> *Dr James wrote to me the other day: 'Your School House trio are* excellent *fellows, good workers, manly, and altogether an excellent element in it, so I am keen to get more.' Give my love to the other two and mind you all three live up to your present character! It is a long time since anything has pleased me so much. Scholarships are* nothing *to it.*[12]

Jack Haldane as Head of School at Eton, 1911

The year 1911 also saw the end of Jack Haldane's time at Eton. In the Summer Term, just as his sister Naomi was taking her leave of the O.P.S., he was in his last year at Eton, where he was now Captain of School (i.e. Head Boy). Despite the difficult early years, Jack had not allowed himself to be pigeon holed academically.

> *I could read Latin, Greek, French and German. I knew enough chemistry to take part in research, enough biology to do unaided research, and I had a fair knowledge of history and contemporary politics.*[13]

To this claim Jack should also have added his considerable knowledge of English and classical literature – he and

Naomi often engaged in a quotations war. His next step was to sit for a scholarship at Oxford and, as the *Isis* Magazine of 1920 was to reveal in a series of 'Isis Idols', plot his own particularly individual path though university life.

> *The story runs that he had intended to take a History Scholarship at New College, but that the Mathematical Scholarship papers were dealt out to him by mistake, so he indolently took a mathematical scholarship instead. He took a first in Mathematical Moderations and then proceeded to take another in Greats. At the same time he managed to publish a paper on the Physical Chemistry of Haemoglobin, and later one on Genetics dealing with his own discoveries with regard to the partial linkages of Mendelian factors in vertebrates.*

* * * * * *

University Life

Robin Laffan

Two other Old Dragons had already been 'Isis Idols' in the summer of 1909. The first was Robin Laffan, President of the Union. He was, the magazine noted, an Oxford man born and bred.

> *'Coming up' was to him no more of an ordeal than being thrown into the briar patch was for Br. Rabbit ...* [having been at] *Mr. Lynam's Academy for young gentlemen, known to us, the Aestivagrians, as 'Dragons'. In this Gegenic environment we may well imagine that he acquired the Spartan traits in his character which have since then been so well developed. Here at any rate he laid the foundations both of his athleticism and of his humaner interests.*

This account goes on to describe Robin's influence up at Oxford.

> *A Boys' Club has trembled at his nod; provincial towns have needed him to goad them into Missionary enthusiasm. As an orator, he is calm, persuasive, imperturbable; his speeches have no lack of humour ... Readers must see him for themselves as he roams the garden quad; must see the Nationalist in his stick and Homberg hat, the dévot in the O.U.C.U. cross on his watch-chain, the Socialist in his pipe, the historian on his brow, the orator in his noble features.*

The second 'Isis Idol' was another Old Dragon of Balliol College, Ronnie Poulton – by this time in the university rugby team. The magazine recorded that he was born in 1889 and drew an amusing portrait.

> *Shortly after this he began to smile; in which he has continued with slight intermission ever since.*

He lives several lives: he has a Science Exhibition, which seems a pity; he has played for England against France, Ireland and Scotland: as he is a member of the O.T.C., we trust he will never be required for his country against Germany.

The piece concludes with the remark that Poulton was 'nearly all things to all men, and they all like it'.

Ronnie Poulton scoring his record-breaking 5th try

Needless to say, there was plenty of O.P.S. support for Ronnie at the 1909 Varsity Match. The Editor of *The Draconian* himself was there to report on the event.

This year's Inter-Varsity match will always be remembered as Poulton's match. After much discussion and a vast amount of 'newspaper' criticism (which means so little and produces so little effect, if 'our special correspondents' would only realise it), Poulton was given his Blue as a wing three-quarter and proceeded to silence his detractors by scoring 5 of the 9 tries in the record score which was piled up against the unhappy Cambridge team …

Most of Poulton's fielding was well done; he kept his position splendidly; his trick of holding the ball with both hands at the full extremity of his reach, his swaying for the feint, his masked pace, and his swerve fascinated everybody, and with it all he was rarely tackled.

Poulton's five tries remains the record number of tries scored in the Varsity Match to this day. A clergyman friend congratulated him, observing, 'You played like an angel, in fact, probably better!'[14]

With Bob Bourne stroking the Oxford boat to victory that year (and indeed for the following three years), Skipper had reason to be pleased with his Old Dragons. When he welcomed many of them back to the O.D. Dinner of June 1910, he was justifiably a proud man. His standards were rigorous, however, and he expected more of his ex-pupils than just rising to the top of their chosen profession or sport.

My dear Old Boys, once again I am very proud to meet you here and to be reminded that I have become the educational father of a great and growing family. To think that my Old Boys are more and more distinguishing themselves in all parts of the world as well as at home, in the realms of literature and art, as rulers of the empire, politicians, lawyers, soldiers, sailors, ranchers, administrators, fills me with a just pride. And still more when I feel that part of their inheritance may be a wide sympathy with poverty, suffering and weakness in whatever

forms they may meet it. I hope and think that in my old days the inclination to climb to the top by thrusting others down is tempered by a willingness to stretch out a strong and unselfish hand 'helping when they see them lame dogs over stiles'.

* * * * * *

Such values were not universal among students of the time. At university Old Dragons encountered many from a much higher stratum of society, and the experience was not always a happy one. Naomi Haldane's family, for instance, had little time for those who came up to university to enjoy themselves, often at others' expense.

> *These were still the days of the Bloods who had, it seems, dominated young University life for a long time, but had only lately come to be resented actively, instead of being accepted as the kind of thing that happened in a class society. The Bullingdon Club and other Blood organisations had been behaving very badly in the early years of the century …*
>
> *They had a class arrogance which was becoming less and less tolerable in a society like Oxford, which was slowly changing into something fairly mobile class-wise. They had broken into the rooms of the intellectuals, destroying books or pictures, knocking the owners about. They had torn up the manuscript – years of work – of a don they did not favour. They were forever lighting bonners in the quads into which they threw things they disapproved of … The College authorities were, by and large, unable or scared to control or discipline the Bloods, many of whom came from aristocratic families with quite a lot of political and social power …*
>
> *There was no sympathy in our house for the Bloods. Aristocrats they might be, but gentry they were not. My father would come back angry at their anti-intellectualism every time the Bullingdon Club went in for one of their antics.*[15]

George Fletcher was one of the few O.P.S. boys of that time to go to Eton, where he became Head of School. He must have known a number of Bullingdon members, but was interestingly remembered as a 'unifier of sets amongst us' by the Master of Balliol.

The Competitive Spirit

Many of this era relied on sport to provide the excitement and challenge in their lives. Talented young sportsmen would not have been short of invitations to represent their university, college or public school, depending on their level of ability. Yet the call of the O.P.S. was still a strong one, particularly for those who had been brought up in Oxford.

Rugby football was not the only sport at which Dragons were excelling. In December 1910 the Old Dragons put out a hockey team to play Oxfordshire; they won by four goals to two, in very poor weather.

Back row (left to right) D. Innes, S. Richter, R. Lucas, C. Hardy (middle row) L. Smith, L. Wallace, C.S.W. Marcon, R.W. Poulton, C.P. Duff (front row) T.O. Thompson, L. Kendall

Lindsay Wallace scored three goals and Lionel Smith one. Joad failed to put in an appearance, and we were soon two goals down, but when Marcon (who did not mean to play because of a bad hand) filled the vacancy in goal, the O.D. side soon asserted its superiority, and gave a good display of hockey despite of a drenching downpour of rain.

(Back row) C.P. Duff, D. Innes
(Front row) J.B. Brooks, C.S.W. Marcon, R.W. Poulton

In April 1911 *The Draconian* noted that there were no fewer than 35 Old Dragon Oxford undergraduates. There were a record five Old Dragons in the Oxford hockey team that year, with Sholto Marcon captaining the side.

Together with Ronnie Poulton, captain of the rugby team, and Bob Bourne being Captain of Boats, the O.P.S. could boast a clean sweep of three of the top jobs in Oxford sport.

* * * * * *

Association football played a comparatively minor role at the O.P.S. However, Alan Haig-Brown, who had gone on to Charterhouse (very much a footballing school), turned out to be good enough to go on to join the London club Tottenham Hotspur as an amateur. He played seven matches for them in what was then the Southern League.

In 1911 the Sergent family, living in France, not only played football, but was also rather good at it. Victor (captain and fullback), Noel (right half) and Dick (inside left) were joined by their Old Dragon friend and brother-in-law Lindsay 'Pug' Wallace (centre half) in playing for Saint-Raphael. The team went on to win the French Championship, with Victor being good enough to play for France five times.

Dick Sergent was lucky to have been available for selection, having been sent to prison for three weeks in Geneva 'for an ordinary "rag" which would have been laughed at at Oxford or Cambridge'. The incident was reported in the press.

> *The trouble goes back to May last, when a crowd of students, of all nationalities, 'vetoed' an objectionable song sung by eight German women in uniform to the march of the Alsace-Lorraine, at the Corso Theatre at Zurich.*
>
> *This song the students thought reflected on the honour of the French nation and people, so they asked for its elimination from the programme.*
>
> *The director of the theatre – a German – refused, and the students showed their annoyance by hissing the turn at the theatre.*
>
> *When this took place, policemen in plain clothes attacked the students, and the latter, thinking that they had to do with roughs, retaliated. The police suffered especially at the hands, it is said, of Mr. Sergent, who has a knowledge of boxing.*
>
> *They were first tried last November, when they were sentenced to various terms of imprisonment and fined, but, backed by their professors, who gave them all good characters, appealed.*
>
> *In their appeal they were very unfortunate, for all the sentences were increased threefold, and the fear exists that in some cases this severity means the ruining of promising careers.*

At least there was no possibility of such an incident ruining Dick's reputation at the O.P.S. Indeed, G.C. Vasssall, as editor, requested an account of his experiences for the next edition. Having successfully knocked out no fewer than five of the policemen who confronted him, a three-month sentence and a 1,000 franc fine made Dick something of a hero. His fine was in fact paid off by subscription from French supporters.

The Draconian later described the event as 'an early example – three years early – of England and France joining hands against German aggression and misappropriation. As in 1914, it seemed to meet with the approval of the British public'.

Taking Stock: The First 35 Years

Throughout his time as headmaster, the Skipper improved the school's facilities considerably. In the 1912 *Draconian Register* he observed with pride that the O.P.S. now at last possessed 'thoroughly adequate buildings'.

School House, 1912 – a new home for the boarders

> *In September 1910, the New Boarding House was ready for occupation. It seems, as it were, to hold out its arms to the sun; the fresh air circulates unhindered through its day rooms, dormitories and corridors. There is a splendid lead-lined plunge bath into which we take 'headers' every morning in the year (even when the ice on its surface has to be broken!). The Dining Room will easily accommodate over 100 people, and the oak floor of it is specially constructed for dancing.*

To pay for these new buildings and necessary equipment, Skipper was helped by his brother Hum, G.C. Vassall, Pug Wallace and another member of staff, Leslie Eastwood. Between them these colleagues contributed £8,000 towards the cost.

It was noted that the boarders in the Summer Term of 1910 now numbered 59 out of a total of 136. This led to concerns about the school becoming more of a boarding school, but Skipper explained to the day parents that they had no reason to complain.

> *It is the existence of the boarders that enables the Day School to be run at comparatively low fees. The Oxford resident graduate is notoriously badly paid and has a considerable position to maintain on a small income. The day school fees at Liverpool and outside Birmingham and London are double mine.*

The School was now clearly doing well financially. This was due to the Skipper's appointment of a Bursar, as finance was not one of his personal strengths.

> *The Skipper was no financier. He dealt with money matters by 'methods' all his own, which gave rise at the time to many surprising rumours, destined to pass into the realm of Legend. Did he in fact make out the boys' accounts on his way north to join* Blue Dragon *with no other data than his own guess at the wealth or otherwise of the parents? And when Bills and Reports all went to the bottom of Oban Harbour, did he really substitute a short note to each parent saying, 'Your boy is doing splendidly. Please pay what you think you owe'? And was any difficulty over Staff salaries dealt with by the simple expedient of borrowing from one master to pay another?*[16]

In 1911 the Skipper had completed a quarter century at the helm of the O.P.S. and over the next couple of years might well have been weighing up the results of his labours. A register of everyone who had attended the school since its opening in 1877 was compiled and favourably reviewed by an Old Dragon, Francis Duckworth. His uncle, the Rev. Robinson Duckworth, had accompanied Charles Dodgson on the boat trip down the Thames in July 1862 with Alice Liddell and her sisters, which inspired Dodgson to write *Alice's Adventures in Wonderland.*

> *The* Draconian Register *enables you to trace the fortunes of some hundreds of men who from this one preparatory school have passed into almost all the public schools …*
>
> *The number of boys who entered from the foundation up to the end of 1894 amounts to about three hundred. I looked among this number for those who had attained to a distinguished position in the career they had taken up. Nor is 'distinguished' too strong. Notice I do not use the phrase 'those who had done particularly well'. And I find that I marked over fifty names.*
>
> *I am glad that among O.D.s are to be found a bicycling half-blue, and the basketball champion of Cascadilla.*

To that could be added 41 Blues and internationals in this first 35 years. There was also an Olympic Silver Medallist in 1912, when Bob Bourne stroked the New College eight into second place for Britain.

* * * * * *

Loyal Old Dragons were proud not only of turning out for their teams, but also of attending regular reunion dinners, reinforcing the ties that bound them to both the O.P.S. and the Skipper.

One such occasion, the O.D. Dinner of 31 May 1913, was a thoroughly enjoyable evening, according to Francis Duckworth's *Draconian* article.

> *The host himself* [Skipper] *was absolutely at the top of his form. I had a glimpse of him just before the dinner, sketchily attired and hurrying off to his tent to change for the photograph. So he's living in a tent! Why does he live in a tent? You wouldn't ask the question if you had ever visited his study. I visited that apartment, and through all the consequent bewilderment and admiration one question persists unanswered – 'Why trouble to have cages?'*

> *Fresh from sweeping the highroads of Oxford like a pirate on his L.M., where multitudes scatter and flee at the sound of his horn, this man who is on intimate terms with the Arctic circle and lives in a tent, and has for a study a grotto where birds pour forth divine oracles ... spoke of handing over the reins.*

A London Midland cycle car of the type purchased by the Skipper

> *However Hugh Sidgwick got up and reassured us by proving that this talk of resigning was all nonsense ...*
>
> *Last time I attended an O.D. Dinner, co-education seemed to permeate the atmosphere. On this occasion there were vague and scarifying allusions to Eugenics.*
>
> *I cannot remember the speeches in their right order. Haldane had pink plaster across the bridge of his nose, but we forgave him that for his wonderful revelation of the use of paper-fasteners as a substitute for shirt studs.*
>
> *Hum's speech fairly sizzled with epigram, paradox and apophthegm. I liked 'We continue to receive our parents in a glorified dustbin' and 'We continue to excuse idleness and loafing on the plea that this is developing individuality', and the climax 'We know that he (Skipper) will be safer on the high sea than on the high road'.*
>
> *One of the staff, as a matter of fact, propounded a very pretty solution of the problem of the L.M. cycle car: 'You see, he forgets he's not at the wheel of the B.D.* [Blue Dragon] *and keeps on thinking he's got to keep steerage way on her'.*

There can be no doubt that Skipper had built up a very successful school. When he took over in 1886, the school numbered some 50 boys; by the end of the Summer Term 1913 it had grown to over 130, with another 22 in the junior section. He had also raised the money to establish the excellent facilities that the school could now boast.

More importantly, he had created a generation of Old Dragons who appreciated that their old preparatory school had been not only successful, but also rather different. They were proud of the school and had not only respect but also a deep affection for their old headmaster, who for many of them had grown into a lifelong friend.

These were halcyon days in which all seemed to prosper and the future was bright. Yet the events of 1914 were to divert these young men from their intended paths and to test their resilience to the full.

The Dragonian
No. 80.
December, 1914.
Leonard Campbell Taylor O.D 1900

Chapter 4
1914: The Clouds Descend

The first half of 1914 saw life at the O.P.S. carrying on very much as normal; even the news of the event said to have triggered the war, the assassination of Archduke Franz Ferdinand of Austria on 28 June, would have made little impact on most in Oxford. It was a lovely summer – just right for cricket matches, and swimming and diving competitions in the river. Life was being enjoyed.

Only a couple of weeks earlier, on 13 June, the usual gathering of Old Dragons for a Boarders *v.* Dayboys cricket match had taken place, followed by the annual dinner. According to the toast list, six speeches were made that evening, including three entitled 'The Past', 'The Present' and 'The Future'. The last was made by Hugh Sidgwick, who recalled with pleasure the quality of conversation at such dinners.

> *On no other dining occasion does one seem to converse on a wider range of subjects – from theology to ragtime: on this steep descent one snatches at stray topics in an attempt to check the fall – eugenics, co-education, light cars and cycle cars, the Russian Ballet.*

There were numerous other contributions too, including some musical items. Francis Duckworth remembered through 'the golden mists of recollection' that 'at one point fourteen enthusiastic Wykehamists rose to their feet and sang a long and joyous chorus in praise of the present subjunctive'.

The Skipper came in for his fair share of both respect and ribbing, the latter in the form of comment on his love of the L.M. cycle car.

> *The firm have ordered to be placed on all their cars a plaquette with the inscription 'similar to the model supplied to C. C. Lynam, Esq.'. Two theories have been advanced in explanation, (a) that they regard this as a testimonial worth many medals won in less strenuous trials, (b) B. W. Watson's theory – that the Skipper is their only customer.*

Of the 65 Old Dragons present that day, 45 were to answer the call to arms; ten of them were never to return.

* * * * * *

Term time it might be, but, true to his belief in finding time for diversions, Skipper decided on a day out to sample the world of Royal Ascot – in his own particular style.

Left: Cover of *The Draconian*, designed by the artist Leonard Campbell Taylor (brother of Brigadier General Stuart 'Fluff' Taylor)

The Skipper defies convention at Ascot, 1914

I must tell you of a great day Mrs Wallace and I had at Ascot on June 17th. We started in the L.M. about eleven, had a ripping drive by Nettlebed and Henley, Wargrave and Wokingham, through lovely woods and by the cool shining river. We got a paltry lunch at Bracknell at a tea-shop, left the car and walked up to the course. We thought we would 'plunge' on paddock tickets, paid a pound each, for paddock enclosure badges, much better than busting the money on bets! Of course I was not dressed up to paddock point. I think there was one other straw hat amongst thousands of toppers: however, nobody took any notice of us.

The last month of the term seems to have progressed perfectly normally and the speeches at the end of term Prizegiving made no mention of national, let alone international, events. There was one ground-breaking piece of news, however. For the first time a girl, Norah Jolliffe, was chosen to be Head Boy, giving the Skipper another opportunity to champion the cause of co-education.

Norah Jolliffe

Why shouldn't boys see something of, and be intimate with, girls at school in the same natural way that they do at home? I feel that in the years to come some of the boys in VIa will look back with pleasure on the remembrance of Norah as their schoolfellow, and she will remember with kindly feelings her time at the O.P.S. I have seen no sign of jealousy of her success, indeed I feel sure that her good influence and good fellowship have made her deservedly popular.

He also took the opportunity to show appreciation for his long-suffering staff.

My staff, male and female … one and all have my heartiest thanks for their hard and loyal work and their very considerable and much tried forbearance towards a Headmaster who most unconscionably interferes with well-established rules, alters dates and arrangements in a horribly whimsical fashion, gives holidays when the staff specially want to work hard with their forms, torments them with the braying of macaws and the pelting of parrots and the odours of Benzol, and generally plays the cat and banjo with all that is seemly and decorous in school institutions.

In response to the headmaster's speech, one of the parents, a Mr Barker, attempted to summarise what it was he thought made the school tick – a version of a tonic wine of the time called Sanatogen.

I am rather tempted to think of it as a Sanatogen establishment, which dispenses, on much more generous terms than most owners of patent medicines, a sort of elixir of boyish life, cunningly compounded and admirably administered. How ordinary Sanatogen *is made I do not know. How this super-Sanatogen is made I can guess. You take three parts Skipper, and two of Cheese*: you add some turtle (Tortoise* will serve your turn, if turtle cannot be procured); you get Wallace* (who loves any sort of exercise) to stir it hard till it Hums*; and then, when it has been sweetened to taste by Higginson* with a dash of music and a spice of art, you serve it piping hot. It is an infallible tonic; and it has this peculiarity that the more you take of it, the better you are.*[1]

As always, such a speech ended with a clear message to the young Dragons as to what was expected of them in the future.

All the same, let us remember that there is nothing here for self-conceit. Much has been given you; but that only means that you will have to give much back … Just because you have been nurtured here so well, and thriven so strongly in body and in mind, the world expects and has the right to receive a great deal from you.

Just what was about to be expected of them, or more especially the generation above them, could not have been easily guessed that day.

* * * * * *

The term ended on Saturday 25 July, after which everyone departed for two months of summer holiday. For Skipper that could only mean one thing – a return to his boat, *Blue Dragon II*. It had wintered in Norway, where he had been sailing the previous year.

His crew consisted of his 26-year-old daughter Kit and her friend Gwen Brooks, a member of his staff, Leslie Eastwood, and two boys who were leaving the O.P.S. that term, Amyas Ross and Arthur Gaitskell (both aged 13).

As the world rushed into war, the log shows that news, if not always accurate, travelled fast.

Monday 3 August
We heard all sorts of horrible rumours about war and mobilising; how much is true, I don't know; but rumour says the Germans have sunk the Russian fleet and invaded France.

Tuesday 4 August
We were immediately boarded by the British Consul, who brought us a telegram – 'English vessels warned not to put into German ports'. Then a gloomy day ended with the awful news that England had declared war against Germany. We do not know what we shall do, and it is too hideous to contemplate …

Wednesday 5 August
It seems that the Germans have invaded Belgium and that England sent an ultimatum last night. Everything seems in chaos. That we should go to war with Germany because the Serbians will not apologise for the murder of the Archduke of Austria appears too idiotic, but the fat seems to be in the fire with a vengeance.[2]

By Tuesday 11 August the crew was heading for home, leaving Skipper alone on his boat. He finally returned on 2 September, his plans of sailing to Bergen being put on hold 'till the war is over and the monstrous German terror [is] a thing of the past'.[3]

Preparing for War

All through the early months of the war, Old Dragons were answering the call to arms. With the next *Draconian* not due until December, events demanded an emergency edition, which was duly printed in November. This issue shows some 225 Old Dragons and staff already in uniform and a further ten in training for Army or Navy service at Sandhurst, Keyham or Osborne.

In the war of words, Frank Sidgwick contributed a poem to the *Saturday Review* and, of course, *The Draconian*. The final verse of *The People's Gift* clearly expressed the expectations for all Old Dragons on the outbreak of war.

Take the lesson, then, young Englishmen, when the war-cloud lowers black,
Let no man shift his burden of gift on to the next man's back;
Answer today what part you will play, when your country gives the sign –
What gift will you bring to your country and King – is your blood water or wine?

Part of the explanation of why people joined up so quickly and in such large numbers lies in their upbringing and training. However privileged their background, however rich their families, they had not been brought up to expect a life of total self-indulgence. From an early age they had been educated in schools, often as boarders, to accept discipline and routine, while also learning about responsibility, duty and leadership. Many of the public schools that were started in the mid-nineteenth century saw it as their role to train up those needed to go out and run the British Empire. Boys needed to be brought up to be robust and to lead.

On his arrival at Clifton College from the O.P.S. in September 1893, Tankred Behrens had received a letter from his father. It clearly expressed a father's ambition for his three sons.

It is a great joy to me to have you and the two small boys, I long to see you all thoro' men, every one of you has his points and I want to see the three brothers well knit together, must stand like a rock, the protectors of their country and family.[4]

Both Oxford and Cambridge had founded Volunteer Corps in the 1860s. Numerous public schools, led by Eton, Harrow, Rugby, Rossall, Felsted and Hurstpierpoint, also formed Corps. The Boer War (1899–1901) added further impetus to such early training.

In 1905 Jack Haldane's uncle, Lord Richard Haldane, had become Secretary of State for War. He immediately set about reforms that were to account for the country's state of readiness in 1914. It was clear that there could be a shortage of trained officers, so Sir Edward Ward had been given the job of studying this and producing a report. Given that Cadet Corps already existed, one obvious answer was to bring them under the control of the War Office to regulate the training and make it more systematic.

By this stage Alan Haig-Brown had forsaken the pets of his O.P.S. childhood for the schoolmaster's life at Lancing College. In 1906 he had taken command of the Lancing Corps, and in that capacity attended a meeting at the War Office at which Sir Edward Ward presented his suggestions for change. Alan clearly felt further discussion unnecessary:

> *The whole matter had been carefully thought out; the actual details were waiting for us – there was really nothing to discuss, but where many schoolmasters are present lack of discussion is improbable, and if there are headmasters amongst them, as in this case, impossible.*[5]

The structure was easily agreed, but the question of how to attract volunteers to join the Corps required more thought. Up to this point, the prospect of ever needing to repel an invasion seemed a very remote possibility. Alan amusingly noted that 'as for examinations, so for war, it is a British custom to prepare overnight or early next morning'.[6]

An Officers' Training Corps was much easier to promote, with the proviso 'that there really was a need for officers, and that every member was to be trained to fit himself as a leader of men and as an important and desired servant of the Empire'.[7] At Lancing, one way or another, Alan Haig-Brown had persuaded every boy to volunteer, making it the only school, he claimed, with 100 per cent participation.

Lord Haldane had not been the only person concerned to prepare the nation for the possibility of war with Germany. In February 1906 Lord Roberts of Kandahar V.C. addressed the boys at Rugby.

> *I want the country to bear in mind that, however little we might wish it, we might one day, through no fault of our own, find ourselves in a serious war with a great nation trained to arms, and if we had not taken the trouble to be prepared we should not only deserve defeat but most assuredly experience it. I want every boy to feel that it is his bounden duty to his country to fit himself for its defence.*[8]

Ronnie Poulton informed his mother in a letter that 'it was quite an interesting occasion'.[9] Against the background of an arms race with Germany, Ronnie did indeed join the Oxford University O.T.C. soon after it was formed in 1908. So did another Old Dragon at Balliol with him, George Fletcher. After he came down from university in 1912, Ronnie joined the territorial battalion of the Royal Berkshire Regiment. He was by then convinced that war with Germany was inevitable.

In the years leading up to the war, a number of articles appeared in *The Draconian* concerning the O.T.C. The December 1908 issue had an article on *A Week with the Public School Brigade*; it introduced Dragons to, and attempted to enthuse them about, the annual camp, encouraging them to join the O.T.C. at their public school in due course. The article did not hide the fact that this would involve hard work, but stressed there was also much to enjoy.

Towards the end of camp there is some ragging, such as letting down other peoples' tents over them, and rotting the guard ... When the last day comes you pack up the tent boards, and get ready for going away. You feel that you have thoroughly enjoyed yourself, and go back home jolly fit, in spite of the fact there is much less skin on your face than when you started. As a camp song says, 'There's not an idle moment, from Reveille to Tattoo'. And it is this which makes the week such a ripping one.

The Painful Call of Duty

Per Mallalieu was only aged six when war was declared in August 1914. As was the case most years, his family had assembled for their summer holiday in the seaside town of Nevin in North Wales. It was a large gathering of the extended family, all of whom had children who either were or were about to be Dragons.

Percy Campbell was up at Hertford College, where his father was Senior Tutor and Bursar. He had been a keen member of the O.T.C. at Clifton College and, like Ronnie Poulton at Rugby, he had been impressed with a speech by Lord Roberts. Percy immediately applied for a commission. On 22 August he received news that he should join the Wiltshire Regiment.

Two days later he was off.

The whole family – Campbells, Browns, Hardmans and Mallalieus – walked to where the bus was waiting ...

Soon the driver cranked up the engine, the bus began to shake and Percy climbed to the unroofed upper deck. As he looked down at his mother, even Lucy and I stopped showing off. There was no cheerful wave, no brave goodbye, only a long look of scarcely contained misery.[10]

There was no enthusiasm for war shown here, only acceptance of the very painful call of duty.

These families were to lose ten sons to the war. The annual gathering of the clans at Nevin was destined never to be repeated.

Autumn Term 1914

Walter Bye

On returning to school in September 1914, the first thing that would have become apparent to the young Dragons was that four of their teachers had gone. Leslie Eastwood had joined the King's Own Royal Lancaster Regiment, Blair Watson the Queen's Own Dorset Yeomanry, Tom Higginson the Shropshire Light Infantry and Walter Bye the U.P.S. Royal Fusiliers. Maud Wilkinson, the school's nurse, had also left to join the 3rd Southern General Hospital in Oxford. Here she was confronted with some very trying cases, chiefly the dreaded tetanus.

Some pupils were missing as well; two boys who had been holidaying in Austria when war broke out had yet to return. In their places were a Belgian refugee 'whose father was a Professor at Louvain' and several American boys who had been travelling on the Continent.

The Skipper was proud to announce the changes in the December issue of *The Draconian.*

There are many Old Boys and Masters who have not yet gone to the front; these have been undergoing strenuous and trying training, and their time will come. While they are still in England we are delighted to see them, and several often come and spend a hard-earned short leave at the old school. Of all the staff, all of military age enlisted or received commissions straight off, taking it for granted that notwithstanding any promulgations of the Board of Education, their first duty was to their country.

Finding good staff to replace those who had joined up must have been difficult for the Skipper. Some he selected found that training Dragons such as the young Francis Wylie was not for them (as Francis recalled many years later):

> *There were men who came on the Staff for a week, for a month, for a term, and we did not treat them well – nor let it be said did all of them treat all of us well: but that was our fault!*[11]

Per Mallalieu also had some less than satisfactory memories of war-time staff.

> *We could have done without some of the wartime variety of staff – the gin-soaked invalided officer, for example, who emerged from his deckchair on the flat roof outside the classroom only to slap faces when a disturbance threatened to attract Hum's attention; or 'Marmalade' Scott, unfit for the trenches, but capable of fighting off the housekeeper if she tried to get at the marmalade pot before he had met his needs.*[12]

Skipper appreciated some of the replacement staff gave cause for concern and, typically, came up with the answer.

> *As it was obvious that my Staff was no place for 'fit' young men, and I did not want unfit ones, I took steps to supply their places as far as possible with ladies.*

The men who remained were busier than ever. G.C. Vassall and Pug Wallace turned out regularly to drill with the Local Volunteers at 7 a.m. and often put in extra drills and marches out. The Skipper allowed the school field to be used by Oxford recruits as a drilling ground. In this, the first term spent at war, both staff and boys were expected by the Skipper to contribute to the war effort. *The Draconian* recorded their industry.

> *The boys have also sent stamps to the Base Hospital, and indeed have made a very large money collection considering their small incomes! The* Blue Dragon *gramophone with*

> *its lovely old records and many new ones has delighted the inmates of Medical Ward V, where it is guarded most jealously from the raids of other wards.*

Hum Lynam was declared 'almoner-in-chief'; he installed and looked after Belgian refugees at the Lodge and elsewhere. Hum also collected and forwarded sweaters, pipes, pencils and writing books, subscribed for by the boys, to various quarters. These included H.M.S. *Colossus*, H.M.S. *St Vincent* and H.M.S. *Russell* – all ships with Old Dragon officers on board.

As with all well-brought-up Dragons, 'thank you letters' were forthcoming.

H.M.S. St Vincent
First Battle Squadron
20 November 1914.

My Dear Dragons,
Pipes very much appreciated – now smoked by His Majesty's Jollies.
Who owned?

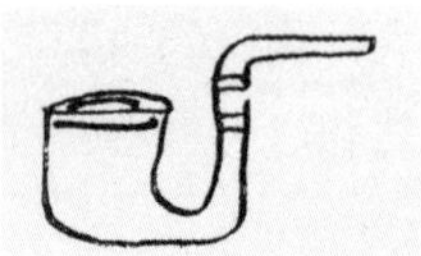

And the other one that might have been made by Krupp?

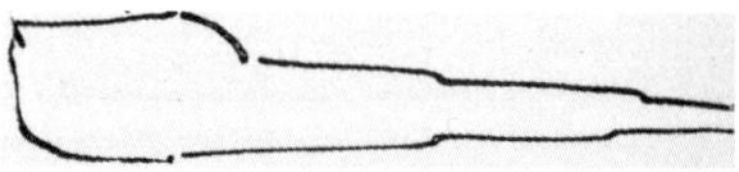

It was a kind thought and entailing some sacrifice I've no doubt – parting with old friends – Censor allows no news.

William Fisher (Captain, R.N.)

H.M.S Russell
21 November 1914

Dear Dragons,
A line to thank you all for sending us that generous supply of briar pipes. The men are no end pleased, and wish me to thank you for your kind thought for them. I only wish I could come and thank you all personally for them! But I shan't be able to do that until they become Pipes of Peace.

Lance Freyberg (Lieutenant Commander R.N.)

* * * * * *

That the Royal Navy would ever see action in a war that was expected to be over by Christmas must have seemed unlikely. Indeed a European war of any sort had been an unthinkable concept for many, including Skipper, who shared this view in the December issue of *The Draconian*.

> *I must freely recant certain views I have held, views held I believe by a great many Englishmen whose ideas of peace and brotherhood have been rudely shattered.*
>
> *I believed that the peoples of the civilised world were too sensible to put their differences to the rude arbitrament of war, that the principles of Christianity, or at all events of moral ethics, were too strongly established to allow it. I was wrong. The enemy has thrown down the glove to challenge civilisation and freedom, and all that is dear to the peace lover, and perforce we had to take it up and to fight our best for civilisation, freedom and peace.*
>
> *And it cannot be said that those connected with the O.P.S. have failed to respond to the call. The lives of some of our best have been given freely; many others have spent untold hours of privation, anxiety, and brave determination; and all are animated by the feeling that no sacrifice is too great for our noble cause.*

Everyone's thoughts were focused on the first 100,000 of the British Expeditionary Force (B.E.F.) that went to rescue Belgium from the German onslaught. It was not long before the Old Dragons involved in this adventure were thinking of the needs of the editor of their school magazine. A stream of letters and articles flowed back to the O.P.S. and *The Draconian*. The December edition featured communications from 17 Old Boys engaged in the war, among them Rupert Lee and Victor Cowley, professional soldiers both and part of what Kaiser Wilhelm had described as a 'contemptible little army'.

Chapter 5
'Over by Christmas'?

War Diaries

Rupert Lee (Lieutenant, Worcestershire Regiment) was one of the first Old Dragons to make it over to France, landing on 15 August. Summer holiday diaries were something of a Dragon tradition, so it may have been natural for him to record the events of the opening months in this way and submit them to the Skipper. Rupert started with a caveat: his narrative, he stated, 'was written in strange postures and places, in varying frames of mind'. He understood the shortcomings of an individual's account, concluding that his journal should be seen as 'merely a conglomeration of statements of happenings as they appeared to me at the moment'.

It was an enormous logistical challenge to get an army armed, provisioned and transported over to France in such a short time, but war plans swung quickly into operation. Rupert and his men left their barracks at Tidworth at 4.45 on the morning of 13 August. This was followed by a long wait at Southampton docks, an event surrounded in secrecy.

Rupert Lee

13 August 1914
The embarkation and departure of over 100,000 men and their attendant stores, horses, guns etc., was, I believe, carried out without the people of Southampton realizing that more than a few train loads had gone.

It was not until midnight on 14 August that he and his battalion finally set sail. From Southampton the boat crossed the Channel and made its way up the River Seine to Rouen.

Directly on arrival at the Quay we started on the work of disembarkation, which was soon accomplished; we got all the men into a long shed within 50 yards of the boat and they started an impromptu concert. Ragtime, speeches, patter and the like, the only instrument a mouth organ; the reason for it was, I think, hunger.

I notice that whenever everything is most miserable, wet and dejected, then Tommy starts to sing.

From left: Gen. Sir Douglas Haig, Maj. Gen. Munro, Lt. Col. A.J.B. Percival with an unidentified companion following the retreat from Mons

From Rouen they moved by train and marches by way of Amiens and St Quentin to Mons, destined to be the location of the first British engagement of the war.

Following his entry for 19 August, writing became impossible for Rupert. He put his diary in his kit bag (which was evacuated) and did not see it again until 24 September. The British Expeditionary Force was bound up in a fight for survival. On taking up their position near Mons, they found that the French on their flanks were being forced to retreat. They had no choice but to do likewise to avoid being surrounded. Although there were many times when the positions and numbers of enemy troops were far from clear, the British managed a successful 'fire and retire' withdrawal.

It was not until late September that Rupert had some time to bring the diary up to date. He started with the Battle of Mons (23 August).

> *I stood to arms at 4 a.m. of the morning of 23rd August … I assisted T's platoon; my trench was an improved railway cutting, bullet proof, bomb proof shelters, stores, ammunition, water supply etc etc., capable of all-round defence and easy communication under cover with main road in rear of position. It had a fairly good field of fire.*

The land in front of them was then cleared of as much cover as possible and a trench, deep enough for their horses to stand in, was dug. Rupert noted with relief that 'ranges were taken and before dusk everything was ready'. A tense night followed, and it was not until dawn that the silence was broken by an artillery duel.

> *My trench was apparently unseen, as few shells came near us and only occasional rifle bullets. The South Lancs., about 300 yards to our left, however, had a jolly time …*
>
> *We sat watching the fight for some time; apparently some German observation party had got up on top of one of the slag heaps which was a peak; when our gunners had finished it was a plateau. I do not know what happened to the observation party during the transition.*

Rupert and his men remained in their trench until midday, when they were ordered to retire.

> *Well, we retired over the sky-line under fire, and down the next hollow we all walked – slowly for morale – and kept quite a decent line. There were no serious casualties and no disorder in my platoon.*

Expecting that the retirement would just be over the first ridge, he was surprised to get instructions to withdraw further. However, it soon became apparent that this was a general withdrawal.

Nearby was another O.D. diarist, Victor Cowley (Lieutenant, Royal Irish Rifles). On the night of 22/23 August, he and his men were sleeping comfortably in billets behind Rupert Lee's position. Roused at 1.30 a.m., they marched towards the village of Bavay, where they eventually dug in. Before the men had dug more than one foot, the first shell burst over them.

Victor Cowley

The ground was soft and the earth flew as we burrowed like rabbits to get cover. It was the first time we had been under fire and we were all anxious to know what it felt like. The relief was wonderful when we found that though the air seemed thick with shells, we were still alive. The men began jeering at the shooting and singing 'It's a Long Way to Tipperary'; however they were quietened down a little when two shells burst in the trench, one in the parapet and the other knocking the gun back into the trench and nearly taking off the head of No.1, who was working it.

For the rest of the day they were under incessant bombardment. Out of Victor's section of eight men, one was killed and another wounded.

When the German infantry eventually attacked, however, 'they were met by a fire which cannot have left many unhit'. Much to Victor's relief, the order to retire came around midnight. The French on their right flank had already retired and, given that the Germans had started a powerful enveloping movement round Victor's left flank, they were in severe danger of being surrounded.

We had to march night and day fighting a series of rear-guard actions the whole time, but the weight of the pursuit was relieved by the cavalry.

The men suffered terribly from sore feet and want of sleep; so much so that after a temporary halt two miles outside Le Cateau it was found impossible to wake some of the men when the regiment moved on again.

Between 23 and 29 August they marched 140 miles (225 km) and fought two big battles (Mons and Le Cateau). Lack of food and sleep made it a perfect nightmare. Victor felt the worst aspect was marching at night, as it was impossible to keep awake; he used to arrange with someone to lead him while he went to sleep, and then in turn led them. It was, he said, 'no use riding my horse, as when I went to sleep I used to fall off, which woke me up too suddenly'.

Food had to be grabbed whenever the opportunity arose.

At every place one halted, excursions were made for eggs, bread and chickens, but one never knew if you would have time to cook them. I became an excellent cook, my forte being 'aeroplane duck'. The recipe for this was after having caught, killed and plucked your duck, to truss it with sticks like a man on the rack, then hang it from a tripod over a wood fire, turning it over when the underneath was cooked. The basting was done by filling its inside with bacon fat which melted and oozed through, giving it a delicious flavour.

The retreat from Mons finally came to an end some 200 miles (322 km) later on the River Marne, with the British then supporting a French counterattack on the Germans. This finally ensured the failure of the Germans' plan to envelop the Allied forces. With a gap opening up in their line, the German troops were themselves forced to retreat to the line of the River Aisne, where they dug in and regrouped. The Battle of the Marne (6–10 September) was followed by an Allied advance and a further battle at the Aisne (12–15 September). Victor Cowley saw action in both. On 5 September Victor found himself near Crécy, a site famous for a British victory over the French in the Hundred Years' War. As it transpired, this was where his retreat ended and the British and French, now allies, turned on their enemy.

> *From then onwards began our advance on their heels, capturing prisoners and transport every day. Plenty of fighting, especially crossing the Marne, but we were advancing, so what did it matter to us? …*
>
> *It was here we made a big haul of prisoners, all of whom were only too glad to be captured. On being questioned, they said they had been marched off their legs and been given no food. They had certainly had enough drink, as one was able to trace where they had been the night before by the hundreds of bottles they left empty. The first remark one of them made on being captured was 'Thank God, at last I am amongst friends'.*

It turned out that this Anglophile had been a waiter at the Criterion in Piccadilly before the war. When he joined up, he soon became 'fed up with it' and was delighted when he got the opportunity of being made a prisoner.

By 13 September Victor Cowley had arrived at Braisne, only to find that the Germans had destroyed all the bridges. After several unsuccessful attempts, the Sappers rectified the situation.

> *During the night they put the pontoons in the river and some planks across on the debris of the railway bridge, over which we started to cross in single file. Only a few had got over when they opened a terrific fire on us which literally churned up the water all around us, and we were lucky in not having many hit. After crossing the river we had to cover 400 yards of open* [ground] *which was ploughed up by shells, there being a regular canopy of them overhead; a fragment of one of them got me on the arm but did no more damage than cut it a little.*

This required a visit to a dressing station, but Victor soon returned to his men, only to find that two fellow officers had been killed and seven men wounded in his brief absence.

> *The Germans were entrenched 500 yards away and a battery of their artillery 1,200 yards. They kept up an incessant bombardment all day and it was a perfect inferno. Their 'John Willies' used to sing overhead, followed by the most awful explosion which very seldom did much damage except churning up the ground. However, they affected the men's nerves a little, which was a good thing as they had got rather callous about other shells, and it made them keep under cover more.*

The conditions were appalling. Incessant rain caused a quagmire and, as no fires were permitted at night that might give away their positions, there was no hot food, just bully beef and biscuits. The troops were all on 'short rations'. Extraordinarily, that did not stop the postman delivering some cheer.

> *The postman managed to get up to us one day, which made us forget all the attendant discomforts of shells and rain. One's letters were very precious possessions, as they whiled away many a weary hour in the trenches.*

However, this was no time for relaxation and the reading of letters that allowed the soldiers to think of the life back home. There was a full-scale battle going on around them.

The worst day was the 19th September, as they had the range to an inch and we cringed in our trenches while the shells shrieked and burst around us, in the parapet, knocking down trees in the wood just behind us, trying to frighten us into submission, but so well had we entrenched ourselves that very few got hit. Unfortunately the Colonel and Adjutant were both very badly hit, but that was about all. They kept it up from dawn till about 6.30, when hordes of infantry were launched at us. We were just the reverse side of a slope so could not fire at them till they got within about 50 yards of us. I worked one of my machine-guns and they went down like corn cut by a reaper. I got through 1,200 rounds before a bullet picked me off through the neck, a most horrid sensation!

This was what the soldiers referred to as a 'Blighty one'– a wound sufficiently serious to have to be returned to 'dear old Blighty', England. The journey was not a comfortable one for Victor, who spent three days in a cattle truck getting to Saint-Nazaire, every jolt causing pain. In comparison, the journey across the Channel on a Union Castle liner seemed like luxury. The whole episode left him somewhat confused as to his feelings about what he had experienced:

It was hard to believe that one had been one of the actors in the world's greatest tragedy, and the whole experience seems like one gigantic nightmare.

Whatever the result may be, what success can recompense one for the loss of those good friends and comrades who fell never to rise again?

A Surgeon's View

One Old Dragon to cross over to Belgium at this time was not in fact a professional soldier but a surgeon: Henry Souttar. In September 1914 he was appointed Surgeon-in-Chief at a Belgian field hospital in Antwerp. Here he had to deal with casualties of war for the first time.

Unfortunately his stay there was cut short when the Germans turned on the city and laid siege to it at the end of September 1914. The order to evacuate came shortly afterwards. Henry saw his patients disappear on tramcars, ordinary trams and some specially equipped 'stretcher-cars'. He then heard that British Marines were coming to the rescue. 'That was good enough for us,' he wrote, rather optimistically. The patients were returned to their beds, 'and a more jubilant set of patients I have never seen'.[1]

His confidence was misplaced, however. On 6 October the Germans gave notice that they were going to bombard the city. The Belgian government left and general evacuation took place the following day. Henry's patients were evacuated again, this time by bus. On 10 October Antwerp surrendered, before the Marines could get to them.

They reached Ghent in a state of exhaustion, with Henry having 'slept a sort of nightmare sleep on the top step of a bus which boldly announced its destination as Hendon'.[2] From there he travelled to Ostend, before returning to London.

A week later Henry was setting up another field hospital in Furnes, a town 15 miles (24 km) east of Dunkirk. It was here that Marie Curie, Nobel Prize winner and the discoverer of both radium and polonium, visited him, accompanied by her daughter.

> *She brought her large X-ray equipment to Furnes for work amongst the wounded, and we persuaded her to stay for a week. One of our storerooms was rapidly fitted up as an impromptu radiographic department, the windows painted over and covered with thick paper, a stove introduced and a dark-room contrived with the aid of a cupboard and two curtains. Electric current was obtained from a dynamo bolted on to the step of a twenty-horse-power car, and driven by a belt from the flywheel of the engine. The car stood in the courtyard and snorted away, whilst we worked in the storeroom alongside …*
>
> *Madame Curie was an indefatigable worker, and in a very short time had taken radiographs of all the cases which we could place at her disposal …*
>
> *Mademoiselle Curie developed the plates, and between them they produced photographs of the greatest utility to us.*[3]

Marie Curie was determined to bring X-ray facilities to as many hospitals as possible. At her own expense she converted a number of vans (nicknamed 'Petites Curies') and trained radiographers to operate them.

As a result of her work it was possible to see more of the shrapnel and bullets that needed removal in the operating theatre. Prior to this, it was often necessary to open up a patient a number of times if post-operative infections revealed the existence of further foreign bodies. Developments such as these were to save many a life in the war years.

From a War of Movement to Trench Warfare

With the failure of the Allies to break through on the Aisne, there followed a period of about a month during which the Allies and the Germans tried to outflank each other in what was referred to as a race for the sea. Following this, the trench warfare for which the First World War is famous emerged.

Another Old Dragon involved in these early stages was Roderick Haigh (Lieutenant, Royal West Surrey Regiment), the elder son of a Fellow and Tutor of Corpus Christi College, Oxford. He had won an Exhibition to Winchester from the O.P.S. before going up to his father's college. He took up his commission with the Royal West Surreys in 1911. War was what Roderick was trained for, and he displayed all the fervour and enthusiasm associated with the opening months.

Roderick Haigh

1 October 1914

I am extremely fit, and thoroughly enjoying myself. We are all inspired with the justice of our cause, and by the fact that we are fighting for the cause of honour and liberty throughout the world. The question at stake is whether liberty and justice or military despotism and tyranny are to prevail. It is a great privilege to fight in such a struggle. I look forward to seeing you all again one day in England. But if I do not return, remember that it is the highest honour to which a man can attain – an honour which is open to officers and men alike, a higher honour than all the honour that can be showered on those who survive – to die for one's country.

These extracts were sent to the O.P.S. by Roderick's sister. He had written to her (in pencil) on sheets taken from his Field Message Book.

St Crispin's Day (25 October 1914)

This has been no St Crispin, but a quiet, peaceful Sunday in Reserve after a week's very heavy fighting. On Tuesday last I was wounded by a shrapnel bullet in my thumb. These bullets are about ⅓ to ½ inch in diameter. The bullet was ¾ covered. I at once bit the bullet out, and Capt. Weeding put on my 'First Field Dressing'. It is a very slight wound indeed, and is healing up well. I am remaining with my unit, and can even write orders, although, as it is my right hand, I cannot write as fast as usual.

I cannot tell you how much I enjoy it all. There is something so noble and something so grand about the whole show, which places it on a far higher plane than any other scene in which one has acted in this life.

* * * * * *

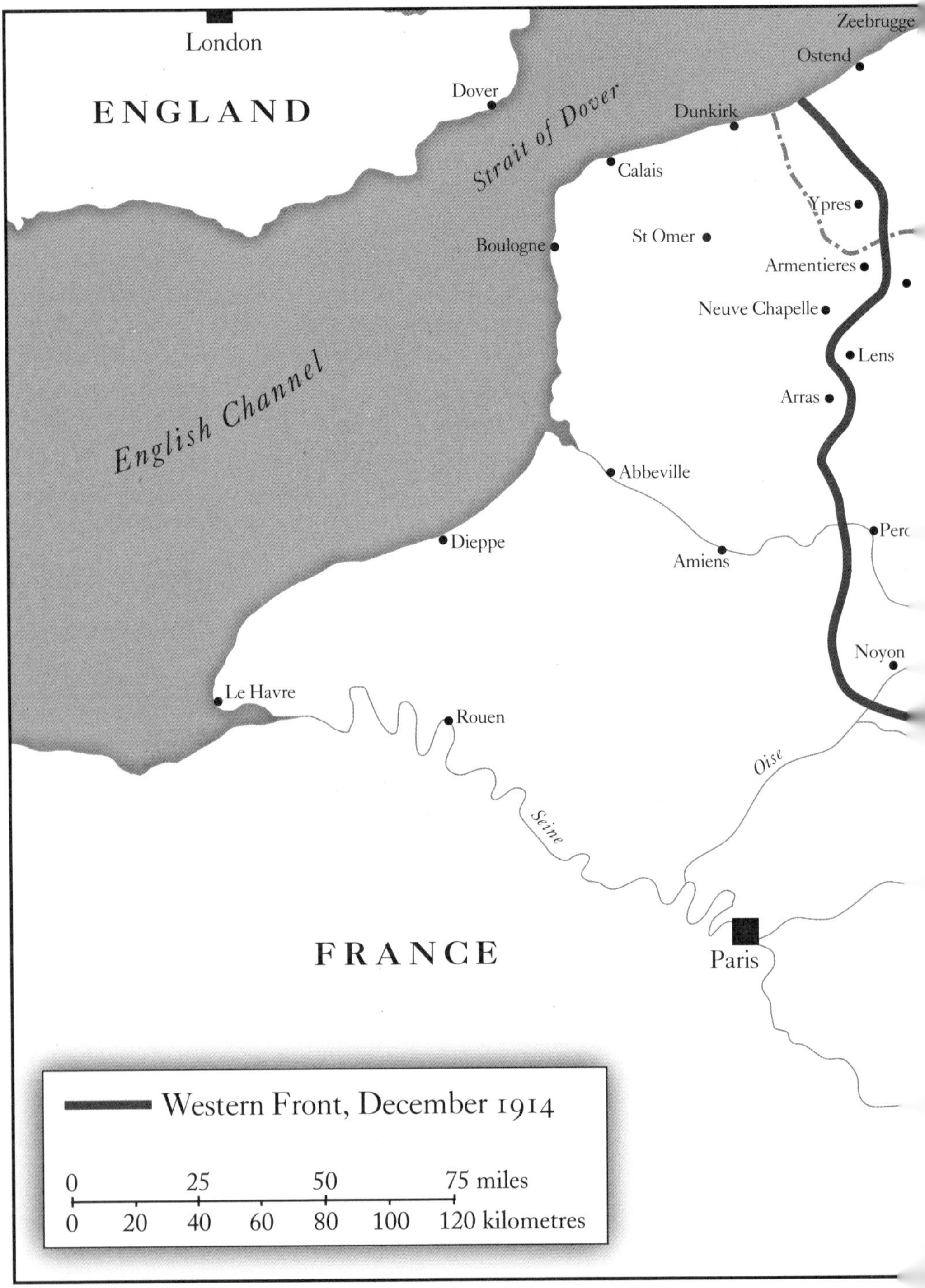
London
ENGLAND
Dover
Strait of Dover
Zeebrugge
Ostend
Dunkirk
Calais
Ypres
St Omer
Boulogne
Armentieres
Neuve Chapelle
Lens
Arras
English Channel
Abbeville
Dieppe
Amiens
Noyon
Le Havre
Rouen
Oise
Seine
FRANCE
Paris
Western Front, December 1914
0 25 50 75 miles
0 20 40 60 80 100 120 kilometres

WESTERN FRONT, 1914
Antwerp
ent
Brussels
BELGIUM
HOLLAND
Cologne
Aix-la-Chapelle
Liége
Rhine
Meuse
Mons
GERMANY
Cateau
LUXEMBOURG
Moselle
Luxembourg
N
Craonne
Aisne
Reims
Verdun
Metz
Marne
St Mihiel
Nancy
Epinal

As months passed, other Old Dragons, who were not regular soldiers, began to join the forces in France. George and Regie Fletcher were among the first of this category. George had been joint Head Boy at the O.P.S. with Robin Laffan and in 1900 George and Robin had the distinction of becoming the first Dragons to win scholarships to Eton. The two remained great friends at the O.P.S., Eton and at Balliol, Oxford. George went on to become a schoolmaster, first at Shrewsbury, before moving back to Eton in 1913.

While his brother Regie joined the Royal Field Artillery in 1914, George joined the Intelligence Corps. With two other masters at Eton who spoke German, he was quickly signed up by the War Office and sent over to France. He went through the retreat from Mons and the first battle of the Marne, never enjoying it as he was not involved in the fighting. At the invitation of its Colonel, he was delighted to transfer into the 2nd Battalion Royal Welch Fusiliers during the Battle of the Aisne.

Shortly afterwards he found himself involved in the first of three battles that were to be fought at Ypres. The fighting started on 18 October 1914 and continued through until 22 November amidst mud and exhaustion on both sides. George soon became aware of the unpleasantness of war and high rate of casualties.

George Fletcher

> *2 November 1914*
> *Imagine the conditions: trench just wide enough for two men to squeeze by: parapet just high enough to fire over comfortably, and so necessitates continual crouching while walking along. Perfect quagmire whenever rain falls, as it did in torrents for several hours one or two nights, drenching wet clothes, of course, and covering you with a perfect plaster layer of yellow mud, especially about the hands. Squashed frogs underfoot, and all around stinks.*

The carcases of cows and sheep were deemed the main cause of the stink of which George complained. He believed that the cows' deaths were part of a cunning plan.

> *They came browsing within thirty yards of us, and the Germans fired at them on purpose, as I believe, to leave them there and stink us out.*

But it was the bodies of the fallen men – in some cases right in front of their entrenched position – that were the biggest problem, having been there many days. The soldiers could do nothing about them.

> *Of course, whenever we attempt to remove them they fire on the parties, even those bearing the Red Cross, so I believe it is also part of their object to stink us out with the dead bodies of their own brothers and comrades.*

There were attacks every night, but there was one particularly big one that George Fletcher describes in detail.

> *There began on this occasion, soon after dark, a terrible musketry outburst on our right. It rolled along, and soon the enemy began firing from in front of us. There was a*

continual rattle of pellets on our parapet, and on looking out, or rather, bobbing the head up for a moment, one could see the flashes from their rifles ...

At about 2 a.m., the fire slackened, and there were rustlings in the turnips ahead, and callings, and rallyings among the Deutschers. 'The rally for the charge,' said I to myself. And it was ... Then a pause again, and suddenly, 'Alle Fertig! Vorwarrts! – Los!!' and they came on. They got as far as the open ground and near our wire, thirty yards away, and then fell face-forward on the ground with heads to the enemy like the good men they are. Of course, it is a terrible thing to attack a strong entrenchment full of thoroughly armed defenders, and they never got nearer than thirty yards.

... Well, this attack waned again at dawn, and 'in the morning they were all dead corpses', like Sennacherib. We saw 200 in front of our Company. Add to those the number of dead in the turnips which we did not see, perhaps 200 more = 400. Add to these the number of wounded which must have been removed (six wounded to one dead) = 2,400 + 400 dead = nearly 3,000 out of action in front of our Company, if such calculations are worth anything.

Captain J.C. Dunn, the Medical Officer of Royal Welch Fusiliers, described another of George's exploits, in which he put his German to effective use.

He was patrolling a decent way along a willow-lined ditch, up which one of our machine-guns fired, when he saw an attack coming. He shouted an order in German to the attackers to halt, and make their way by the line of the ditch. Having seen that they were doing so, he hurried back and got our machine-gunners and the riflemen near them to open fire, with what good effect the morning showed.[4]

In the course of a battle, it was not always possible to help the wounded who lay out in no man's land, between the opposing trenches. They would have to await the cover of darkness. Sometimes British soldiers risked their lives to help the German wounded – as George did.

We were fortunate in being able to rescue one wretched man. He was one of the advanced party in the charge, and had seven bullets in him. He stopped for a day in front of us shouting, but we were getting such a peppering from snipers all that day that we were not allowed to fetch him. At night I got two volunteers to come and fetch him, and just as we were getting out such a hail of bullets came that we nipped back. I kept up a conversation (shouted) with him next day – he told me the Germans had been practically up to him in the night, but had refused to help him. I told him to hang on till night, and we would try and rescue him again. So at dusk I got two volunteers again, and we pulled him in successfully, and doctors say he will live in spite of his seven wounds. Funny thing, war.

Roll of Honour

The Old Dragons all pulled though the opening weeks of the war and only one, Robert Pringle, was killed in September. But by the end of the October, with the Battle of Ypres in full swing, the school's luck changed dramatically; 31 October, sometimes referred to as Ypres Day, was to prove particularly dark. Just as it seemed the British line had been broken, Rupert Lee's Worcestershire Regiment counterattacked and

Reginald Fletcher (2nd Lieutenant, Royal Field Artillery)

retook the nearby village of Gheluvelt, saving the day. It was a pivotal moment in the battle, but one that cost the lives of two Old Dragons. One of them was George Fletcher's brother, Regie. Like George, Regie had won a scholarship to Eton (in 1905) and had gone on to Balliol College, Oxford. He rowed in the 1914 Boat Race for Oxford. Skipper recalled his strong character.

> [Regie] *loved to sleep in the open air, and would sleep quite comfortably under several degrees of frost. As in face and colouring, so in his fierce independence of character, he seemed like some old Norse Rover; and it was this same independence that made one of his schoolmasters compare him to Achilles ...*
>
> *Extraordinarily well-read as he was for a man of twenty-two, in the best modern literature, his highest delight was in Greek poetry; he knew enormous stretches of Homer and Aeschylus by heart, and would chant them, to the amazement of his crew, in the Balliol barge.*

Regie was second-in-command of the artillery section of the Oxford University O.T.C. (1913–14) and obtained his commission in the R.F.A. on the day war was declared. He sailed for France on 20 August, and so only saw just over two months' service before he was hit by shellfire as he was dashing for cover. Skipper later found consolation in the fact that his service had been so brief.

> *Regie was spared all the extremity of horror endured by so many in later months and years of the war; he saw only the glory and the glamour of it.*

* * * * * *

The second of the deaths of 31 October was that of Arthur Percival, son of the late Bishop of Hereford.

Arthur Percival (Lieutenant Colonel, Northumberland Fusiliers)

Arthur Percival had arrived at the O.P.S. in 1879, only two years after the school was started. Skipper remembered him as a determined boy.

> *A resolute and sturdy little fellow, who went his own way regardless of what others might think of him, not afraid to stand up to anyone who tried to bully him, however big his opponent.*

Arthur was present at the Battle of Omdurman in 1898. He also fought in the Boer War and in 1901 became the first Old Dragon to win a D.S.O. In the First World War he served as General Staff Officer to Major General Munro (2nd Division of the First Army Corps). The *Church Times* reported that 'on the day on which he met his death it had been decided to recommend him for the command of a brigade with the rank of Brigadier General'.

Arthur and Major General Munro, together with a number of other staff officers, were conferring with the Divisional Commander, Major General Lomax, when a shell hit their office in the Hooge Château. Munro was only concussed, but Arthur and six others were killed outright. Lomax died of his wounds a few months later.

* * * * * *

A third O.P.S. death occurred on the fateful day of 31 October. Alan Leggett was killed near Armentières, to the south of Ypres, where his regiment had been engaged in action. His trench received a direct hit from a shell. A fellow officer and friend wrote that 'His death, I trust, was almost painless, for he was asleep when he was hit, and he became unconscious almost immediately'.

Alan Leggett (2nd Lieutenant, North Staffordshire Regiment)

The day before he died, Alan had written a postcard to his family in Kent.

> *I am at present in some trenches. I have been here for over 24 hours now, and expect to stay for four or five days before being relieved. We live like rabbits, keeping out of sight and under cover. The German shells have been peppering us a good deal and we get smothered with earth and get buried now and again; however, thank God, I am still fit and sound, the ground regularly trembles when it is struck. It rained a bit last night, so we had an unpleasant time of it. One's feet get chilled to the bone, however, with all you sent me, I am warm enough otherwise. It will be a mercy when this is over – it is awful. Well no more now, keep cheery, and don't be anxious. Very best of love.*

Alan's parents arranged for his body to be repatriated and he was buried in St Martin's churchyard, Cheriton, Kent, near his home. In March 1915 such repatriations were banned, for sanitary reasons and the increasing numbers involved. The last was that of the grandson of William Gladstone, by special permission of George V. It took place in April 1915.

Alan Leggett's funeral procession

* * * * * *

Roderick Haigh (Lieutenant, Queen's Royal West Surrey Regiment)

Within a week of these three deaths, Roderick Haigh's crusade had also come to an end. He was in the last charge of the 22nd Battalion of the Queen's Royal West Surrey Regiment at Klein Zillebeke (afterwards called Hill 60) near Ypres on the night of 5/6 November 1914. The Brigade, only 700 strong, attacked and carried the German trenches, capturing three machine guns.

A private in his regiment wrote to describe the attack in which Roderick was killed. They came under rapid fire almost as soon as they left their trench. Nonetheless, 'through a terrible hail of bullets' they managed to take two enemy trenches before attempting a third one, which turned out to be a running stream.

> *The Adjutant* [Roderick Haigh] *with myself and 14 others got into this ditch only to find that the Germans were only 10 to 15 yards away, strongly entrenched. We were firing point-blank range at each other, and all the time the Adjutant was standing up in the trench, head and shoulders showing. I actually stopped firing to look at him and admire him. He was using his revolver with great effect, and kept saying to encourage us, 'That's another one I hit'.*
>
> *We kept firing for half-an-hour afterwards; then the brave Adjutant was shot through the temple. He died a noble death.*

This unnamed private, finding himself the only one of the 15-man platoon still alive, beat a hasty retreat. He was a lucky man – he subsequently discovered three bullets in his pack, close to his head.

Christmas 1914

After the end of the Battle of Ypres on 22 November skirmishing continued. The two sides jockeyed for the best positions, from which the British hoped to launch another offensive in early 1915 – by which time new and fresher troops would have completed their training and be in the line. Greville Drew (Captain, Royal Engineers) described this period from his dug-out:

Greville Drew

30 November 1914
Here I am just behind the firing-line, with plenty of shelter, plenty of charcoal fire, and plenty of food. Also, incidentally, plenty of bullets flying about, but fortunately not many shells except our own. Our guns do much more firing than those of the Germans, and we seem to have many more of them. This is my fourth day in the trenches.

2 December 1914
The novelty of this job soon wears off. I got very tired a night or two back, and also lost one of my best men, shot on the road by a sniper, poor chap. It made me feel 'fed-up' and nervy, but a good sleep put things right. I have seen Jack Smyth once or twice; he is a little way along to my right.

A couple of days later Greville wrote to report on a rain-free week and comparative luxury.

All our troops are fed absolutely tip-top. We get bacon, fresh or tinned meat, jam, cheese, tea, sugar, every day, with butter and tobacco and matches occasionally. Of course, we buy our own butter, of which there is any amount about. In fact, one of the things that strikes one is how the civil population is staying right up near the firing-line. It seems foolish in a way, as the number of spies and snipers is prodigious.

There was still some business to be transacted, however, in a comparatively quiet period in operational terms. On this occasion the British managed to catch the Germans napping.

During an attack on a German sap-head we lost one officer killed, one wounded, and six men killed and wounded, but we accounted for over forty Germans, who were stuck through with bayonets whilst fast asleep in their covey-holes!

By all appearances we are just sitting tight in our trenches until we get all our new troops trained and ready.

Greville's interpretation was indeed correct, as the volunteers who answered Kitchener's famous call would not be ready for the fray until the following summer. In the meantime there were still many skirmishes, as he reported in a letter on Christmas Eve.

24 December 1914
They tried hard to get into us with their trench mortar. It throws a 10 lb shell about 400 yards. Luckily one can see the thing coming, so it gives you time to get under cover, which I can assure you we did. There was one poor wretched fellow lying wounded between the two sap-heads. One of these beastly mortar bombs dropped right on him and afterwards there was absolutely no sign or trace of him left. He just disappeared …

We had another officer casualty: he was shot along the head and was quite all right, but apparently it bruised the brain and he has to go home and rest. That makes our casualties in officers up to 200% which, I believe is almost unique, five killed and three wounded in a company of four officers!

Casualties among officers – often too easily identified at the head of their troops – were alarmingly high, and they often adopted a rather care-free attitude to the danger. Despite this, the death of a friend or even acquaintance was a cause of considerable personal grief, as Greville revealed.

Everyone takes up a cheery attitude, 'For tomorrow we die' sort of thing – and very often it is true. I was very upset the other day as I met the body of a Captain coming along a narrow communication trench. I had been 36 hours in the same carriage with him coming up from Rouen and he was a topper.

* * * * * *

Another Old Dragon who had sailed with Skipper on *Blue Dragon* was Treffry Thompson. On these voyages Skipper had insisted on a log being kept, and Treffry, now a Captain in the Royal Army Medical Corps, determined to keep a similar log of his time at war. Having been a casualty house surgeon at the Radcliffe Infirmary in Oxford, he joined the R.A.M.C. in 1914 and was attached to the headquarters of XV Brigade with the Royal Horse Artillery. For Treffry, the first year of the war ended on a very relaxed note.

Treffry Thompson

30 November 1914

Resting ... A typical day is as follows. I wake lazily at 7.30 when my servant brings me coffee and hot water. Down and walk sedately up to Mess for comfortable breakfast. Smoke a pipe and look at papers. Start off at 9.15 on horseback to do morning rounds. Trot along canal through woods for 1½ miles. Woods very pleasant and many pheasants about. See the sick of C Battery, then go on to K down the road. Chat with officers and then go off for a short gallop across country to Ammunition Column ...

Trot back to lunch. After lunch either the General or some of the Staff come and we go off to the woods with two borrowed 12-bores. We then spend the afternoon waking up pheasants in the more open parts of the woods and get, say, six brace. Back to a cosy tea and much chatting. Change, read papers, and write letters. At 7.30 an excellent dinner of pheasant, venison etc. Pipes and more reading and off to bed at 10. And this is War!

* * * * * *

As famous as the expectation that this was to be a war that would be 'over by Christmas' is the unofficial truce that reigned on certain parts of the Western Front on Christmas Day 1914. The Royal Welch Fusiliers were involved in this unscripted drama and one of their subalterns was a certain Lieutenant E.L. 'Fuzz' Francis. He may have had no knowledge of the O.P.S. at this stage, but he was destined to join

Skipper's staff and spend nearly 30 years at the school after the war. He later recalled the Christmas festivities with amusement.

> *My own platoon Sergeant was a very cheerful reservist in his mid-thirties and well earned his nickname of 'Chirpy'. He added a good deal to the informal Christmas party by going out to meet the Germans wearing a large skirt which he had found in a deserted farmhouse; this led to some earthy Teutonic byplay and caused plenty of laughs.*[5]

It was, perhaps, not surprising that there were some Germans who tried to take advantage of the situation. The Lieutenant continued to keep a watchful eye – and was right to do so.

> *Both sides seemed to be imbued with the Christmas Spirit until I noticed a German officer who was walking up and down between the trenches and gradually getting nearer to ours. I pointed this out to my friend and fellow subaltern, Frank Strawson, and we started to walk parallel with the German officer. We rode him off in true polo style and he returned disgruntled to his own trenches.*[6]

George Fletcher, also with the Welch Fusiliers, was particularly keen for Christmas Day fraternisation with the enemy, envisaging a 'beer and sausage evening' in no man's land. George kept up regular contact with the Germans in the trenches opposite his position, although his company commander was not impressed. On the other hand, the Germans were; they rolled two large barrels of beer over towards the British lines. Out came soldiers from both sides and various goods such as food and cigarettes were exchanged. Unfortunately, the company commander continued to be a party pooper; George was ordered to get the men back to their respective trenches.

Old Dragons Remembered

Each term, from December 1914 through to the end of the war, *The Draconian* recorded the deaths of all Old Dragons under the heading of 'Our Sacrifice'. After the war the Skipper personally assembled a Memorial Book recording all the Dragons who died. In this poignant testimony he often commented on the men's characters, as well as detailing their school and military careers.

It was not until late September that news of the first Old Dragon to die would have reached Oxford. Robert Pringle (Lieutenant, Queen's Royal West Surrey Regiment) had been in the army since 1907 and his death would certainly have been a shock to the school – but to lose Regie Fletcher within six weeks of his arriving in France and then Roderick Haigh a week later were still heavier blows. Skipper recalled of Roderick that 'he was at every Old Boys' dinner, and constantly visited us when at home'. Roderick left £500 to the O.P.S., of which £200 was immediately spent on making a rifle range at the bottom of the playing field, on the banks of the River Cherwell. It was also decided to fund an annual shooting competition for the Roderick Haigh Cup. Skipper determined too that some of the legacy should be spent on 'educating the son of a brother officer who was also killed'.

Roderick Haigh's will revealed a man of some means – and notable generosity. He left £6,701 net, of which £500 was left to the officer commanding 2nd Battalion, Royal West Surrey Regiment, 'for … the purchase of instruments, music etc., for the drum and fife band, or for any other purpose he may determine'. Furthermore, there were bequests of between £10 and £50 to warrant officers, non-commissioned officers and men of his regiment 'as a token of gratitude'. If they were no longer alive, then it was stipulated that the money should go to their next-of-kin.

* * * * * *

As the first term at war came to an end, and with it the realisation that the war was not going to be a short one, the Skipper offered some headmasterly advice for his Dragons as they departed for Christmas.

> Keep fit – *don't stop in bed late and don't go to bed late. Take a cold bath every morning, don't frowse over the fire, take a good walk or have a game out of doors every day.*
>
> Be kind and amiable to those at home, including servants. *Remember the description of the boy (not a Dragon) who whines 'I don't know what to do!', who bags the best chairs, who won't play with younger brothers and sisters, who is rude and says 'I shan't', 'I don't want to', who says 'Oh bother' when asked to do anything, who 'bags' the best things for himself, who at a party gets excited and 'barges' about and plays the fool generally, often ending up by stodging to such an extent that he is ill in the night. For heaven's sake, be all of you as far from and as different from this sort of ass as you possibly can. You can make the holidays very happy ones if you try your best to do so. And I hope you will all have very happy ones.*

But for the Mallalieus, Browns, Hardmans and Campbells it was not going to be a happy Christmas. Percy Campbell, armed with the training he had had in the Clifton College O.T.C. and a further five weeks on being called up, had been in action for only three weeks. Then he went missing, and the signs were ominous.

> *No official news has yet been received …* [Percy Campbell is] *reported to be missing … he is believed to have lost his life in Flanders, on Saturday 24th October, while attempting to bring in a wounded brother-officer.*

Yet no one was sure.

Chapter 6

The Western Front

The British Tommy

It is sometimes supposed that public-schoolboy officers would have had little knowledge of the background of the men they were to lead in war. Many, however, wanted to reach out to those less fortunate than themselves and boys' clubs, backed by public schools, proliferated. Ronnie Poulton was involved in such work from the age of 16, when he first went on the Rugby School Mission Camp weeks at New Romney in Kent. When up at Balliol he worked with the Balliol Boys' Club in Oxford and then, after going down, with the Reading Boys' Club. Ronnie was said to be equally at home 'with all sorts and conditions of humanity'.

Those officers who were professional soldiers had, on the other hand, worked alongside 'the ordinary man' for some time. They were quick to draw the Skipper's attention to the merits of 'Tommy Atkins'. Tyrrell Brooks (Major, Duke of Cornwall's Light Infantry), for example, was a career soldier who had gained nine years' military experience before the war. Like other serving Old Dragons, he knew and appreciated the troops' fortitude and good humour:

Tyrrell Brooks

Dear Skipper,

A strange mixture of sentiment and pathos is Private Thomas Atkins. A splendid grouser when in clover, when really up against it he faces with equanimity the longest of days and most trying trench work.

In letter writing he uses the most pious and well-rounded phrases which would delight the soul of a cleric and give him hope, and afterwards you will hear the same hero expressing to his friends his grievances in language that even a bargee would resent.

Tyrrell, censoring his men's letters, noted a propensity for Tommy to write of bayoneting Germans – something that he stressed was 'not a daily occurrence'. However, he accepted the boasting as understandable, given the mix of tedium and fear that characterised trench life:

Left: Jack Smyth on horseback, with the 15th Sikhs in France, 1915

> *After all there is little to write about when you live in a trench for four days at a time, having shrapnel for breakfast, high explosive for lunch, and rifle fire when you should be having your evening glass of ale in the canteen.*

He also observed that Tommy was inclined to have exaggerated thoughts of home, 'his best gal' and the glory that awaited his return home when victory had been won. If he was wounded, 'well somebody else will take his place and he will become a 'Ero'. Above all, of course, was Tommy's ability to use humour, as in the naming of the shells that regularly visited his trenches. These were duly designated 'Little Willies', 'Dirty Dicks', 'Black Marias' and 'Jack Johnstons', according to their size and other features.

In his letter, published in the April 1915 edition of *The Draconian*, Tyrrell also included a story that was to become very well known.

> *Just after Ypres, a troop train full of enthusiasts pulled up opposite a hospital one in a siding. Those in the troop train were longing to perform deeds of valour and longing for blood. Those in the hospital train had already shed much in the lowlands of Flanders. Those in the troop train were hanging out of the windows and trucks joking with each other. Suddenly the hospital train started slowly forward and a troop train enthusiast shouted out 'Are we downhearted?' and the chorus answered 'No' – but again he shouted 'Are we downhearted?' and again the chorus bellowed 'No'. This was more than a figure in the hospital train, swathed in bandages, could stand. Propping himself up he retorted 'Ain't you? Well you bloody soon will be!' which said, he returned to a prone position.*

Other Old Dragons were similarly impressed by the men under their command. Not being a man of great private means, Jack Smyth had joined the Indian Army in 1912, which 'offered better pay, a bigger pension, cheap and excellent polo and big game shooting, and almost certain prospects of active service on the Indian frontier'.[1] Now serving as 2nd Lieutenant in the Indian Army, he too held the British Tommy in high regard.

Jack Smyth

> *The British Tommy is simply magnificent … One in a regiment close to us the other day came up very pale, and saluted, and asked if he could go to the rear. 'Whatever for?' said his officer. 'Well sir, I've been 'it three times,' he said.*
>
> *Before we came under fire for the first time I asked a sergeant who had been at Mons what it was like. 'Perfect 'ell, sir,' he replied, and he wasn't far wrong.*

Jack Smyth's 15th Sikhs had arrived in France in October. His first taste of action had been on his 21st birthday on October 24th, when his regiment was thrown into the First Battle of Ypres. From then until the spring of 1915 and the Battle of Neuve Chapelle, he and his regiment endured long spells in action, discovering the reality of trench warfare.

15 February 1915

I am writing this in a German trench and am too filthy and muddy and disreputable for words. As I expect you saw in the papers the Indian Corps captured a German position the other day, and here we are holding on to it for all we are worth. It is more interesting here in a place where the Germans have been for about four months; the place is quite dry, a captured pump tells us the reason why; they did themselves pretty well as all the dug-outs are littered with old bottles of champagne etc., and photos of the Kaiser, and letters and food, etc. Our men rather fancy the German boots and I have one of their haversacks.

There are about 100 of their dead lying just outside my trench where they were discovered creeping up to try and recapture the place and were promptly laid out by a machine gun.

I haven't taken off my boots for five days and am a sight for the gods.

The Battle of Neuve Chapelle

By January 1915 the war of movement had come to an end. The two sides found themselves facing each other in what was to become a system of trenches stretching some 400 miles (644 km) from the coast to Switzerland.

Although trench warfare was not new – it had been practised extensively in the American Civil War of the 1860s and the Russo-Japanese War of 1905–6 – it was not a form of combat for which European armies had trained. General Haig had to develop tactics that were detailed and innovative to meet this new state of affairs. There would be a preliminary artillery barrage, lifting to coincide with the advance of the infantry. Given the limited amount of both guns and ammunition, the barrage lasted only 35 minutes, but it proved pretty effective in clearing a path through the German barbed wire. The infantry attack that followed succeeded in taking the German frontline trenches and capturing the village of Neuve Chapelle.

Several Old Dragons were involved in this battle. Nevile West (Captain, Royal Berkshire Regiment) had decided on a military career, having gone through the United Services College in Windsor and Sandhurst after leaving Marlborough. Given that he had only taken up his commission in January 1914, however, his experience was still minimal. It left him ill-prepared for what was to happen at Neuve Chapelle.

Nevile was ordered to take out a party the night before the battle to remove the wire from in front of their trenches, in preparation for the infantry attack the following morning. As the German trenches were only 100 yards (91 m) away, this was dangerous work.

His account of this first attack (on 10 March) is dated just nine days after the event.

Nevile West

19 March 1915
The attack commenced the following morning with half-an-hour's terrific bombardment of the Hun trenches, which, being so close, proved a terrible ordeal for us sitting cramped in the wet trenches, several shells pitching short in amongst us; any way it blew all their barbed wire entanglements away, and their trenches and themselves to blazes.

The bombardment lifted. With only one German machine gun causing them any trouble, they were able to make their way across no man's land with minimal losses. Just how effective the shelling had been was evident in 'the masses of horribly mangled remains, and the whole air full of picric acid fumes from the lyddite shells' that the men discovered in the German trenches.

The troops advanced over three lines of German trenches, at which point they dug in. They had done their job and another regiment passed through them to take the fight forward, leaving Nevile to try to recover his thoughts.

It was a terrible day, horrible sights. May it be a long time before I see such another, and when quiet came not with darkness, but about midnight, one's nerves were all over the place. During the actual proceedings one has little time to think.

The following day was a considerably quieter one. However, it saw Nevile's 'skipper' wounded by a shrapnel shell, leaving Nevile in command of his company. He admitted that 'being alone like that, at such a crisis, a horrible feeling of loneliness came over me, and does come now'.

There was no time for further reflection, as the next morning Nevile had to face a German counterattack. They tried to impersonate the Highland Light Infantry who were stationed nearby, shouting in good English, 'Don't shoot, we are the H.L.I'. The ruse was discovered just in time and rapid fire was opened, with the result that 'the ground in front of our trenches now is heaped with their dead, and those that were wounded crawled into our lines'.

Nevile's ordeal was not yet over, however, as the Germans decided on revenge. This took the form of an hour-long artillery bombardment. It was fearsome, and Nevile was surprised to have lived through it.

The bits of shell and the fumes were horrible; it is impossible to get away from either, and I saw two men blown quite 30 feet in the air.

The tit-for-tat continued. No sooner had the German bombardment finished than a British one began, preparatory to another infantry attack. This time it was the turn of the Rifle Brigade to launch an attack from their trenches. Nevile described the results.

They fortunately hadn't gone far before (I should think) about 12 German machine guns opened fire, and God knows how any of them escaped; I was right in the open at the time and it was hell. Those that remained crawled back at dusk. A great friend of mine who was in the 1st Battalion with me was riddled with bullets, and killed instantly. A bullet hit my camera which was in my coat pocket, and just turned its course enough, otherwise, 'I shouldn't have gone no further'. My luck has been extraordinary, may it long continue so. We have just been sent two more 2nd Lieutenants. Apart from that we have only five Officers left.

Here Nevile's account ends. Despite his initial self-doubt at being suddenly in charge, having experienced what he described as 'real hell on earth', Nevile West clearly rose to the challenge. Not long afterwards he was awarded the M.C. for conspicuous gallantry on 9 May 1915, at Fromelles. The citation could almost be describing a different person:

When the leading line of his battalion was unable to advance, all the senior officers having been shot down, he rushed forward and attempted to lead his men on. He was almost immediately shot down, but picking himself up went forward again until he was hit a second time.[2]

However, his luck did finally run out. In January 1916, when moving into position prior to another attack, Nevile fell victim to one of the many shells hurled by the enemy into British positions. His parents received a letter of condolence from a fellow officer. In it he commented that up to that point Nevile 'appeared to have led an almost charmed life'.

* * * * * *

Jack Smyth and his 15th Sikhs were also involved at Neuve Chapelle, where they occupied captured German trenches. He was rather impressed by both their strength and comfort, and took note of the empty wine bottles and cigar boxes. It was clear that the Germans had been very reluctant to surrender them.

They must have lost very heavily indeed, as there were rows of dead bodies in front of our trench when they made a counter attack to try and get the place back and came under the fire of our machine-guns.

By 24 March, when Jack was writing this, the battle was over and the enemy at a safe distance.

It was a relief having the trenches a good way apart so that we could have patrols out at night and sleep comparatively comfortably instead of the jumpy nights when the trenches are 50 and 80 yards apart, as we have been having lately …

We brought in three of their wounded who must have been out there for five or six days. They [the Germans] *seem very callous about that sort of thing and never made an effort to bring them in although they were nearer their trenches than ours more than a good deal.*

* * * * * *

Geoffrey Buck had made remarkably quick progress to join up. In November 1914, although not yet 18, he was serving as a 2nd Lieutenant in the 1st London Regiment, Royal Fusiliers. He must have been one of the youngest officers in the army. Geoffrey was at Neuve Chapelle barely a month after the battle had finished and witnessed the devastation.

Geoffrey Buck

We spent about a fortnight at Neuve Chapelle and had rather a rotten time. The whole place is a complete ruin; dead bodies are lying all over the shop, and they smell bad, but the dead cows smell far, far worse! We were often engaged in burying our own and German dead; but this was much more pleasant than burying cows of neutral disposition and some six months seniority on the Roll of Honour. I employ most of my time in the trenches by sniping, and have had some minor successes. One day a German fellow smashed my periscope and cut my face a bit with glass, but otherwise I have not been touched.

Geoffrey went on to bemoan the lack of exercise and the frightening nature of being under shellfire, admitting that 'one gets downhearted sometimes'.

'We Must Each do our Bit'

John Betjeman recalls being told this, but this expectation did not only apply to the boys. It must have been practically impossible to sit at home doing nothing while your son was risking his life on the Western Front. Many an Oxford mother offered her services locally, preferring activity to hours of fruitless worry. Mrs Grundy was instrumental in the organisation of the food for the 3rd South General Hospital, catering for several hundred patients. Mrs Poulton was involved with the Union Jack Club, which provided a time and place for mothers and wives of serving soldiers to meet and comfort each other. Lady Osler organised a group making bandages and other medical necessities. Mrs Gamlen started a branch of the Needlework Guild devoted to war work. Mrs Kingerlee started the idea of having Flag Days to raise money in Oxford to finance the war, and Mrs Vinogradoff raised money for Russian prisoners of war. All were mothers of Old Dragons.

Meanwhile, the Skipper was endeavouring to maintain 'business as usual' at O.P.S. He declared the Easter Term of 1915 to have been 'a prosperous and successful term, unmarred by illness'. Looking around them, however, the young Dragons must have become more and more aware that they were all to some extent involved in this war. Staff were to be seen busy instructing squads in Morse code and semaphore signalling; many white handkerchiefs were apparently sacrificed as flags. The fields were also no longer just the province of the boys for their sports. The new shooting range, paid for from a legacy in Roderick Haigh's will, was now ready for use.

Hall, our groundsman, with the assistance of some outside labour, made an excellent range; and later, Anderson, our carpenter, put up two sheds, one at 25 yards, and one at 50 yards. As a result we have a really good range at which one can fire under cover at either 50 or 25 yards in any weather. I don't know what value shooting may be to small boys; I feel sure it can't do much harm and most of them enjoy it and take great pains to improve. The range has also been very useful to the 4th Territorial Battalion of the O.B.L.I. and to the Oxford T.C. Officers home on leave from the front and others in training have also used the range for revolver practice. In fact it has been a great success.

There was still money left over from Roderick Haigh's legacy. Skipper decided, with typical generosity, that the rest of it could be used 'to help the sons of Oxford dons attending the school who, on account of the war, or for other reasons, may need it'.

Among all the depressing war news, there was at least one cause for celebration. Kit Lynam, Skipper's daughter, now aged 27, decided to get married. After leaving the O.P.S. at the age of 14, she had spent five years at St Leonards School at St Andrews in Scotland (said to be the inspiration for Enid Blyton's Malory Towers). Kit excelled in sport and had played hockey for Oxfordshire and Staffordshire. The marriage took place early in 1915.

On February 27th we had a whole holiday in honour of Kit's wedding. All who know him agree that Lieut. Marshall, the bridegroom, has only one fault – and that is that he is not an Old Dragon. A wedding under the auspices of about a hundred schoolboys, mostly armed with confetti and old shoes, is an ordeal severe enough in all conscience. But the bride and bridegroom took it all smilingly.

Kit was not alone: numerous hasty marriages were made before soldiers went off to war. Naomi Haldane, rising only 17, had become engaged to one of her brother Jack's best friends, Dick Mitchison, on the outbreak of war. They were not to marry until 1916, leaving Naomi to wonder and worry. She also contributed a moving poem to *The Draconian*.

In the grey evening after I come home
I draw the curtains to shut in the light
– One never knows what cruel things may roam
Through the wet cloud-banks in the hostile night –
And when the fire's lit, and throwing wide
Streamers of flame light, dancing as I look,
And I am reading at the fire-side,
Now and again I glance across the book
To think if you were sitting in that chair
Your eyes and mouth, your forehead, oh my dear,
And the red glow reflected in your hair …
Only you're out in Flanders, and I am here.

Roll of Honour

However much he might have tried to focus on school matters, there can be little doubt that the events of the war, and the loss of two more Old Dragons, dominated Skipper's thoughts at this time. On 15 January, after nearly three months of uncertainty, the Campbells finally learned of Percy's fate. Skipper paid moving tribute to him in the Easter 1915 edition of *The Draconian.*

Percy Campbell (2nd Lieutenant, Wiltshire Regiment)

> *In the last* Draconian *we were unwilling to mention, as there was still some hope that he might be a prisoner, the death of Percy Campbell in action; but from what has been gathered from eye-witnesses there seems to be now no doubt that he was killed in the trenches in the neighbourhood of Armentières in October. His loss has been a great grief to us.*
>
> *Though by all his instincts he was one who hated war, he had volunteered for the Special Reserve as soon as the war broke out. Gazetted to the Wiltshire Regiment, he went to the front at the beginning of October and was the second of my Old Boys to fall, near Ypres, on 24th October 1914, at the age of 20.*

Skipper's words summarise Percy's tragically brief military career, which lasted less than a month. A fellow officer described his end:

> *When he heard that a brother officer was wounded on the road, he asked me to go back with him ... but before we got within fifty yards of the wounded officer, Campbell was hit. It was absolutely necessary to leave him, and for some time hopes were entertained that he might have been a wounded prisoner in the hands of the enemy, but eventually that hope had to be given up.*

* * * * * *

Confirmation of Percy Campbell's death was swiftly followed by another. Only five months after the death of Regie, the historian and academic C.R.L. Fletcher heard he had also lost his second son. 'We regret to have to chronicle the death of a very dear Old Boy, George Fletcher,' Skipper announced in the same edition of *The Draconian*.

George Fletcher (2nd Lieutenant, R.W.F.)

Robin Laffan, who had known George all through the O.P.S., Eton and Balliol, wrote a heartfelt appreciation of his close friend.

> *His letters from the trenches abound in the fun which kept himself and his men cheery in the midst of their hardships. Knowing his enemies, he had an intense admiration and even affection for them.*
>
> *He used to relieve the tedium of the trenches with friendly sarcasm shouted at the opposite lines. 'It ain't 'arf a joke being in Lieut. Fletcher's trench,' said his men. ''E talks to the b*****s in their own b****y language.'*
>
> *Of George's courage it is superfluous to say much. Readers of* The Times *will have seen how an officer described him as 'the bravest man I ever saw'. He was mentioned in dispatches on Feb 18th and he was again recommended for distinction after his reckless feat of crawling through the German lines and recovering from a tree a captured French flag.*[3] *By such deeds of daring he restored the jaded spirits of his men. But those who were lucky enough to see him in February, when at last he got his leave after six and a half months at the front, realised that the strain had told heavily on him. His light-hearted gallantry was not the result of mere animal vigour, but the triumph of spirit over bodily and mental exhaustion.*

George Fletcher is mentioned by Frank Richards in his book *Old Soldiers Never Die* (written with the help of another Welch Fusilier, Robert Graves). He remembered George as not only 'the bravest man in France',[4] but also as possessing 'more brains than all the Battalion officers put together'.[5] George's deeds had become legendary.

> *He had done some brave and brainy deeds at Fromelles, where he was always out on night patrols, along with the men of his Company. He could talk German like a native and once or twice mixed with their patrols, for the fun of it and to pick up what information he could. When we were in the Houpimes trenches he had planted a British flag right on the enemy's parapet. We soon agreed with B about Mr Fletcher, but he was not long with us. One morning when we were in the line he was informed that he had been awarded the Distinguished Service Order, and it happened that only a few minutes after he took a sharp quick look over the parapet and got sniped through the head. During the whole of the War I never saw men so cut up over an officer's death as in this case.*[6]

Only one other officer compared with George, as far as Frank Richards was concerned, and that was 'young Sassoon'. He described the latter as 'the best officer I have seen in the line or out since Mr Fletcher'.[7]

* * * * * *

It was on 6 May 1915 that what was to be the biggest bombshell for Skipper dropped. That evening Professor and Mrs Poulton received the telegram notifying them of the death of their son – and one of Skipper's 'particular favourites'.

Ronald Poulton Palmer (Lieutenant, Royal Berks)

Ronald Poulton's death was not only a personal blow to his family, Skipper and the O.P.S, but also a great loss to his country. In 1914 he had become captain of the England Rugby XV, and to this day he shares the English record for the most tries (four) scored in an international match. Ronald was a difficult man to stop. One of his opponents is reported to have declared, 'How can anyone stop him when his head goes one way, his arms another, and his legs keep straight on?'

Bullets, tragically, proved more difficult to dodge. Ronald survived barely six weeks at the front with the Royal Berkshire Regiment before becoming the third of what were to be nine Old Dragons killed who had also attended Balliol College, Oxford.

The news of his death spread rapidly. Jack Conybeare (Captain, Oxfordshire and Buckinghamshire Light Infantry) had been at both the O.P.S. and Rugby with Ronald; he had indeed seen him only a few days before in the trenches, when the Royal Berkshires were taking over from the Ox. & Bucks. He passed on these details of Ronald's death.

Jack Conybeare

5 May 1915.
I have just heard that poor Ronald is dead. He was shot through the heart, in the early hours of this morning, and was killed instantaneously. This is the first real shock I have had since we have been out here. There always are a certain number of bullets flying about, but they never seem to hit anyone one knows, and in consequence, I, at any rate, had half forgotten that a friend might at any moment be killed. This is rather a rude awakening …

It seems, indeed, hard lines, that a stray bullet should light on one who had both the power and the inclination to do so much good in the world …

Apparently he was standing on top of the parapet last night, directing a working party, when he was hit. Of course, by day, anyone who shows his head above the parapet is courting disaster, in fact if one is caught doing so one is threatened with court-martial. At night, on the other hand, we perpetually have working parties of one kind or another out, either wiring, repairing the parapet, or doing something which involves coming from under cover, and one simply takes the risk of stray bullets.

There could be no greater sacrifice, surely, both for the O.P.S. and for the Skipper himself, than that of Ronald Poulton. Nor was the grief confined to Oxford: the rugby playing world had lost its leading light. Alfred Oliphant contributed this poem to *The Spectator* of 22 May 1915.

Ronald is dead; and we shall watch no more
His swerving swallow-flight adown the field
Amid eluded enemies, who yield
Room for his easy passage, to the roar
Of multitudes enraptured, who acclaim

Ronald Poulton, England Captain, 1914

Their country's captain slipping toward his goal,
Instant of foot, deliberate of soul –
'All's well with England; Poulton's on his game.'

Aye, all is well: our orchards smiling fair;
Our Oxford not a wilderness that weeps;
Our boys tumultuously merry where
Amongst old elms his comrade spirit keeps
Vigil of love. All's well. And over there,
Amid his peers, a happy warrior sleeps.

On 9 May 1915 Rugby School held a joint Memorial Service for Ronald and another of its old boys, who had died of blood poisoning following a mosquito bite on his way out to Gallipoli – Rupert Brooke.

Another Memorial Service, attended by some of the O.P.S. boys and staff, was held in St Giles' Church, Oxford, on 29 May. The Rev. William Temple (a mentor and friend from Ronald's time at Rugby School, later to be Archbishop of Canterbury) gave the address, which he started by saying, 'There are many of us who, if asked to point to a life without blemish, would have pointed to Ronald Poulton'.

In 1913 Ronald had inherited a fortune from his uncle, G.W. Palmer of Huntley & Palmer, the biscuit-makers, who required him to change his name to Poulton Palmer. Huntley & Palmer were the world's largest biscuit firm, employing some 5,000 people in 1900; Ronald, after completing a three-year apprenticeship, would almost certainly have found himself on the Board of Directors. He now had an income of £4,000 p.a. (over £400,000 in today's money), to which he reacted by observing, 'Yes, but what troubles me is the responsibility of how to use it for the best'. Remarking that he had not been brought up to spend large sums of money, he had decided simply to save 'till some really worthy object comes along'.

In the opinion of William Temple, Ronald, with his charisma and leadership qualities, would no doubt have found 'a worthy object' in the business world after the war.

> *Many of us believed that with his ready sympathy, his utter freedom from selfishness, and his courage to follow what he saw to be right, he would grasp the causes of our labour unrest and class friction, and by removing them from the great industry in whose control a large part was to be his, set an example which would prove a great force in our social regeneration … What he hated most in our usual manner of life was the artificial barriers that hold people apart, and the suspiciousness of one class towards another. It was because he found spontaneity and fellowship in the Workers' Educational Association that he was drawn to help that movement.*

Temple's last meeting with Poulton confirmed both Ronnie's religious convictions and also his belief he would not return from the war.

> *We were silent for a long time. 'What do you suppose it's like (life after death)?' I said one had no ground for even guessing, but that no doubt there was both activity and growth: the only thing we knew was the Love of God, and perhaps the reason why everything else was hidden was just to make us concentrate on that. Then there was another long silence. Then he said, 'I don't want to be killed yet: there is such a lot I wanted to do, or try anyhow.' I asked if he felt he would be killed; 'Oh yes,' he said, 'sure of it.' I said nothing and again there was a long silence. Then he suddenly said, 'Of course it's all right; but it's not what one would have chosen.'*[8]

'Particular Favourites' – Mixed Fortunes

Of the other three 'particular favourites' highlighted, if Ronnie's luck had run out all too quickly, Jack Smyth was blessed with a charmed life in the 15th Sikhs. He readily acknowledged his good fortune.

> *23 May 1915*
> *We had the most extraordinary luck as a regiment up till the end of April, as, although we have had several officers wounded, we had not one killed, but during the last three weeks we have had six hit and out of these five were killed, which is real bad luck. Losing five officers makes an awful gap in a small community like ours, where we all mess together.*

Jack had also survived a period in the Ypres salient – held, he felt, 'for sentimental reasons more than anything else'. During this time he was under artillery fire from three sides. On top of that, his trench was one only partially captured from the Germans.

We have just been in a very nasty bit of trench which was captured from the Huns, and we and the Huns were in the same trench with a barrier of earth in between. Most unpleasant!

It was clear to all fighting in these conditions that heavy losses were inevitable. Jack was amused, and impressed, by his men's ability to resort to humour in such circumstances.

A Corporal of the Shires made a grand remark the other day when the regiment was ordered to attack, 'Now then No.3 Company, fall in for the thinning out parade'.

The battle in which Jack had been involved was the Second Battle of Ypres, where the British suffered about 60,000 casualties in a month. He ended his letter with a remark that brings into sharp focus just how lucky he had been thus far.

I am now the only one in the regiment who has been right through the show without being either wounded or invalided sick; the Quartermaster, who was the only other one, went down with measles last week!

Well I must end up now, the best of luck to the O.P.S.

This was not a full account of Jack's exploits at this time. A fellow (anonymous) officer provided *The Draconian* with the details of the heroism that led to Jack being awarded the Victoria Cross.

Jack's company of 15th Sikhs had moved into a treacherous section of trenches in which there had been furious fighting – only to find that part of one of the trenches was still in German hands. Here an impromptu barricade separated them from their foes. This much Jack had mentioned, but not what happened next.

On the following morning the Germans had attempted to reinforce their troops and the bombs (grenades) began to fly. By noon the Sikhs were running out of ammunition, and it was decided that a bombing party should be brought up from the reserve trenches. Two unsuccessful attempts were made, before Jack was ordered to get together a group of volunteers to try again.

Lieut. Smyth and his little party of ten men started at 2 p.m. to cover the 250 yards which intervened between them and our trench, taking with them two boxes of 96 bombs. The ground to be covered was absolutely open, devoid of all natural cover. The only possible shelter from the frightful fire which met the party as soon as they were over our parapet was an old broken-down trench, which at the best of times was hardly knee-deep, but now, in places, was filled almost to the top with the dead bodies.

Some were pushing the boxes of bombs; others had attached *pagris* (turbans) to pull them along. After struggling 100 yards (91 m) under a deluge of rifle and machine-gun fire, only six of the sepoys remained unwounded.

> *They crawled on and on, until just before they reached the end of the trench, the party had dwindled to two – Lieut. Smyth and Sepoy Lal Singh. The second box of bombs had, therefore, to be abandoned.*

Sepoy Lal Singh and Jack Smyth continued with their box of bombs, often in the open, until they reached a stream, which they found too deep to wade. They crawled further on until they found a point where the stream was fordable.

> *Across this* [stream] *they struggled with their valuable burden, and in a few yards they were among their friends in our trench, both untouched, although their clothes were perforated with bullet holes. Shortly after reaching the trench the gallant Sepoy was killed.*

This sealed Jack's reputation with his men, who had observed in him the qualities of a super-hero.

> *The men in the regiment believe that Lieut. Smyth bears a charmed life, for he has had his cap blown off by shells five times, has had bullets through his clothes, and lately, while lighting a cigarette, the match was taken out of his fingers by a bullet.*

Nonetheless, Jack was very aware of just how easy it was 'to get knocked out', as Ronnie had been. He provided *The Draconian* with this explanation of the nature of modern warfare.

> *Modern Warfare*
> *(Or how to get knocked out without seeing a German).*
>
> *Ten British Officers sitting in a line:*
> *One stopped a 'pip-squeak', and then there were nine.*
> *Nine British Officers – What's to be their fate?*
> *One dropped a live bomb, and then there were eight.*
> *Eight British Officers looking up to Heaven:*
> *Down came a German bomb and then there were seven.*
> *Seven British Officers leaning on their sticks:*
> *A sniper drew a bead on one, and then there were six.*
> *Six British Officers very much alive:*
> *One smelt a 'stink-bomb', and then there were five.*
> *Five British Officers sitting round a tree:*
> *'Maria' bagged a brace of them, and then there were three.*
> *Three British Officers – All that had got through:*
> *One sat on a bayonet, and then there were two.*
> *Two British officers basking in the sun:*
> *Our gunners had a premature, and then there was one.*
> *One British Officer still fighting with the Hun*
> *Picked up an unexploded shell, and then there were none.*

* * * * * *

Jack Haldane

If anyone could be said to have been enjoying the war it was Jack Haldane, serving as Lieutenant in the Black Watch. Not many admitted that they liked killing and that life in the trenches was an enjoyable experience. Jack was also quite prepared to risk his life unnecessarily, and to boast of this.

I once bicycled across a gap in full view of the Germans, having foreseen that they would be too surprised to open fire till I was under shelter again.[9]

Jack discovered the joys of teaching bomb-throwing. He noted in a letter to his father that those who were the best at it were 'the reckless kind, who are always breaking rules and things in peacetime'.[10] Clearly kindred spirits. 'Bomb-throwing is the next most exciting thing to being under fire,'[11] he told his sister Naomi.

Having wished he could kill his tormentors as a child (see p. 16), Jack now had plenty of opportunities to kill Germans. His detachment was allowed to roam along the line, firing off trench mortars and experimental devices at will. This was generally not popular with those around them at the time, as another Old Dragon, Charlie Childe, a Captain in the Gloucestershire Regiment, explained:

Charles Childe

These trench mortar people are a little tribe of pariahs, who stalk up and down other people's trenches, drink their whiskey, and make themselves quite pleasant. Meanwhile their satellites stealthily fire the beastly things, knock in some Hun dug-outs, put out a few of their cook-houses (you can see the smoke coming out of their trenches here and there), and thoroughly annoy the Hun over his lunch – a most ungentlemanly thing to do. Fritz then urgently telephones to his gunners, and the creators of all the fuss have meanwhile gone away somewhere else.

No doubt this was all water off a duck's back as far as Jack was concerned. He had always been something of a maverick and his men had to adapt to his ways.

> *His small unit enforced no particular discipline, ordered no routine guard-duties. Officers and men lived on one meal a day. For three weeks in 1915 Haldane did not take off his boots, and it was probably during this period that he was first described by Haig as 'the bravest and dirtiest officer in my army'.*[12]

Jack's group even had its own workshop. Here they experimented with different fuses, undertook their own repairs and made improvements to their weaponry. Contrary to the accepted wisdom, Jack made smoking compulsory, on the basis that it would instil confidence in each other and the weapons they were handling. 'We had no accidents and few casualties,' he maintained.[13]

Jack's experiences of helping his father in mines, where the dangers of gases were still being understood, turned out to be of particular help. During the war there was a lot of tunnelling to place mines under enemy trenches, and his father's idea of using canaries to warn of the build-up of gas was adopted. An aviary was even set up in Calais to breed more birds.

Thus, when the Germans released a gas attack on Allied troops at Ypres, on 22 April 1915, it was not surprising that Lord Kitchener should turn to Professor Haldane for advice. The Professor went straight over to France to investigate the situation personally, returning with a dead soldier's lung to dissect in the laboratory at his Oxford home. It was imperative to confirm the exact nature of the gas and develop an effective respirator as soon as possible. Here, with Aldous Huxley, a long-standing family friend, taking notes for him, he carried out numerous tests on the effects of chlorine gas on himself and other volunteers. Meanwhile, the soldiers in France were warding off further attacks with nothing more effective than urine-soaked handkerchiefs.

In May Professor Haldane was back in France, where he set up a laboratory in Saint-Omer. Jack was summoned from his bombing duties to assist him. The Professor could think of no one better than his son to have in his gas chamber, reporting on the effects of the gas he was inhaling, as Jack explained:

> *We had to compare the effects on ourselves of various quantities, with and without respirators ... It stung the eyes and produced a tendency to gasp and cough when breathed. For this reason trained physiologists had to be employed.*[14]

But why did it have to be Jack in the gas chamber?

> *An experienced physiologist has more self-control. It was also necessary to see if one could run or work hard in the respirators, so we had a wheel of some kind to turn by hand in the gas chamber, not to mention doing 50 yard sprints in respirators outside. As each of us got sufficiently affected by gas to render his lungs duly irritable, another would take his place. None of us was much the worse for the gas, or in any real danger, as we knew when to stop, but some had to go to bed for a few days, and I was very short of breath and incapable of running for a month or so.*[15]

Then Jack, on learning that his troops were about to go into an attack, returned to the trenches. Here he suffered wounds from shellfire and found himself being given a lift by the Prince of Wales to the clearing station. 'Oh, it's you,' the Prince is reputed to have said.[16] They had met in Oxford the previous year, where one of the Prince's tutors was another Old Dragon – Lionel Smith.

Jack's wounds were 'blighty' ones. Before he knew it, he was back home at 'Cherwell' in Oxford, recovering from an operation to remove a shell splinter.

His war was almost over, however. Having recovered from this wound, Jack was sent to the Mesopotamian front. Within a month he was wounded in the leg when a bomb exploded as he was trying to put out a fire in his camp. The remainder of the war was spent recovering in India. Jack never lost the thirst for battle though; aged 70, his ambition was to die in battle aged 100.

* * * * * *

Hugh Sidgwick, another 'particular favourite', had moved seamlessly from Winchester to Balliol College, Oxford, winning the inevitable scholarship. There he achieved a first class in Mathematical Moderations (1902) and a first class in Classical Moderations (1903), followed by a first in Greats and a Fellowship at University College.

In 1906 Hugh had joined the Education Office. His work was considered too important to spare him for the war effort, so instead he became a Special Constable – much to the amusement of another Old Dragon, who wrote to ask whether he would arrest suspected spies in Greek verse.

Hugh Sidgwick

Special Constables – by one

The Editor has asked for an article on Special Constables, and the motto of the force being obedience I can only comply. But one thing must be made clear at the outset. This nation at present consists of (a) the armed forces of the Crown; and (b) the rest. Special constabling is one of the forms of consolation for (b), who are small beer, and don't matter much; it stands on a level with knitting socks, and putting on a light green uniform and gesticulating in Hyde Park on Saturday afternoons. It is miles away from the activities of (a), and must not be spoken of in the same breath ...

Special constables are amateurs who in their spare time assist the police in their lighter duties. They are sworn in for the period of the war – to carry out their duties without favour or affection, malice or ill-will, to preserve the King's peace and guard the persons and property of his subjects, and so forth. They are provided with an armlet and a truncheon and a note-book and a warrant and a whistle and a badge; (I am going to make a song some day with this refrain). They may also provide themselves with a uniform. In our detachment it is a long blue overcoat and a yachting cap, in which we look like well-intentioned tram-conductors: but I am told that elsewhere there are variations in head-gear. Thus equipped, the special constable goes forth upon his duty.

So far the terror of our name has kept the malefactors away, and we have arrested only a bronze statue and a cat. But the moral effect has been enormous. The criminal classes and the foreign agents stand appalled at the reserves which the Executive has brought into play; they argue, a fortiori, *that if respectable elderly gentlemen take such a lot of trouble about a little thing like that, what will happen if matters get really lively? Further, the ascendancy of the male sex is now re-established. I know of at least one dinner invitation which has been refused on the ground of constabulary duty. The dinner was on Tuesday and the duty on Thursday: but who could know that?*

Such an article, typical of Hugh Sidgwick, must have been welcome light relief to all those who read the April 1915 edition of *The Draconian*. This issue also contained lengthy obituaries for Percy Campbell and George Fletcher.

With the death of Ronnie Poulton on 5 May 1915, the O.P.S. Roll of Honour now numbered eight. No further casualties were recorded for the rest of May, June or July. Following the end of the Second Battle of Ypres (25 May) the war continued with less intensity, giving Old Dragons more time, perhaps, for their correspondence.

Chapter 7
Summer 1915

Potholes, Dug-outs and Gas …

News from serving Old Dragons on the Western Front continued to build up over the summer of 1915. There were others who had been involved in the Second Battle of Ypres (21 April–25 May). Donald Innes – another of the five Old Dragon hockey blues of 1911 (see p. 54) – had enlisted immediately in 1914 as a dispatch rider and served as Sergeant in the Motor Cycle Corps. He subsequently gained his commission in the Royal Engineers.

Writing on 1 May 1915, Donald described the town of Ypres as 'smashed up', but noted that the cathedral had been miraculously spared. He was impressed by the philosophical attitude of the town's inhabitants, remarking that 'where the shops [were] absolutely smashed, the owners sell their goods in the street outside'. A 'more or less patched up café' even managed to provide him with an excellent dinner.

Donald appreciated that the infantry had it worse than dispatch riders – for whom there seemed to be only three principal dangers.

Donald Innes

1 May 1915

For an infantry man, a modern attack can only be described as 'Hell let loose'. I thanked God I was a Dispatch Rider. Our troubles are rather neatly put by one of the D.R.s in what he called the D.R.'s prayer.-

From holes, shells, and motor 'bus
Good Lord deliver us.

* * * * * *

Meanwhile extracts from the war diary of Treffry Thompson – a Captain in the Royal Army Medical Corps, now attached to the 18th Hussars as their Medical Officer – revealed that he was experiencing certain domestic difficulties with the building of safe dug-outs in such sodden ground.

Left: Jack Smyth with the Skipper, G.C. Vassall and the pupils of O.P.S., July 1915

Treffry Thompson

18 May 1915
In afternoon started building sumptuous H.Q. dug-out with great beams for roof with magnificent table and fine brocaded chairs out of neighbouring château. My experience at O.P.S. in fort-building in the School hedge was of untold value. Just before dark, Capt. O. was in his dug-out and saw a bit of entrance beginning to fall in. He started to walk out shouting 'Hi! Who's walking on the roof?' It was supported by a large iron bedstead, which collapsed and broke his neck.

Treffry was at the other end of the trench at the time and there was nothing he could do. No sooner had he returned to his dug-out than he was summoned to attend to a subaltern who had apparently gone mad.

> *I found L. who was one of the few who had come safely through the bombardment on the 13th, and he was completely off his head from the shock of hearing of O.'s death on top of the previous strain. Gave him some morphia and got him quiet and put him in a dug-out.*

On returning to his dug-out a second time, Treffry was summoned again, this time to a man with a broken leg buried in another dug-out. That was the final straw.

> *After this series of collapsing dug-outs, we turned everybody out of any dug-out that wasn't absolutely sound.*

Shortly after this, Treffry experienced the effects of gas for the first time, and then became a casualty himself.

> *24 May 1915*
> *At 2.30 a.m. we were awakened by one of the subalterns who was blue and coughing madly, dashing into the cellar shouting 'Gas! Gas!' We nipped up and shoved on our respirators and put on our kit. The captain of one of the squadrons came down with his respirator on, looking very bad, and said the men were retiring. The colonel immediately sent a telephone message along the trenches to say that they were not to retire, with what result I do not know.*
>
> *We all went outside and immediately got our first impressions of gas; even through the respirator there was a sense of fearful choking suffocation …*
>
> *The gas was awful and gave one a feeling of absolute terror and helplessness. We went outside the château ruins and, just as I got beyond the wall, there was a loud crash just in front of me and I thought my arm had gone and had to look down to see that it was still there.*
>
> *The whole place was a hell of shrapnel and rifle and machine-gun fire. I got in a blue funk and bolted, still however holding on to my mackintosh with my left hand. I fell into various ditches and lines of trenches, got tied up in the wire, fell again into the trenches where the Territorials were and was promptly kicked out on the farther side.*

> *Beyond this was a long open slope, swept by shrapnel fire and thick with gas. I fell into a shallow ditch and fainted. Somebody came and pulled me out by my wounded arm, which brought me to my senses. I made for the dug-outs down by the stream; there some men tied up my arm and I became less of a raving lunatic.*

After the shelling had calmed down, four men put Treffry on a stretcher and took him down the Menin Road in search of a dressing station. However, they came under more shellfire and had to take shelter in a ditch at the side of the road. There were between 30 and 40 wounded men collected there and all had to remain in the ditch for two hours. Treffry recognised the soldier lying next to him, in a pitiable state.

> *K______, the new machine gun officer, was lying beside me dying from gas. He was a ghastly sight, turning from white to blue and back again. He had been caught asleep in his dug-out by the gas without a respirator on.*

From here Treffry was moved to the G.H.Q. line of trenches, but there was a general withdrawal going on such that he might again find himself in the front line. So, on he went, eventually making his way back to the railway south of Ypres – but if he thought he was now out of trouble, he was wrong.

> *There I found a battery and asked for a drink. While drinking some red wine, which made me sicker than I ever hope to be again, a 'crump' fell beside one of the guns and killed two men.*
>
> *I again thought it was no place for me and went along the railway towards the Lille gate. I was staggering along when a subaltern in charge of a working party saw my condition and helped me along to his medical officer, who made me lie down and finally packed me off in a motor ambulance to the dressing-station.*

Treffry's ordeal was finally over. His was a 'Blighty' wound that ensured that he was shipped back to England, where he thankfully recovered quickly. Within a couple of months he was back at the O.P.S. to share his stories with the editor of *The Draconian*.

G.C. Vassall with Treffry Thompson on the O.P.S. playing field, 1915

Summer Term

On returning to his old school, Treffry would have noticed the absence of Pug Wallace, who had recently joined the Oxfordshire and Buckinghamshire Light Infantry. Having been at the O.P.S. man and boy, the young Dragons were part of the family he was leaving behind him, as he went off to be Lindsay Wallace (2nd Lieutenant, O.B.L.I.).

'Pug' Wallace

6 Park Town, Oxford.
June 27th 1915

Dear Fellow Dragons,

I am writing to thank you all very much indeed for the present, or should I say presents, which were thrust into my hands about ten days ago. Whenever I use them, and, as soon as I leave Oxford, that will be very frequently, I shall be reminded of the O.P.S. and all of you and of the many happy days spent there both out of doors and indoors.

I first came to the O.P.S. in January 1885, as a boy, and left in July 1890. I remember crying hard when my last summer term was finished. During the next ten years or so when I was at Winchester and Balliol, I was always to be found at the O.P.S. if I had a chance, in fact at the time I came too often and was a nuisance. In my Varsity days I used to cadge a tea as often as I could from Hum or Maurice Church, in order to stay for the whole afternoon. In 1901 I returned as a master, and I've been there ever since.

I have stated this in detail to try and make clear to you how heart-broken I felt when I spent my last day with you as a genuine member of staff. I want to make it plain that I didn't want to go, I don't want to go, and I shall always want to be back.

I am going to play a new game, and I mean to play it for all I am worth, but, when that game is over, I shall change and come home as quick as I can. I don't know whether I have made myself clear; thank you again very much for your present. Don't forget

'Pug'

* * * * * *

Pug would surely not have been forgotten, but others stepped into his shoes to ensure that school life for the boys carried on much as before. One can also imagine Skipper channelling any sense of loss on the boys' part into some positive action, such as fundraising activities for good causes.

The members of the school have sent in the course of the term £13 7s 3d (last year £13 2s 0d) to the Fresh Air Fund, after being asked to decide among themselves whether they would support the Fund again or devote their contribution to some War Fund. They have also sent £5 1s 0d to the Base Hospital Tobacco Fund, and £1 to the Red Cross Fund. £2 of this represented what would have been spent on ices on the Fathers' Match Day, but the boys asked to give up their ices.

While these good causes were certainly in need of money, Skipper was feeling the pinch too. School fees were more affordable to middle-class families in 1915, but the Dragon was not a school that attracted the smart or particularly rich set. Skipper knew many parents struggled to pay the fees, both at his school and then at their public schools. Often he found ways to subsidise children rather than let them leave. There was clearly some pressure on him from the parents to make reductions, whereas in reality the fees should have gone up. Skipper resisted both equally.

As is well known, the expense of 'keeping school' has gone up very considerably – at least 33%. The Preparatory Schools Association suggested two courses, (1) to give a week extra holiday three times a year, (2) to increase the fees.

I do not think either of these proposals is to be commended, but I would ask parents to remember the circumstance, and not to ask for reductions for epidemic absence or lost time! Of course we do our share in taking sons of fallen officers and of Belgian refugees free or at nominal terms – but this is only possible if parents will remember that the schoolmaster suffers quite as much financially by the War as anyone else.

A stream of Old Dragons and ex-staff continued to visit the school and no doubt the latter were given a particularly enthusiastic welcome by the boys. They probably did not need too much encouragement to show off their weaponry.

Blair Watkins and 'Higgy' arrived more than once, and the former firing blanks from his revolver on the field was only defeated by Jack Haldane exploding German bombs in his garden along the road. Jack at any rate satisfied us that the school range is a far safer place for the neighbours than is the Cherwell garden.[1]

* * * * * *

The Dragons were also becoming aware of the human suffering involved in war. Wounded soldiers were regularly welcomed into the school, as *The Draconian* recorded.

Mention must be made of two visits of parties of wounded soldiers from the Base Hospital and Somerville. On the first occasion, the soldiers played cricket in the nets, and in spite of bandages and crutches, bowled and batted with much skill. VIa were their hosts and bowled at them till tea-time; after tea hosts and visitors mutually entertained each other with songs and recitations: one professional comedian, just home from the trenches, seems to have been well enough to stand on his head and sing until he was 'as-you-wered' by a companion, who was afraid the strawberries and cream wouldn't stand the inverted position any longer. A match was to have been played on the second occasion, but it was so wet that a sing-song was held in the School Hall.

* * * * * *

The undoubted highlight of the term was the visit of Jack Smyth, who had just been invested with the Victoria Cross by George V the day before. The events of the day were written up for *The Draconian* by one of the boys, 14-year-old Cyril Harvey.

Jack Smyth's V.C. medal (front and back), dated 18 May 1915

At nine o'clock on Tuesday 13th July, the school photograph was taken, and Jack Smyth was photographed with us. When the business was over we went into the Hall and sang a hymn. It was then the embarrassing duty of one of the boys to make a short (extremely short) speech, and he felt much more comfortable after it was finished.

Jack Smyth was then requested to tell us exactly how he won the V.C. He climbed on to the platform to the accompaniment of thunderous cheers, and drew a map and explained all about it. In conclusion he said, 'Needless to say, this is the first and last time I am ever going to say anything about this, and I would not have done so today unless I had been bullied into it by G.C. [Vassall]'. *At this we nearly took the roof off with shouting.*

Jack Smyth got down from his perch and, standing between the parallel bars, produced his Victoria Cross. The whole school filed by one by one to examine it.

He wound up by asking the Skipper for a whole holiday. After more cheering, Jack Smyth stepped boldly from the school buildings to face an enormous body of photographers. This latter ordeal ended the morning's proceedings.

In the afternoon we played a most exciting cricket match against Jack Smyth's team: it is doubtful which was the most enjoyed, his innings, or winning the match, or the subsequent bathe with him (his first since he swam the stream with his bombs) and several members of his eleven.

In his autobiography, Jack Smyth recalled meeting three young Dragons that day he got to know well in later life, when he served as an M.P. They were Lance and 'Per' Mallalieu and Hugh Gaitskell, all future Labour politicians.

* * * * * *

As the first year of the war came to an end and the long summer holiday of 1915 loomed, Skipper was determined to send the boys off with a few thoughts for the weeks ahead, along with clear instructions on what was expected of them as Dragons.

We seem to have been living in a dark shadow all this year. Just a year ago we were all looking forward to bright and cheerful holidays. I was off to the Blue Dragon *to 'Narroway' over the foam and you were off to the seaside or the country and none of us had any thought of the dread horror that has befallen the world and yet the silver lining does appear at times shining through the dark cloud.*

The horrors of the trenches, the hideous wickedness that our enemies show in their ways of warfare, the utter absence of anything like the old chivalry that made war romantic, all this blackness shows up with more beautiful contrast the gleams of light that come through – the brave and noble deeds of so many of our dear old boys and of others who have put on the armour of light and fought against the powers of darkness.

The question we who have to stay at home all have to ask ourselves is what have we done, what are we doing, what shall we do to help – and it is very difficult for you and me to say that we are really helping as much as we possibly can those who are enduring so much for us and for our country and for the cause of right. It is a question that each of us must answer for him or herself – personally I find it very hard to get out of the ordinary way of living and thinking and I really don't know whether it is right or wrong to enjoy oneself in ordinary ways – ought one for instance to refuse to eat meat, salmon, new potatoes? Ought one to give up driving a car because it is a pleasure to do so, ought one to give up the pleasure of giving tips or presents and buy war vouchers instead? Ought you boys not to spend any money on grub, on presents, on holiday excursions? It is very difficult to answer …

Try then, my dear boys and girls, to help and be good to others, to work hard and do your very best to help your parents, to be brave in refusing when other people try to make you do wrong by 'daring' you or jeering at you, or by threatening to lick you if you don't. You little boys and girls try to be specially good to your parents and brothers and sisters and to make the holidays happy ones.

What cowards boys sometimes are to be actually ashamed of their parents, to tell them not to come to the field, to be angry if their mothers kiss them before other boys, to be ashamed to take their sisters by the arm and proudly show them round – nothing is more despicable than such false shame. Be chivalrous and truthful and kind and prove that the Germans are wrong and that the true Christian spirit which is I believe the spirit in which we and our allies are fighting is for ever right.

Skipper

With these inspiring words, the children returned to their families to enjoy, as best they could, their summer holiday.

Summer Holidays (of sorts)

Living just round the corner from the school, on Chadlington Road, was the Childe family. Charlie Childe had left the O.P.S. with a scholarship to Clifton in 1909 and when the war broke out was reading Medicine at Pembroke College, Cambridge. He enlisted straight away and was commissioned into the 8th (Service) Battalion of the Gloucestershire Regiment. To judge from his early letters, Charlie too seemed to be enjoying something of a holiday:

Charles Childe

6 August 1915
I can't plead the excuse of being at war for not having written before. As a matter of fact, there is evidently a war on, as I have seen aeroplanes shelled and bombs dropping from a German aeroplane – also the guns can be heard. But, for my part, I live, eat, sleep and feed in perfect comfort and feel no more uncivilised than at a garden party at home.

One day Jack Smyth turned up to lunch here and his regiment was then in the trenches quite near. However, the trenches are on the reverse slope of a hill, so once out you can get on a horse or motor-bike, or your flat feet and go wherever you like. He chose the motor-bike, lunch here, and an afternoon's shopping in a town quite handy; then in the evening he went back and took on the role of cannon-fodder for a bit during the evening 'hate' period.

Charlie was in a comparatively quiet sector where neither side tried to shell incoming supplies 'because it's a case of both or neither being knocked out, and "live and let live" is more satisfactory when possible'. In such circumstances it was even possible to take time off:

Tomorrow the Padre and I are lunching in the town. A pal of his in command of a motor-ambulance is calling for us and bringing me back in time for an afternoon's parade.

Daily life was relaxed enough for his 65-strong section to enjoy swims in a nearby river before breakfast and after lunch, although this did provoke some criticism (rather trivial in the circumstances).

The bathing has apparently offended some august swell's senses, as an Army Order now insists on pants. The Padre is a very good sort and has a pair of very shrunken and minute ones which he uses for diving in. He keeps them on the bank to put on when he gets out again, and so the order is complied with.

By a strange coincidence, the Curators of the Oxford University Parks at this time issued an edict that 'All those who bathe in the river after 8 a.m. will, for the future, be required to wear bathing costumes'. This was a time of less self-consciousness, communal showers and very uncomfortable woollen swimming trunks; certainly the early morning swims of young Dragons were *au naturel* then and for many years thereafter.

This relaxed tone of war was too good to last, however. Later in August Charlie found himself in a far more combative area, where life was much less comfortable.

My four guns covered a frontage which included the 'Glory Hole'. The average distance across to 'Germany' is 450 yards, but 40 yards at the 'Glory Hole', jutting out into a sharp salient.

A salient – described by Charlie as 'always a cheerful spot', where you 'get potted from all directions' – attracted all manner of weaponry for short-range warfare. The worst of these, in his opinion, was the 'Minenwurfer'.

This throws a bomb of very high explosive, 3 feet long by 12 inches diameter. The bomb goes vertically up to a great height and then curves over and falls with a soft heavy 'wop', and then just as you put yourself on [your] *back and say 'it isn't going off this time', you hear a roar like absolutely nothing on earth, and it shakes the ground for two or three acres or more. The effect though is extraordinarily local, just a hole varying from 15 feet by 6 feet to 10 feet by 5 feet. A thick oily column of smoke goes straight up in the air, and that's about all.*

Sketch by Charles Childe, 1915. He described the scene as showing 'German Trenches (open country behind) 40 yards from ours at "Glory Hole". Our barbed wire in the foreground'

* * * * * *

Philip Frere had left the O.P.S. in 1912. Although the normal age to leave a preparatory school is usually assumed to be around 13, it was not unusual then for boys to stay on rather longer. Philip was actually 15 in the month he left the O.P.S. The following year he spent in Hildesheim learning German, before going on to Westminster School in September 1913. He stayed there for just one academic year. By August 1914 Philip had become an Articled Clerk to a solicitor and was a member of the Inns of Court O.T.C.

He gained his commission in September 1914, having turned 17 only two months before; his strapping frame of 6 ft 2½ in (1.89 m) may have assisted in this regard. By November 1914 Philip is listed as being a 2nd Lieutenant, 8th Battalion, East Surrey Regiment. He was not yet 18 when he found himself engaged in one of the most terrifying spots on the Western Front, vividly described in a letter dated 13 August 1915.

Philip Frere

We are in trenches ten yards from the Germans. They have mined our front trenches and we have mined theirs, so we have but to touch the button, and so have they, for everyone to go heavenwards.

This was not his greatest nightmare, however.

The barn in which I now sleep is infested with rats, and you hear them squealing in the hay at night and they also run over your feet. I hate the beastly things and am far more afraid of them than of the Germans.

Rats were indeed constant and entirely unwelcome guests everywhere there was human flesh on which to feast. Soldiers fought a continuous battle with them in the trenches. There were even attempts at a scientific approach to their extermination – the subject of a *Draconian* article by Douglas Rose, a Captain in the Oxfordshire and Buckinghamshire Light Infantry.

Douglas Rose

It was at the Field Ambulance that I met O.C. Rats. I had come in that afternoon, not wounded this time but with a silly leg and foot which I hardly possessed it seemed, a result of sciatica. The medical officer for the day was looking round for the night and brought a companion with him whom he introduced as O.C. Rats.

I had been keenly interested in this appointment ever since we received the order in the front Line to look out for any Rats that appeared to have died from natural causes and to send any such, duly labelled, to Brigade Headquarters for examination by a Bacteriologist.

'Well,' I said, 'how's business?'

'Nothing doing,' he replied. 'I have only had two carcasses to examine: one of these had most of its ribs broken and the other appeared to have died of senile decay.'

'B', in the next bed, said he had fired 72 rounds with his revolver at the beasts, and generally had a shoot at night, but had never seen a naturally deceased rat. I related my experiences with a cane and how I had once made the mistake of moving my foot too soon when I trod on one in mistake on the duckboards.

O.C. Rats said we must let some of them die naturally, otherwise how could he judge the effect of the serum which had been given to the rats by a thoughtful Government with views to exterminating them entirely.

I explained to him that when a Platoon Sergeant lost his upper denture completely, rats having taken it off from the shelf in his dug-out whilst he slept, and the Company Sergeant-Major had all the vulcanite bitten off his lower denture when having a siesta, one could hardly expect a truce between the men and the rats, so that the serum could work out to a scientific conclusion.

We all promised to secure some remarkably fine specimens for the Rat Commander and I fancy he will find some lively corpses when he opens the bag I intend to send him. Curiously enough, I have just heard from the Quarter-Master Sergeant that the dirge which the infants sing about fifteen times day in the schools adjoining is Fontaine's fable, 'The Lion and the Rat'.

* * * * * *

After a tour of duty of 16 days, soldiers generally could expect a similar period of rest. Sport and entertainment were often organised by officers, perhaps remembering their school days. *The Draconian* received details of 'Aquatic "Spasms" at the Front', organised by an anonymous Old Dragon Royal Engineer in August 1915.

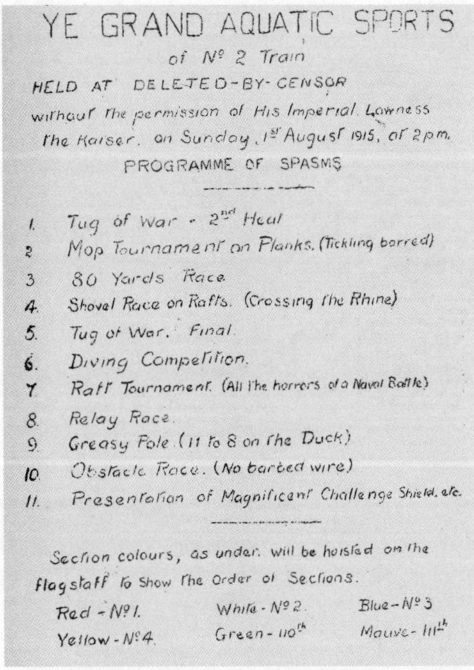

YE GRAND AQUATIC SPORTS

of Nº 2 Train

HELD AT DELETED-BY-CENSOR

without the permission of His Imperial Lowness the Kaiser. on Sunday, 1st August 1915, at 2pm.

PROGRAMME OF SPASMS

1. Tug of War - 2nd Heat
2. Mop Tournament on Planks. (Tickling barred)
3. 80 Yards Race.
4. Shovel Race on Rafts. (Crossing the Rhine)
5. Tug of War. Final.
6. Diving Competition.
7. Raft Tournament. (All the horrors of a Naval Battle)
8. Relay Race.
9. Greasy Pole. (11 to 8 on the Duck)
10. Obstacle Race. (No barbed wire)
11. Presentation of Magnificent Challenge Shield, etc.

Section colours, as under, will be hoisted on the flagstaff to show the Order of Sections.

Red - Nº1.	White - Nº2.	Blue - Nº3
Yellow - Nº4.	Green - 110th	Mauve - 111th

A programme of 'Grand Aquatic Sports', August 1915, published in *The Draconian*, December 1915

Yesterday we organised a Regatta, or rather some Water-sports on the Canal basin, by the side of which our train is stabled. Everything passed off most successfully, and it was a very laughable affair as well as a big success. The greasy pole was however too easy, and the expert came too soon among the competitors and released the coop which held the duck, who fell into the water, where it was chased and captured by one of the competitors.

We wound up the programme with a surprise for the spectators. A mock telegram was read out as from the Kaiser saying he was sending a submarine to stop the sports. A submarine with U.29 painted on it was then pulled in by wires, and as a wind-up, we exploded a mine under it. All events were held in the water; and the instability of the rafts (which were made of sleepers lashed to drums) was a source of constant amusement.

The very last item on the programme was the presentation of prizes, among them being a Challenge Shield made out of a German shell.

Such jollity did not mask the fact that in the past year the O.P.S. had lost eight of its Old Boys; a further 26 had been wounded. This seemed no doubt a lot to Skipper and his small school, but worse was to come as the war spread its tentacles across the world to the Dardanelles.

GALLIPOLI CAMPAIGN, 1915

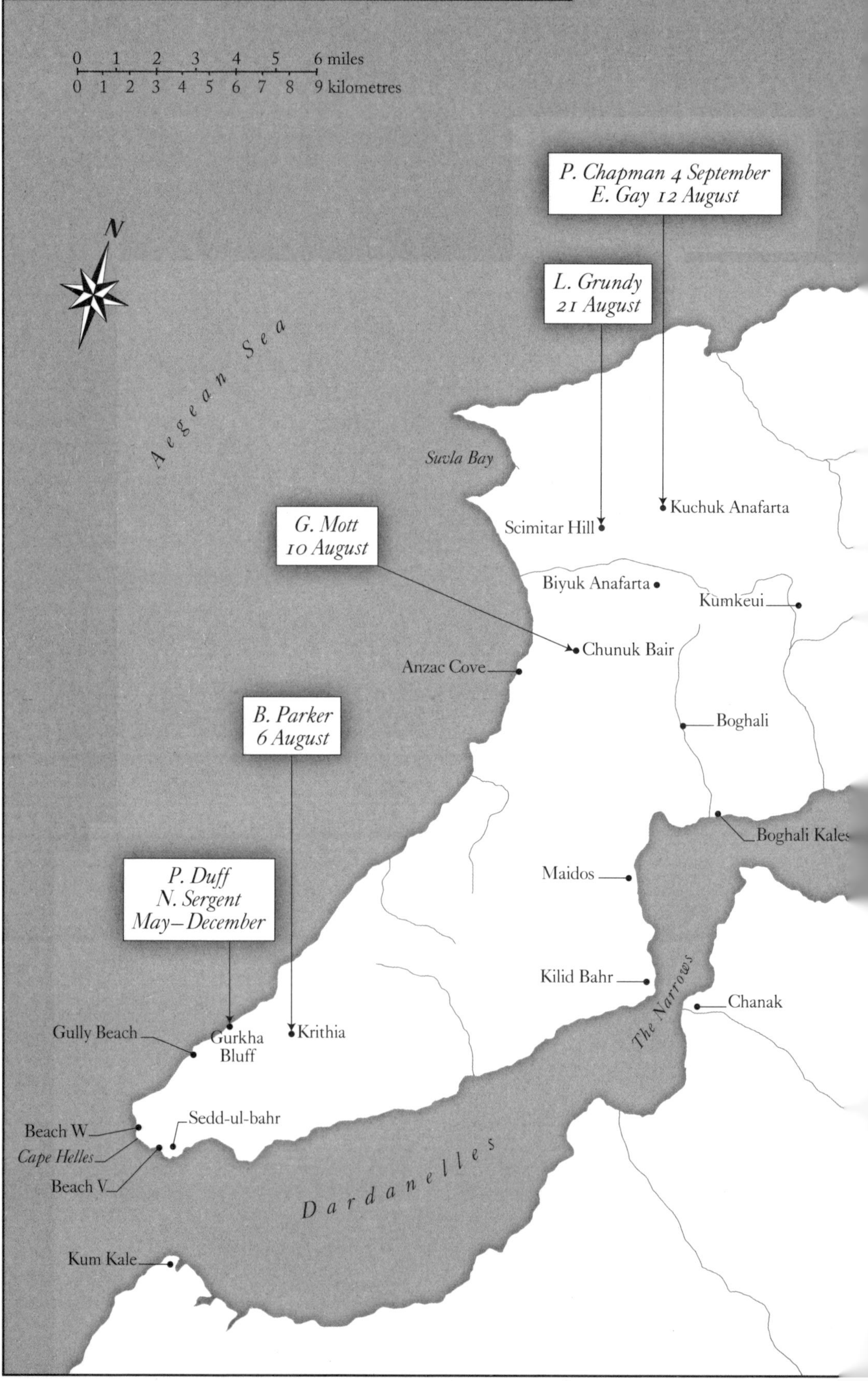

Chapter 8
The Gallipoli Campaign

By the end of 1914 the Allies had suffered nearly one million casualties and the trenches stretched over 400 miles (644 km), from the North Sea to Switzerland. With the lack of a breakthrough on the Western Front, thoughts turned to the idea of opening up another front. Winston Churchill, First Lord of the Admiralty at this time, was very keen on attacking Constantinople, bringing help to the Russians. Following an unsuccessful attempt to force their way through to Constantinople with the navy, the decision was taken to commit the army to a land operation. The first landings, at Anzac Cove and Cape Helles, took place on 25 April 1915.

Although these landings were successful, the hoped-for joining of the two forces and advance on Constantinople did not materialise. As a result, a war of attrition similar to the trench warfare on the Western Front emerged.

Life on the Peninsula

Pat Duff, now a Captain in the Royal Field Artillery, had been another of the five O.P.S. hockey blues in the team of 1911 (see p. 54). In 1915 he was serving with the R.F.A. in the Cape Helles sector. Pat kept a diary throughout the campaign and sent instalments home for publication in *The Draconian*. Some were entertaining, but others were sober accounts of what became a disastrous campaign. Apart from the Australian and New Zealand forces, the British also found themselves fighting alongside a French division. Pat was clearly not too impressed by some of their troops, who he believed were too easily rattled.

Pat Duff

9 May 1915
One dashed into my lines two nights ago (being nearly shot by my guard); I shouted 'Français, venez ici'. He was a little man with a huge rifle and bayonet, and looked as if he were supporting a lamp post. I asked what was happening, and where his comrades were.

He gesticulated and danced about saying 'on crie, sauve qui peut. Rien ne va plus; les Turcs do this, that, and the other and I am a most miserable soldier'.

So I replied, 'Courage, comrade; revanche, Marseilles, Paris attaque, grande attaque'.

This apparently did the trick and the Frenchman returned whence he had come. Pat admitted to being a little disconcerted but, believing that the Frenchman had 'got the wrong end of the stick', he held his ground.

Six days later it was the turn for the French to be unimpressed by the behaviour of their British allies.

> *15 May 1915*
> *There was rather fun the other day, though I didn't see it. A hare got up and all the English, of course, leapt to their feet with fearful yells. Presently a French General came to complain of this behaviour: 'à la guerre, comme à la guerre, et à la chasse comme à la chasse!' He explained that his enfants think it is the Turks who arrive when they hear the row.*

Part of Pat's job was to join the infantry in their trenches to identify targets for the artillery, not all of them of great importance. On one occasion, peering through his field glasses, he spotted little puffs of smoke, indicating that the Turks were brewing up some tea.

> *22 May 1915*
> *This was more than we could stand, so we telephoned down to the Battery, 'Action', and gave various angles and elevations with the result that the Turkish trench was heavily shelled, causing, as we hoped A.A.D. (which being interpreted means 'Alarm And Despondency').*
>
> *It is rumoured that the above condition prevails in the English Press regarding this expedition; not surprised.*

There was some time for recreation and the occasional acquisition of luxuries. On one of his visits back to the beach where all the stores were landed, Pat managed to intercept and board an incoming ship. There he was able to buy, duty free, a bottle of whisky and a bottle of Heidsieck champagne.

Kind families also sent out welcome supplies – although sometimes these were disappointments.

> *2 June 1915*
>
> *I had some plum pudding the other day which G's people had sent; also the waiter at Buol's* [an Oxford restaurant] *had sent him a slab of turtle soup. This slab was watered down to make soup for all of us, and consequently tasted as if it was water that a turtle had had a bath in.*

* * * * * *

Another Old Dragon, Noel Sergent, being half-French, had joined the French Army on the outbreak of war. He served as a Sous Lieutenant in the French Artillery and in 1915 was sent to Gallipoli as part of the 51e Batterie, 10e Artillerie, E.N.E. Secteur

194, Armée d'Orient. Noel was in fact stationed quite close to his Old Dragon friend on Gurkha Bluff, and the two men managed to meet up.

> *Pat Duff came and saw me the other day; he is very thin owing to a touch of dysentery, so I gave him the pomegranate skin which had just reached me. He brought me over papers* – Sphere, Tatler *etc and I was delighted to see him.*

Like Pat Duff, Noel kept a diary. In August he described his part in an attack.

> *We have two 9½-inch coast guns, and we had a job hauling them up in three parts each, the piece itself causing the greatest difficulty owing to its weight (16 tons). We put 100 men on either side and hauled away; then, when we got them up, 25 of us had to put them in place. We were at work for four nights from 6 p.m. to 5 a.m., with just a cup of caffeine at eleven.*
>
> *Our guns were ready for firing yesterday, so we started today. We topped our drive, put our second shot over the green, on the green in 3 …*

Noel Sergent's gun and crew in the Cape Helles sector, Gallipoli campaign, 1915

> *On August 6th we assisted at an attack. It was a tremendous business and the best way I can describe it is by comparing it to a terrific thunderstorm when the thunder and lightning come before the rain, and directly the rain comes the thunder and lightning stop. The thunder and lightning are the flash and bang of multitudinous guns, and the*

patter of the rain is the rifle and machine-gun fire. What a fearful noise they make once they are started! I believe we took two trenches – hardly seemed worth the ammunition.

Noel sent back a photo of one of his guns being fired, which duly appeared in *The Draconian* of December 1915. Most of what looks like smoke was in fact dust, 'rammed down one's throat and between one's teeth by the force of the explosion'.

Noel Sergent's photograph of his guns in action in 1915, which he sent to *The Draconian* for publication

It was unusual for junior officers to see anything of their Commander-in-Chief. However, at one point – probably in September, although no date is given – Noel found himself in front of Sir Ian Hamilton, who asked him how long he thought the war would last. Noel was wary in his response.

I wasn't going to make an idiot of myself by making a wild guess, so I said we have had so many surprises that I couldn't possibly tell. So he told me that in his opinion the war would last about another year, and that the Germans weren't counting on having to go through another winter campaign, and that next spring something decisive would happen, and that decisive something would come from this side.

* * * * * *

Geoffrey Smyth, a Captain in the 6th Loyal North Lancashire Regiment – and no relation to Jack Smyth V.C. – had landed on the Gallipoli peninsula in July 1915. He spent a brief spell in the trenches, but by the end of the month had been wounded in the foot by some shrapnel. It was not until September that Geoffrey was able to rejoin his battalion – only to experience an even closer shave.

> *29 October 1915*
> *I was reading in bed about 7.30, when a shell came into my dug-out and burst … I could not see anything for about half a minute for smoke, but I climbed out through where the roof had been … a box of provisions was badly wounded, but most of it has survived luckily, although broken glass foretells loss of whiskey. My rifle had the wood stripped off it and the barrel was twisted; the bayonet left the rifle and quitted the dug-out before I did. By the curve on the pieces of shell found among the ruins I should say it was a 5 or 6 in. shell.*

By some miracle all Geoffrey suffered was a couple of scratches on the back of the neck.

Geoffrey Smyth

* * * * * *

Basil Parker (Captain, Royal Hampshire Regiment) had volunteered to serve in the Boer War in the Imperial Yeomanry, Paget's Horse, but transferred to the Hampshires in 1901. Basil was also sent to the Dardanelles, and arrived on W Beach at the beginning of May.

Basil Parker

1 May 1915
This life seems to suit me, I never felt better in my life. Reveille at 4 a.m. and bed at 8 p.m. daily. I drink unlimited tea, no sugar or milk in it, and eat biscuits; can't get bread at any price.

7 May 1915
Got myself into trouble and a bullet into my head, or very near it. It came in absolutely in the centre of my cap (fired from the right), and came out where the top of the cap and the part that fits your head join. I have had luck because, on its way through, it took a piece out of my head as a cheese-scoop would do, down to the bone without damaging the skull.

I could not at first make out what had happened. I felt a huge bang on the head, as if a polo ball had hit me, and asked the man next to me, 'What on earth is that?' 'You're hit in the head, sir.' It began to bleed badly, so I went back a little and got it tied up.

Given stalemate at both Anzac and Helles, plans were made to open up a third bridgehead at Suvla Bay, north of the Anzac position. On the night of 6 August, without a preliminary bombardment to warn the enemy, some 20,000 troops were put ashore at Suvla Bay. They were intended to push on inland to gain the vantage point of the hills, and then join up with the Anzac troops.

Meanwhile, in one of the diversionary attacks that took place both on the Anzac and Cape Helles fronts, Basil Parker was involved in the charge of the 2nd Hants at Krithia, on 6 August 1915.

An unattributed account of this action was printed in *The Draconian* of December 1915.

Exactly at 4 p.m. Captain Parker, who was in command, called out, 'Time's up, my lads', and those in the first trench immediately leapt out, those in the second at once taking their places and leaping out a minute later, and those in the third line doing the same. All were well up in a good deal less than 5 minutes, and with a cheer they rushed forward. It was a glorious charge and everyone showed splendid courage.

The Turks were startled, and took a minute or two – not much more – to get their machine guns (of which they had one for about every 5 yards, and which during the bombardment they had hidden in the trenches) into position, so that our men got some way across the open space. Apparently, however, none reached the Turkish trench. All were mown down.

Of the second line, a few got across. Of the third line which had fewer men, more than half got through, and those who were left of the battalion held the trench until they were relieved by the R. Scots and R. Fusiliers. A private said positively that the Turks were driven from their front trench which remained in our hands, as perhaps did some others.

The open ground was so heavily swept by gun fire that it was impossible to bring in the wounded or the dead, even at night. Some may have crawled in, but the severely wounded must have died. As none could be recovered and identified, they were posted as missing. In the evening of the 6th only 250 out of 900 of the Hants answered to their names.

It was an expensive diversion.

What was left of the 2nd Hants after their charge on 6 August 1915 receive the congratulations of the G.O.C. Division

Basil Parker (Captain, Royal Hampshire Regiment)

Amongst those killed was Basil Parker – a victim, it could be said, of smoking. An unattributed letter to the family revealed that he had left his trench to visit another, when he was hit by a bullet in his left side. It exited near his left breast, but unfortunately then deflected off his cigarette case back into his body.

> *He died four minutes afterwards with his head resting on the leg of a lieutenant. He was brought back to the dressing station and buried at 7.10 a.m. on the following morning about 50 yards behind the firing line.*

* * * * * *

The troops who landed at Suvla Bay had taken too long to organise themselves and advance inland, allowing time for Turkish reinforcements to take up defensive positions. Fierce counterattacks followed both there and in the Anzac sector. In the latter Geoffrey Mott – a Major in the South Lancashire Regiment and one of three Old Dragon brothers, all of whom had also served in the Boer War – found himself up against the Turkish counterattack at Chunuk Bair on 10 August 1915. It lasted nearly six hours, with the Turks advancing in wave after wave. Many were cut down, both by shrapnel shells from the battleships offshore and machine-gun fire from positions to the rear of Geoffrey Mott. He commented that he had never seen 'greater pluck than that displayed by the Turk, particularly on this day'. It is not clear exactly where Geoffrey was hidden. Wherever it was, the Turks had not spotted him and he was ideally situated to do some sniping:

Geoffrey Mott

> *How many rounds I fired during all those hours I should be sorry to count. By my side lay a man who passed me ammunition and my field glasses as required – fresh rifles were handed on to me as each one got too hot to hold, and another man kept record of my score.*

He noticed a machine-gun detachment, commanded by a German officer only 150 yards (137 m) away.

> *I picked him off with my second shot, and shortly after two of his gunners, and then opened rapid fire on the remainder which must have dispersed them as that gun never came into action, at least not from that position or anywhere near it.*
>
> *With regard to the bushes, I let a dozen Turks or so bunch together behind them before pouring in the contents of my magazine, or sometimes two; this had the effect of making a few men bolt in all directions to get clear of such false cover, but how many I hit in this way it would be impossible to say, and not one could be fairly included in the 'bag'.*

Geoffrey ended with a 'bag' of 47 Turks plus the German officer. He was reasonably pleased with his 'score'.

> *A fair day's work, though very trifling, of course, in comparison with the wholesale slaughter effected by our guns and machine guns whose handiwork would beggar description, for the Turkish dead must have amounted to thousands.*

Suvla Bay Operations

Among the troops who had landed at Suvla Bay were Edmund Gay and Philip Chapman – Captain in the Royal Norfolk Regiment and Private in the 8th Battalion of the Royal Hampshire Regiment respectively. On 12 August Edmund was involved in the unsuccessful attempt to break out from the landing area and take the high point of Tekke Tepe at Anafarta. *The Draconian* included Sir Ian Hamilton's own dispatch regarding the events that led to Edmund's death.

> *In the course of the fight, creditable in all respects to the 163rd Brigade, there happened a very mysterious thing. The 1/5th Norfolks were on the right of the line and found themselves for a moment less strongly opposed than the rest of the Brigade. Against the yielding forces of the enemy Colonel Sir H. Beauchamp, a bold, self-confident officer, eagerly pressed forward, followed by the best part of the Battalion. The fighting grew hotter and the ground became more wooded and broken. At this stage many men were wounded or grew exhausted with thirst. These found their way back to camp during the night. But the Colonel with 10 officers and 250 men kept pushing on, driving the enemy before him … and were lost to sight and sound. Not one of them ever came back.*

As one company hailed from the King's Sandringham estate, their loss was newsworthy, with talk of their being a 'lost legion'.

The Dragon School's *War Memorials* book recorded that, after the war, the remains of 180 soldiers were discovered some 800 yards (732 m) beyond the Turkish front line. Of these, 122 could be identified as 5th Norfolks and three of them were officers.

Edmund Gay (Captain, Norfolk Regiment)

The fate of Edmund Gay was unclear.

> *Private information supplies the fact that Edmund was last seen getting over a fence or wall into the farm with a sergeant and another man. The man who last saw him was wounded and lay out all night beside the body of another 1/5th Norfolk soldier, and managed to crawl into our lines the next day.*

The Skipper remembered Edmund as a 'tall, thin, pale, bright-smiling boy, not very fond of work, but a tremendous "slogger" at cricket'. That said, he had been academic enough to go on to Winchester and New College, Oxford.

* * * * * *

Philip Chapman was one of a handful of Old Dragons to serve in the ranks. On leaving Clifton College, he studied music with the aim of becoming a college organist. When war broke out he joined the 8th Battalion of the Royal Hampshire Regiment and landed in Suvla Bay on 10 August, as did Edmund Gay. Without realising it, Chapman and Gay fought alongside one another, as the 8th Hants were on Gay's left flank when the Norfolks outstripped the Hampshires and disappeared.

Philip Chapman (Private, Royal Hampshire Regiment)

Philip survived this engagement, but was wounded when his trench was shelled on 24 August. He was hit by splinters which shattered his right forearm and exposed a large area of muscle in his back. These wounds were at once dressed and his arm amputated just below the elbow. Philip was then evacuated to Malta, which he reached five days later.

By an extraordinary quirk of fate, he was admitted there to the care of a Mr Charters Symonds, one of the surgeons in charge, who happened to be his godfather. On 5 September Mr Symonds wrote to Philip's family with sad news.

> *All our efforts failed, and the dear boy passed away last night at 10 o'clock …*
>
> *Yesterday it was obvious that he could not live long and I was with him in the morning and again in the afternoon and later on till he died. He asked for me and seemed so relieved when I was near. Then I left a little before six to operate on an urgent case some distance away, and got back about 8.45.*
>
> *He welcomed me again and asked if he would 'pull through' and again 'would he be here tomorrow?'*

I said a few words, and later 'Goodbye', and he, as bravely as anyone could do, replied 'Goodbye'.

I said 'You must give me a kiss that I may give it to your mother', and he did so.

I said we should meet again, and he said 'Yes, we shall', and then he fell on a little sleep. Waking, perhaps from the oxygen that we were giving to relieve his breathing, he said 'I was quite prepared to die, and does not this bring it all over again?'

When I said it was to ease his breathing, he said 'All right' in that quiet, satisfied and resigned way that I had so much learned to appreciate. I gave a little morphia, which relieved his back pains. Never did he wander for a moment or utter one unclear word; he was fully conscious and knew his end was near.

Then most wonderful of all, he fixed his eyes looking outward as he lay on his side and said slowly and with halting breath, each word separated, and some syllables also: 'This is the most be-a-utiful moment of my life … Oh! What a su-p-erb mo-ment'. Then he smiled so sweetly and with so satisfied an expression that we knew he had seen a vision …

I shall ever be grateful to a kind Providence who guided our wounded boy to my care, and that I was able to help him in his last moments.

Skipper remembered Philip as a boy for his devotion to music, and the fact he was always to be found at the piano in his free time. However, had he survived his wounds, with only one arm there would have been no future for him as a college organist.

Scimitar Hill

A contemporary of Philip's at the O.P.S., Leslie Grundy, had been commissioned as Lieutenant in the 6th Battalion of the York and Lancaster Regiment in September 1914. Two weeks after landing at Suvla Bay he found himself taking part in the biggest battle of the campaign – a dual assault on Scimitar Hill (known by the troops as Burnt Hill) and Hill 112. The object of the attack was to unite the Suvla forces with those of the Anzacs.

Leslie described his part in the attack of 21 August in some detail. He had come up from the beach with his men the previous evening, finding his way eventually to dug-out 5 on Hill 50 (also known as Green Hill) just before dawn broke. His account for *The Draconian* describes a battle that he was very lucky to have survived.

During morning spotted a Turkish gun with telescope and sent news back to headquarters. All very tired but fairly cheery. Plans come up showing Turkish trenches – had found them out ourselves two hours before. Had quick lunch of boiled bacon and biscuits and went out to watch preliminary artillery bombardment. Big shells bursting all over trenches in front of Hill **C** (112), *but few seem to get the mark. Noise terrific, generally four high explosive shells bursting at a time. Four fell into redoubt marked* **K** *and must have done a lot of damage. Turks obviously 'lying doggo' at the bottom of their trenches until storm over.*

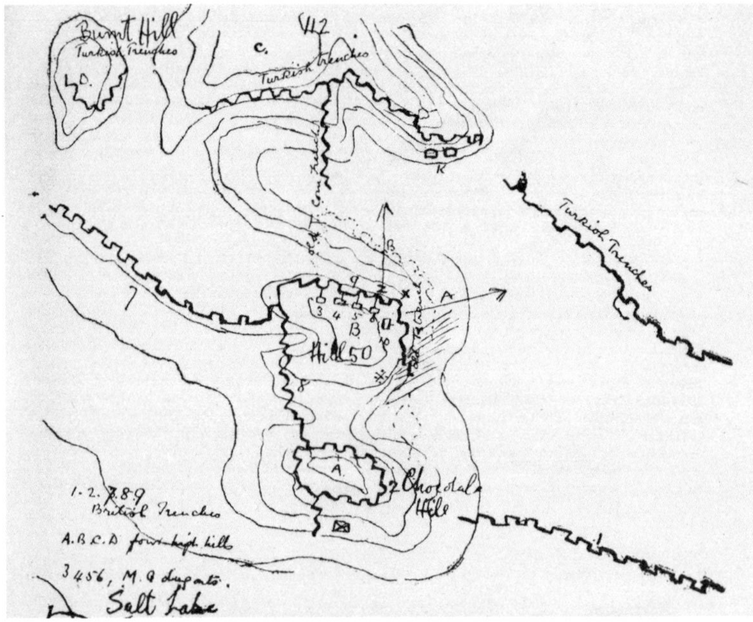

Leslie Grundy's handwritten diagram, made to accompany his description of the events of 21 August 1915

We then opened fire with our guns. Mine were at points **X** *and* **Y**. *We first of all fire at points on the Turkish trenches in direction indicated by arrow* **A** *until our own troops advancing from trenches* **1** *seem to be near the Turkish trenches. We then switched round on to the trenches half-way up Hill* **C** *(112). We kept up a continuous fire on these, the Turks returning our fire with interest. The men in the trenches were now beginning to fall. I myself was with gun* **X** *observing the firing with a periscope when my No.1 (the man firing the gun) fell on top of me, shot through the head. He died almost instantly. The best man in the section.*

Our men meanwhile advanced to a point about **A** *of the arrow* **A**, *and men came into our trenches to go to their support. A great many were shot coming over the back of our trench, and the trench was full of wounded. After a few minutes they made a rush over our front parapet down the hill through the scrub. Only half got over the parapet, the rest fell back into the trench wounded or killed. An officer passed me with three fingers blown off and a hole in his chest.*

*About this time a fire started at point marked * and swept in direction of arrows. The thick scrub, about 3 ft high, burns very well and it is impossible to put out. There were any amount of wounded in it and only about six were rescued – the rest burnt to death. It was the same all over the place in the valley – heath fires and wounded.*

A heavy shelling (shrapnel, thank Heaven!) started about this time (5 p.m.) and one lodged right on top of the section dug-out. I had just started along to see what damage had been done, when my periscope (which I had left standing) was blown to pieces by a shell that burst not 3 ft from it …

> *Shell storm ceased, so the Brigade M.G.O. and myself got a gun firing on to Hill* **D** *(Burnt Hill) at 1200 yds., where we could see the Turks standing up in their trenches and firing at our men only 50 yards below them. We had them in enfilade …*
>
> *We got them absolutely by surprise, and we could see them falling like flies over the front and back of the parapets and dropping into the trenches.*

This may well have saved the life of a certain William Wedgwood Benn (Captain, 1/1 County of London Yeomanry), the father and grandfather of Labour politicians Tony and Hilary Benn, who was one of those attacking Burnt Hill. He later described the event.

> *We lay down flat, and then crawled a little higher up the hill, hearing all the time the terrifying rattle of a Maxim which we, of course, thought was the cause of all the killing. We assured one another for our better comfort that it must be one of our own guns covering the advance, and this, in fact, turned out to be true.*[1]

This action drew the fire on to Leslie's men – but luckily he had a premonition.

> *We had fired for about 15 minutes when something warned me to make him sit down in the trench, so we sat down for a minute. It must have been some sort of premonition, for the next minute a shell storm started, the first shell sending its bullets right on to our gun, smashing the telescope which I had left on the parapet – about as narrow an escape as you could well desire.*

Overall this attack was not successful. There were some 5,000 British casualties, many of whom were wounded and then burned to death in the bush fires. Not long after this battle Leslie was himself invalided home, suffering from sunstroke and dysentery.

Naval Support

Meanwhile Charles Mayhew, a Major in the Royal Marine Light Infantry, was on board H.M.S. *Swiftsure*; he spent this period lying off Suvla Bay. Charles had arrived on 13 August 1915, just a week after the landings took place, and wrote to *The Draconian* to explain 'something about the Naval side of the Dardanelles campaign, as far as is possible without coming under the ban of the Censor'. The chief work of the Royal Navy, Charles wrote, was the landing of men, munitions and a considerable amount of general stores; only once that had been achieved could they turn their long-range guns on Turkish gun emplacements. However, these were well concealed and air observation was needed to spot them, so the navy often focused on the Turkish camps, some six miles distant, instead. Cooped up in the narrow confines of a ship meant that ways for the men to get some exercise required some thought. A game of hockey on the quarterdeck was a popular option and one that Charles enjoyed.

> [It makes] *up in vigour what it lacks in science and observance of rules, and causes more casualties among officers than all the shelling; this is occasionally interrupted by a visit from a Taube commonly called Cuthbert, which at one time made a positive*

habit of flying over in the evening and dropping bombs at us; one of which actually got within 200 yards of the ship.

One evening Charles was startled by a tremendous bombardment unleashed by the Turks on the Allies' lines, finding 'the sight of the shrapnel and star-shells bursting with the noise of the continuous rattle of maxims and rifle firing most awe-inspiring'. It was not heralding a night attack, however.

The real explanation was that our men in the trenches had just heard the good news from the Western Front and a Scotch regiment started playing the bagpipes and cheering lustily, which so alarmed the Turks that they started all down the line loosing off anything that came to hand.

The Evacuation

The Gallipoli campaign had never enjoyed overwhelming support and, with the departure of Churchill from office and continued lack of success, the Dardanelles Committee began to consider the prospect of evacuating the peninsula. Sir Ian Hamilton estimated that as many as 40,000 of his troops might not get off in such an event, but in October he was replaced by General Sir Charles Munro – the same man who had survived the shelling of Hooge Château that killed Arthur Percival in 1914 (see p. 83). Munro believed, as did many others, that the war could only be won on the Western Front; nothing he saw when he got to Gallipoli changed his mind. The idea of evacuation took root. On 7 December the Cabinet finally agreed that Anzac and Suvla Bay would be evacuated. Kitchener agreed with Munro – rightly, as it turned out – that it would be possible to conduct the operation with minimal losses.

The evacuation of the Anzac and Suvla bridgeheads was carried out on the nights of 18 and 19 December; the final 20,000 troops departed on 19 December. Geoffrey Smyth (Captain, 6th Loyal N. Lancs) wrote from on board the *Hunts Green*, a captured German ship being used to evacuate his men.

Geoffrey Smyth

22 December 1915
I suppose by the time you get this the evacuation of Suvla will be old news. I really believe we did deceive the enemy this time – anyway, about five divisions got away without leaving anyone behind; and in our brigade there wasn't a casualty. For two weeks before, all the spare equipment and baggage was sent away and also the postal service, hence the reason why no letter for a fortnight. I marched the last party but two of our battalion to the beach, starting at 8 p.m., the last party leaving the trenches at 1.30 a.m. They say everything was normal up till the last. The night before half the troops were evacuated, and all the last day the line was pretty thinly held. Everything was excellently planned and worked without a hitch…

* * * * * *

Dick Sergent had been born in England and thus did not join the French Army like his French-born brother Noel. Instead he served as Sub Lieutenant in the Royal Naval Volunteer Reserve. Coincidentally Dick was also at Gallipoli, and he too reported on a successful escape.

Dick Sergent

2 January 1916

We are now in Imbros again after having left Anzac, the whole bunch of us. This is to let you know something of the way we did it … We got some wind of it about a week, or perhaps more, before the evacuation (we were instructed only to speak of it as 'embarkation').

Our men set some automatic rifles when they left, and some mines and barbed wire in the trenches. The rifles were managed by way of billy-cans on the triggers with water dripping into them so they went off when the cans were heavy enough; they were set to go off raggedly, as if we were firing normally, for about 1½ hours after our men had gone.

We were to have boarded the Colne, *but she was not to be found, so we picked up the first destroyer we came across, the* Basilisk *… I went up into the W/T cabin and put on a pair of phones to hear the stations at Suvla and Anzac give their 'dismantling' signals. We heard the two at Suvla do so, but not our own. Finally we got a bunting signal that all stragglers etc had been picked up, including the last field hospital which was to have stayed on to look after the wounded in case we had to fight for it …*

We had the supreme pleasure of seeing John Turk shelling our first line trenches at 6.30 a.m. at Suvla and Anzac, and the beach at Anzac also.

* * * * * *

No sooner had the evacuation of Anzac and Suvla Bay been completed than General Munro immediately recommended evacuation of Cape Helles to complete the abandonment of the Gallipoli peninsula. On 27 December the Cabinet agreed.

With an ever-increasing likelihood of the Turks massing for a final attack, a similar plan was put into operation to remove the 35,000 British troops there. By 7 January a large number of French and 19,000 British troops had been evacuated. It was at this point that the Turks attacked – but with a singular lack of conviction, as witnessed by Pat Duff (Captain, R.F.A.).

In the afternoon they put in the biggest and most intense bombardment they ever made, and their front line and supports were seen bristling with bayonets. When their guns lifted, however, their infantry would not come out, except at the extreme right of their line, where a most gallant crowd of yeomanry stood up and shot them down. A cheer started on the left of our line and went across from sea to sea, and the Turkish attack was finished. After this reverse <******> *they* <******>[2] *confined themselves to shelling the beach as usual…*

* * * * * *

This spirited repulsing of the Turkish troops convinced Otto Liman von Sanders, the German general who served as advisor to the Turks throughout the campaign, that there were no immediate plans for evacuation and no further move was made. Thus on the night of 8 January the final troops were able to depart unmolested, among them Noel Sergent (Sous Lieutenant, French Artillery). He described the process in detail, his account appearing in the August 1916 edition of *The Draconian*.

Noel Sergent

23 January 1916
Mudros. Our battery was the last French battery to go off. They fired up to 5 in the evening, then at 7 the Captain, Lieutenant, another, myself and seven men remained at the guns. We rammed earth sacks down the mouths of the guns, then put 26 dynamite cartridges in each ... Then we got our packs and banged about with a sledge-hammer, put the breeches of the guns on the trucks and started off.

They made their way down to the shore line at Sedd-ul-Bahr, where they emptied the breeches into the water. Just then a horn was sounded, warning of an incoming shell from a Turkish gun on the opposite shore.

> *That meant 40 seconds before the shell came along. We all got behind anything and the shot went just over our heads on to the quay by the* River Clyde [the wreck of a British ship, dating from the time of the landings].

Noel felt that the time had come to evacuate Gallipoli, although he had regrets at how the campaign had gone.

> *It is sickening to think that we have been under fire for six months and that the total result of our fighting is that we have got to go and leave our material and everything, especially some 100,000 dead, in the hands of the Turks.*
>
> *It is a good thing anyway that England has at last realised her mistake and has been brave enough to own up to it.*

* * * * * *

The events of 30 December to 9 January were also covered in Pat Duff's diary.

30 December 1915
I think there is very little doubt that we are going. I write this in the middle of a large expenditure of ammunition on what seems a useless target, just, I take it, to get rid of the stuff.

It is quite exciting and I have no sentimental objection to leaving Gallipoli, as the show is obviously a failure, and we shall see another war in a new country.

The next day Pat had to dismantle two of his guns and transport them back down to W Beach, together with a lot of his men's kit. On New Year's Day he was surprised to receive a wire from his general wishing his men a 'Happy and *victorious* New Year'.

> *A farcical epithet at a moment when we are in the act of sneaking away from a place we've held for eight months and in a deadly funk every minute that the Turk will spot it and jump on us.*

By 4 January Pat was manning his position with just a single gun and 50 rounds of ammunition. A wind had got up, however, and he knew it would be impossible for the force to evacuate in these conditions. Going down to the beach on 5 January, he found a long train of 18 pounders that they had been unable to embark in the conditions, along with 'piles of stuff lying about in confusion'. There was a reason for this, however:

> *Everything is going to be piled up on the edge of the cliff and to be blown to blazes by the Navy the morning after we leave.*

By the evening the wind had dropped and this proved to be Pat's last night on the peninsula. The following evening he was on his way.

> *6 January 1916*
> *Rode out on my little horse with the gun about 8, and thought how I should follow the dim roads of Gallipoli by night no more. Some of the more recent arrivals hail the departure with delight; but we who have been here since the very beginning find it hard to leave the place. One knows it more intimately than any spot on earth, having moved about on it at all hours of the night, and dug ourselves into it in every direction.*
>
> *Frightful crush on the beach. I managed to get a move on and presently brought my gun to the pier. Shells were dropping on the other side of the beach, but nothing close to us. The horses were unhooked and sent away; my saddle was taken off my little horse and put on the limber and off he went in the dark.*
>
> *Got out to a ship and had the gun and limber on it by about 5 a.m., and so now I write this sitting on the floor of a cabin, feeling the wiggle of the screw and beginning to realise that, for the time being, I have saved my soul alive.*

Pat had left nothing behind save his little horse, which he knew would be shot. He asked that a shoe be taken off the animal and saved for him. Whether he ever received it is not known.

The final withdrawal took place over the night of 8/9 January – Z night, as it was termed. His description was censored, but is still powerfully evocative.

> *About 4 a.m. the Chief woke me and said, 'the bonfires are lit'. I went on deck; on W Beach about eight great fires were burning and the blaze lighted up the whole place. <******> suddenly a terrific explosion came <******> throwing up the earth in the shape of a huge fan about 100 feet into the air. Shortly after came another awful*

> *burst, hiding the whole beach behind the falling debris and smoke. Flaming splinters seemed to be flying about everywhere, some falling in the sea.*
>
> *There was another fire on V Beach, and I could see the huge wall of the castle of Sedd-ul-bahr in the glare (reminded me rather of Virgil's description of the fall of Troy when the forms of the malignant gods loomed out above the smoking walls). Just around the corner from W Beach another heap <******> was ablaze, and there was a fire on Gully Beach. For an hour or more I stood watching the flames; the Turks were at first firing shrapnel into the middle of the beach, thinking they had set fire to something and that they would catch those who were putting it out. About 5 a.m. they seemed to realise we were gone, as they started shelling out to sea among the ships.*
>
> *About 5.30 we began to move slowly away and the fires grew smaller in the distance. So we left W beach looking like the gates of hell, as it was when we first came there.*

Safely away, Pat allowed himself a little time to reflect on a campaign that he perceived to have been a total disaster. What would be its place in history?

> *This is the end of the Expedition which was to have opened the Dardanelles, filled up Russia with supplies, and as we fondly hoped, advanced in rear of the Austro-Germans along the Danube. How far the frightful waste of men and materials will affect England's fortunes one can't tell, and just now it is hard to take a dispassionate view; but, results apart, I cannot think there is any enterprise comparable to this, except the Athenian Expedition to Sicily, which started with the same high hopes and ended with total disaster to the troops employed and the ultimate fall of the Empire.*

* * * * * *

The campaign's greatest success was ironically the evacuation. Sir Ian Hamilton had told the Cabinet that such an operation could not in his view be carried out without heavy casualties – perhaps as high as 50 per cent. In the event, however, the losses were negligible. Yet, set against that were the 180,000 casualties sustained by the Allies, over 50,000 of whom were killed.

Of the 20 Old Dragons who had journeyed to the Dardanelles, four did not return.

BONDS

Chapter 9

The Winter of 1915–16

'Dearly Loved Masters …'

A year before the events of Gallipoli, Leslie Eastwood had been teaching young Dragons at the O.P.S. He supervised their sport and took pride in being an 'older brother out of school' – the role that Skipper advocated for his masters. He joined up and was sent to the Dardanelles as a 2nd Lieutenant in the King's Own Royal Lancaster Regiment in the spring of 1915. News of his being wounded in Gallipoli reached the school in early August. It did not seem to be too serious a wound, however, and Leslie was able to update his family and friends on his progress throughout that month.

> *2 August 1915*
> *I hope you will get this letter before you hear from any other source that I am wounded. I have two wounds, one in the arm, quite slight, and one in the leg which may, perhaps, have done some damage to the knee. The bullet is still in and the Doctor has not yet made a thorough examination; it gives me practically no pain now and I don't think it can be at all bad. I am on a new Hospital Ship which had just come out here.*

Shortly after this he wrote to his family from the 17th General Hospital in Alexandria, to which he had been transferred. In his letter Leslie explained how he had received shrapnel wounds in the arm and leg, which he described as feeling as if he had been hit 'by a mighty blow with a sledge hammer'.

> *I was taken to the clearing hospital where I was very uncomfortable for 16 hours, having nothing to lie on but a stretcher; then I was taken on board a hospital ship where I remained 10 days. I was operated on and the bullet taken out of my leg; chloroform is not at all bad, not so bad as gas. I arrived here two days ago and am very comfortable.*

His next letter, while sounding positive, revealed another problem.

> *20 August 1915*
> *I am still lying in bed; what a waste of time it seems to be lying here day after day! I was wounded on the 28th July, so I have been in bed for 24 whole days; what a time*

Left: Charles Childe, *A Corner of the Trenches (Flanders)*, 1915

> *it does seem. This dysentery which I have got takes a lot of getting rid of, but there is no doubt I am getting better gradually.*

On 19 September 1915 – only three days before the start of the new school year – Leslie Eastwood died. The Sister in charge of the Officers' Division of the hospital explained what had occurred.

> *I am afraid he delayed too long before he gave in. One of his brother officers told me he suffered from dysentery since the first few days he came out, but would never give in and report sick, and probably had he not been wounded would not have given in when he did. You may rest assured everything that was possible was done for him.*

Dysentery was a greater problem in Gallipoli than on the Western Front. The disease put some 30,000 in hospital, but the fatality rate was under 3 per cent of this number: Leslie was unlucky.

Leslie Eastwood (2nd Lieutenant, King's Own Royal Lancaster Regiment)

Thomas Higginson (Captain, Shropshire Light Infantry)

The following day – some 2,000 miles away, near Armentières in France – 'Higgie' (Tom Higginson), another member of the O.P.S. staff, was also killed. He was the victim of another collapsing dug-out, as his commanding officer explained.

> *He was sitting in a dug-out with another officer about 1.30 a.m. yesterday morning, the 20th September, when the roof collapsed. He had spent most of the day before altering it and adding more bricks and earth to make it proof against shellfire. He must have put on more than the beams could stand, as it gave way.*

Higgie was not a public school man, but he had made his way via Ludlow Grammar School to Balliol, Oxford. There he paid his way by journalism, making quite a large sum with his contributions to the *Westminster* and *Pall Mall* magazines, among others. In his holidays, accompanied by congenial friends, he used to pose as a tramp. Hiring a barrel-organ, they would sing (in harmony) as they travelled around the country. Skipper wrote a moving tribute to both men.

He and Leslie Eastwood soon became great friends on the staff. Eastwood was the practical, determined, go-ahead character, whilst Higgie was the idealist, the dreamer, the artist, musician, and poet.

Higgie left behind Winifred, his wife of only four months.

* * * * * *

When the children returned for the Autumn Term on 22 September, Skipper had to break the news of the loss of these two popular schoolmasters.

It was a sad beginning of term to have to tell the boys that their dearly loved masters, Mr Eastwood and Mr Higginson, had both given their lives for their country. Leslie Eastwood had been with us since 1907 and had become a first-rate schoolmaster. His form was noted for its 'thoroughness'. Strict without being severe, he won the respect and love of his boys and they would at any time do anything for him. It was very seldom indeed that he had to 'send' a boy 'in' to me and yet he had his form always under control. At games he was most keen and successful in his coaching, and showed a manly and loyal spirit that was most stimulating. As a comrade to me on the Blue Dragon *he was splendid. We all miss him very much …*

*'Higgie' was different in some ways. He was more of the idealist, more intellectual perhaps, a writer and thinker, a musician and artist; but he also endeared himself to us and his special work in inspiring enthusiasm for painting and singing was quite unique. The way in which he conquered the difficulties of the introduction of musical comedy (*H.M.S. Pinafore *and* The Pirates of Penzance*) at once stamped him as a genius in organization and initiative. Well, we are all proud of the part they have taken in our country's hour of need and oh, so sorry that we shall no more have them amongst us.*

Letters of sympathy followed the news of the masters' deaths. One of them was from Tom Whittingham, now serving as a Lieutenant in the Royal Leicester Regiment. He had become an accountant before the war while also gaining a commission in the Leicestershire Territorials.

9 October 1915
I must write to sympathise on the loss of two of the staff. But it is by far the noblest death a man can die, and it does one no good to sorrow about these things. Out here, unfortunately, one rarely seems to be able to realise a casualty fully when it occurs; death seems to come as a matter of course. It is only when a death occurs amongst the men one is always with and knows best that one can grasp the full meaning of what has happened.

Only four days after writing this, Tom Whittingham was himself killed. He died in an attack on the Hohenzollern Redoubt, which came at the end of the Battle of Loos and resulted in over 3,700 casualties.

Roll of Honour

Following a two-hour bombardment, Tom was one of 20 officers (all of whom became casualties) who led their men 'over the top'. When the advance was signalled, Tom mounted the parapet with a walking stick in one hand and a revolver in the other. His final moments were described in *The Draconian* of December 1915.

Thomas Whittingham (Lieutenant, Royal Leicestershire Regiment)

> *They advanced over the 150 yards that separated them from the enemy, through machine-gun and rifle bullets, till they reached the limit of the hand-grenade range of the Germans, where they received a momentary check while our bombers replied. Then Tom called on them to advance, and they were within a few yards of the enemy's trenches when a German officer threw a bomb which hit the ground and exploded right in front of him – killing, it is said, five and wounding others.*

Tom's loss was deeply felt by those who had known him. Various activities had brought him a wide network of friends in the community, and he was held in high regard.

> *As a scout officer he took personal interest in the men under him; he also applied himself to know and help the young fellows in an artisan quarter of a large town parish, taking part in their games and working up a Bible class, and getting to know them in their home life. In a short time he won a considerable influence.*

Along with the news of Tom's death came that of Alasdair Macdonell. He was killed on the same day, 13 October 1915, in an attack barely two miles from where Tom Whittingham died. These two deaths touched Skipper most profoundly.

Alasdair's family lived in Bardwell Road, close to the O.P.S. Skipper described him as 'one of the finest performers (if not *the* finest) in athletic sports'. G.C. Vassall measured his record long jump (at the age of only 13) to be 17 ft 1 in (5.2 m). Alasdair went on to win an Athletics 'blue' in due course.

The son of Professor A.A. Macdonell, Alasdair was academic enough to win a scholarship to Repton before going up to Balliol, Oxford, in 1912. After going through Sandhurst he went out to France with the Cameron Highlanders on 3 October 1915, and was thrown immediately into the thick of it. On 9 October he wrote, 'Part of this trench is held by Germans – barricade between'. On 11 October he heard that he had 'to lead a blooming bombing attack along the trench'.

Alasdair Macdonell
(2nd Lieutenant, Queen's Own Cameron Highlanders)

His Colonel wrote of the predictable result.

> *We only know that he was acting most gallantly with an advanced party of bombers down a trench leading into the German line. The actual portion of the trench where he was, was unfortunately regained by the Germans, and is still in their hands; hence nobody can say what actually happened to him.*

Alasdair had survived a mere ten days on the Western Front. His name, together with Tom Whittingham's, is among the 20,000 on the Loos Memorial of those who died, but have no known grave.

Kit Lynam and the Y.M.C.A.

Skipper's own family were also engaged in the war. One of the first casualties in the family was the new husband of his daughter Kit; their marriage turned out to be painfully short, lasting barely a year. Lieutenant Marshall contracted meningitis and died in hospital in Portsmouth on 12 May 1915 without ever seeing action. Notwithstanding this tragedy, within five months Kit Marshall was in France, 'driving a car and working in connection with the St. Leonards School Y.M.C.A. hut, Camp 18, Harfleur Valley, near Le Havre'. From here she described a royal visit, among other experiences, for *The Draconian* of December 1915.

> *29 October 1915*
> *The King visited the camp yesterday, and he looked ill and worn. Only a few of the soldiers round saw him, as they had been on fatigue the day before in a downpour of*

Kit Lynam/Marshall

rain, and of course were soaked to the skin. They have no change of clothes and consequently could not appear properly dressed, so had to stay in their tents till he had gone.

However, it was not George V who made the greatest impression on Kit but the ordinary soldiers. Many of them asked her to help write their letters or advise on tales of domestic woe.

One man came and told us a most pathetic story yesterday. He had been home on leave and when he got to his house, he found it was shut up and his wife and ten months old daughter had gone off with a Belgian refugee.

The character who surprised her most was a strongly built north country miner. He was able to quote Shelley and Keats to her and wanted her to teach him Latin ('I have got a Latin grammar in my tent,' he told her). Curious, Kit enquired how he had come to be so educated. She learnt that he had been an autodidact, living in lodgings on his own; he claimed he had 'never met a woman who liked poetry'.

Having recently had 23 teeth removed, he could not return to the line until a new set of false teeth arrived. This gave Kit the chance to get to know him even better. She was amazed by his superior knowledge.

> *He floors me completely in all save Swinburne and Kipling, which two he does not know. But what surprises me is that things we have been educated up to such as Milton's sonnets, Dante, Spenser and the like, he has discovered and read for his own enjoyment.*

He later wrote to Kit telling her he had been sent back to Blighty with a head wound, adding that he had just discovered Oscar Wilde and was 'devouring his plays'. Enclosed was a copy of Ibsen's *The Warriors at Helgeland.*

'Home-sick' Leave

During the course of the Christmas Term of 1915 Pug Wallace was able to visit the O.P.S., as he was on what *The Draconian* described as 'home-sick leave'. He found the time to deliver a lecture to 'a most enthusiastic and interested audience at the School House one Saturday evening whilst he explained the mysteries of his machine gun', and also to referee a few rugby matches. These were still a regular feature, although travelling was not without difficulty after dark. The return trip from Eagle House School in Sandhurst, for example, involved a range of incidents.

> *A brief halt in Reading to lay in a supply of provisions for the journey home; some narrow escapes for passers-by, lamp posts and animals; various compulsory halts for interviews with special constables; an uninterrupted bump along the Iffley Road – and we found ourselves back at the School House.*

A Second Christmas

In the last Sunday service of term Skipper gave his end of term address. In it he tried to prepare pupils for the more austere Christmas that lay ahead.

We are in the second winter of the Great War and we do not seem to have gained much; but I believe we really are in a far better position.

But there is a long time before we can beat our enemies and win a lasting and glorious peace. We shall lose and suffer much before that good time comes, and your parents and friends at home will be full of anxiety though they will try to hide it from you, their children. The future is dark, everything will be dear and money short, but you will know they will make great sacrifices for you.

They think that the most important thing is that you should go on and they will give up other things for that; and you must help them. There will be few parties, theatres, etc., and you must employ yourselves usefully, cheerfully and unselfishly. Help them all quietly and show that you feel for them in their many troubles. Don't grumble if you don't have a lot of presents, a large Xmas dinner, etc., but rather ask for the turkey and plum pudding to be sent to the soldiers or Belgians, wounded or unwounded. Think of those who are fighting for us in danger and cold.

There followed the usual headmasterly plea for children to engage in some self-analysis and maybe consider the need for some New Year's resolutions.

All of you know within yourselves whether during this term you have been brave and honest and helpful. You know whether you have lied, cheated, used bad language, lost your tempers, been unkind, wasted your time and your parents' money, given your parents pain by not writing regularly. If you feel that you have done these things, do try to cure yourselves and don't do them again.

Less predictably, there followed an admission that schoolmasters are human too, fallible and not always right.

We masters have doubtless often been unfair, thought you were lazy or inattentive when you weren't, pitched into you when you did not deserve it, but we are only boys grown up and it is best for us all to forgive one another at the end of term. Skipper.

The Draconian (censored!)

There was a lull in the fighting in the early months of 1916; on not every day on the Western Front was fear the prevailing emotion. There were times when boredom struck. Maurice Jacks, serving as 2nd Lieutenant in the King's Royal Rifle Corps, craved for his school magazine.

Maurice Jacks

In a stray Oxford Chronicle *which found its way to this dreary corner of Northern France the other day I read an account of* The Tempest *and a letter from the Skipper about the bad state of the roads. These two led my thoughts to the 'School-house afar' and hence this letter. My* Draconian *has not turned up yet; but I can't get on without it and have written for a copy from home.*

It had certainly made its way to General Headquarters, where Cecil Lucas, a Major in the Royal Horse Artillery, and friends 'simply devoured every word … and look forward to every number like anything'.

With such magazines making their way to front-line trenches, some thought had to be given to security. *The Draconian* of April 1916 clarified everyone's responsibilities.

We are requested by the Director of Military Intelligence at the War Office to state that the matter contained in every War Article or letter in The Draconian *is to be treated as confidential, and that no extracts from them may be sent for publication to the newspapers.*

Some material was consequently omitted and it was stated that 'any vacant or starred space in this number of *The Draconian* has been censored to meet the requirements of paragraph 453, King's Regulations'.

Sometimes this was not necessary, however. Maurice Jacks found a way to tell fellow Dragons exactly where he was, confident that the Germans would not know Shakespeare:

Being more or less conscientious I cannot tell you exactly where 'here' is, but if you remember where Polonius was stabbed, you will be within reasonable distance of the spot.

Many a Dragon would then recall that Polonius was behind a rich tapestry, typically hung to make a screen, when stabbed by Hamlet. Such a tapestry was called an arras.

* * * * * *

Some Old Dragons wished they had been censored more, finding that their views had changed from earlier in the war. One of them was Charlie Childe (Captain, Gloucestershire Regiment), who reread in January 1916 what he had written in the first months of the war. After a year of conflict, he now saw things rather differently.

I have just had The Draconian *and was very glad to get it. I'm afraid some of my letters now display a rather green and enthusiastic spirit. In fact I rather wonder at myself in the first days of August and September as a fierce hero! I see I said I didn't mind shells. However, I am not ashamed to admit that familiarity doesn't breed contempt. Jack Smyth quite agreed with me in this when I saw him last.*

At the time of the March 1916 edition of *The Draconian* Charlie was in reserve, but stationed near to a gun battery, which was duly shelled. He was impressed by the accuracy of the German guns, which landed about 70 shells on target, declaring it 'wonderful shooting at a range of at least six miles, when you consider that all the German gunners could see was their own gun and probably a hedge in front'.

Periods of 'rest' were enjoyed, but they provided only temporary respite.

> *This is quite a good place on the whole. We can get a good dinner and baths, and there are plenty of shops where we can get anything we want. I don't think it will last much longer though, as it is about our turn to be in the line again.*

Mounting Losses

Three weeks later, on 21 March, Charlie Childe was killed. He was 21. Captain W.D. Chamberlain of the Royal Army Medical Corps wrote to reassure the family that he did not die in pain.

> *Poor Childe was hit at 10.45 p.m. The bullet went into his head above the ear and came out over his forehead, as near as I can make out, though I did not see the helmet. I saw him about 11.15 p.m. He was completely unconscious, and at no time recovered any degree of consciousness while in my hands. He died, I believe about 3.30 or 4.00 a.m.*

Charles Childe (Captain, Gloucestershire Regiment)

The Childes were near neighbours of the O.P.S. and Charlie's letters and visits to the school had been a regular feature. The previous October he had sent home a five-leaved clover that he had found near his billet, hoping it would bring him luck.

* * * * * *

The Easter edition of *The Draconian* had two further deaths to report. The final British battleship to have left the Dardanelles on 9 April 1916 had been H.M.S. *Russell*, with Old Dragons William Esson and Lance Freyberg on board. The two men, respectively Major in the Royal Marine Light Infantry and Lieutenant Commander in the Royal Navy, may well have breathed a sigh of relief as the ship pulled away from those shores. However, for them there was to be a cruel twist of fate. As H.M.S. *Russell* entered Malta harbour at 5.30 a.m. on the morning of 27 April, it hit a mine.

William Esson (Major, Royal Marine Light Infantry)

The cabins of both William Esson and Lance Freyberg were immediately over where the mine struck, and they suffered the same fate. In a letter of condolence Admiral Fremantle explained to William's mother what had taken place.

> *At that time all the officers, except those actually on duty, were asleep in their cabins, and it is for that reason that we lost such a very large proportion of officers ... including your son and five lieutenants,* [who] *were never seen again after the explosion. Indeed there are now only two men alive who were in that part of the ship.*

William's sister Margaret, who had married Old Dragon Edmund Gay (killed the previous August in Gallipoli, but listed at this time still as 'missing'), had now also lost her brother. Five months later her father also died – three of her closest family gone in one year.

Lance Freyberg had decided on a career in the navy while at Marlborough, obtaining a cadetship on H.M.S. *Britannia* in 1901, when he was aged 16. The navy had been his life for the past 15 years.

By this time those briar pipes that the young Dragons had kindly sent in November 1914 were probably no more (see p. 68). Even had they survived, Lance could never now share with the Skipper those 'Pipes of Peace' of which he dreamed.

Lance Freyberg (Lieutenant Commander, R.N.)

The Easter Rising

Nevil Norway

Easter 1916 provided a news story from Ireland to rival events on the Western Front, when Irish Nationalists stormed the Post Office in Dublin. Old Dragon Nevil Norway witnessed much of the days that followed. Now aged 17, he had moved from the O.P.S. to Shrewsbury in 1913. However, the family home remained in Dublin, as his father had become Secretary to the Post Office in Ireland the previous year.

Nevil found himself outside the Post Office in O'Connell Street only 10 minutes after it had been taken by the rebels. He and his mother were expecting to meet up with his father for lunch, not knowing that he had been unexpectedly summoned to a meeting at Dublin Castle. Nevil witnessed the arrival on the scene of a troop of Royal Lancers. As they drew up the rebels opened fire; he saw four Lancers go down before he scattered with the rest of the crowd.

Nevil then joined an ambulance service set up by the Royal Irish Automobile Club as a stretcher-bearer. *The Draconian* published an account received by a Dragon family (the Sturts) and written by Nevil's mother, Mrs Hamilton Norway, which included some of her son's exploits.

> *25 April 1916*
> *Nevil did a very plucky thing yesterday. He walked up to St. Stephen's Green and saw a little group of men peering through the railings from our side into the Green. He went to see what they were looking at and found an extraordinary sight. A small gate in the railings had been barricaded by the rebels by putting one of the garden seats against it upside down and on the top of another garden seat right side up, and lying full length on the seat, face downwards, was a man with all his lower jaw blown away*

and bleeding profusely. Nevil immediately climbed the railings and dropped down on the other side, and ascertained the man was alive; he then turned and fairly cursed the men who were peering in, and asked if there was not one man enough to come over the railings and help him move the poor creature, whereupon three men climbed over and together they lifted down the seat with the man on it, dragged away the other seat, and so opened the gate and brought out the seat and man without moving him. Nevil escorted the men till they were close to Mercer's Hospital and then left them to take him in. When it is possible I will go and find out if the man is alive, but Nevil says he does not think he could possibly live. It was a terrible case.

Nevil continued to make himself useful. He filled cans of petrol from casks for Red Cross ambulances and travelled round in one with the Lord Mayor to collect food for 40 starving refugees in the Mansion House. He also went out looking for the wounded. Such experience was valuable as, although still at school, he was in the O.T.C. preparing for a military future.

Escaping the Telephone

Another Old Dragon anxious to do more was Hugh Sidgwick. News reached the O.P.S. that he had managed to escape the clutches of the Education Office in London (see p. 108) and had enlisted as a Lieutenant in the Royal Garrison Artillery. Hugh joined a Siege Battery, which he described in typically humorous terms.

That relatively secluded and comfortable branch of the profession that lives well behind the firing line, and pumps a stream of appalling projectiles into the Hun and his whereabouts from a safe distance.

He was disappointed to find one element of office life was still with him.

Hugh Sidgwick

The most distressing thing to me personally is the omnipotence and omnipresence of the telephone. It was my curse in civil life, and I hated it bitterly and profoundly. I did think that in military life I should escape it. But no: it is more important than ever: you range the country at the end of a telephone wire, and if it breaks you are an exile and outlaw at once: you come back and sit in your battery surrounded by telephones, all talkative and all meaning work. The call to arms is a message dictated over the telephone and taken down on a pink form.

His thoughts even drifted back to the O.P.S. and his lifelong interest in what Dragons should be studying. Perhaps siege gunnery should become part of the curriculum.

When one gets to business, the mathematics of siege gunnery are nothing alarming, and many of the beautiful calculations we learnt in England go by the board. One has to know the difference between + and –, and right and left, and to be able to add and work a slide rule, and read a map and take bearings: but that is about it. I would

> *volunteer to make quite an easy and profitable course of instruction in siege gunnery for VIa, and if they would give us a gun and let us practise on North Oxford from Shotover, so much the better for the cause of architecture. If one of the O.D. airmen would come and observe, we could have a charming afternoon.*

John Betjeman, although later to express similar sentiments about Slough, would not have approved.

Chapter 10
The War at Sea

Great Britain had been the great power of the nineteenth century, presiding over an empire that controlled nearly one-quarter of the world's population. Its power was based on trade, and trade routes were of great importance. Although its small standing army had fought in no major European war since the time of Napoleon, the British navy – the 'Senior Service' – had been responsible for ensuring Britannia ruled the waves, and indeed anyone else who dared to sail upon them.

To be a naval officer was considered not only an exciting career, but one of the greatest importance to the preservation of the British Empire. During the First World War 44 Old Dragons served in the navy or the naval reserve; many of them had decided on this as a career years before.

A Naval Education

Rather than going on to the usual public schools, a number of O.P.S. boys opted at an early age for a naval career. Until 1903, young Dragons so inspired had to join H.M.S. *Britannia,* moored on the River Dart, usually between the ages of 14 and 15. Boys thus sometimes stayed on longer at the O.P.S. than they might otherwise, or joined after a year or two at their public school.

Reggie Tyrwhitt, aged 11

One of the first Dragons to opt for a naval career was Reggie Tyrwhitt. The son of an Oxford vicar, he entered the O.P.S. aged nine in 1879, when Clarke was still the headmaster. He was neither particularly academic nor much of a conformist – but he achieved a certain degree of school fame by 'opening' a small stretch of the River Cherwell as a bathing area for the school. As an intrepid type, he was apparently invited by Clarke to make the inaugural dive (then called a 'header'). Reggie may have rued the spot he chose; he came back up to the surface with visible proof that the new bathing area was not as deep as everyone thought. His face was badly grazed and blooded.

Tyrwhitt later recalled Mr Clarke writing to his father to say that 'Your son Reggie is no good and will come to a bad end'.[1] It is difficult to imagine any modern-day

Left: Martin Collier on his submarine, H10

teacher daring to be so negative, whatever he or she privately thought, but maybe the navy was seen as his only chance of salvation.

Reggie did not go straight into the navy, however. As with many of his generation, he was removed from prep school to attend a 'crammer' that would prepare him for the entry exams for H.M.S. *Britannia*. The crammer succeeded in securing a place for Reggie, albeit at the second attempt. He spent two years there, studying mainly seamanship and navigation, before being sent to sea as a 15-year-old naval cadet on H.M.S. *Alexandra*.

* * * * * *

William Fisher was born in 1875, five years after Reggie Tyrwhitt. He was the eighth of 11 talented children, the eldest of whom was H.A.L. Fisher (the historian and President of the Board of Education, 1916–22). Another brother, Charles, was an academic; he became Senior Censor at Christ Church, Oxford. One of his sisters, Adeline, later married the composer Ralph Vaughan Williams.

At the O.P.S. William proved himself an able classicist, who could well have won a scholarship to Winchester. But when, only three weeks before the exam, he was offered a nomination for a cadetship, he wrote to his father in high spirits.

> *I have just received your letter and I should be very glad if you would accept the nomination – I have been waiting to hear what you thought upon the matter eagerly and am very glad indeed to hear its issue. Please excuse pencil and this short note – I will write a longer one tomorrow but shall not change my opinion.*[2]

He was not an obvious candidate for the navy, being far from the rough or tough type more obviously suited to a hard life at sea. Nonetheless, William scraped a pass – without the aid of a crammer – and so joined H.M.S. *Britannia* in 1889. After two years of seamanship and navigation, together with attempts to cover some of the curriculum of a public school, William was sent to sea on H.M.S. *Raleigh*, aged 15. During this trip, which took in both the east and west coasts of Africa, his training and education continued. While the navy had a lot to teach William by way of seamanship, however, he was already overqualified in more academic areas. In French, for example, William felt he knew more than his teacher – an Irishman who had been 20 years at sea and whom he considered 'ridiculously ignorant'.

It was to be three years before William saw either England or his family again. When the time came, as his train approached his home town near Guildford, his excitement was great, as he realised how much he had missed out on family life.

Cadet William Fisher, aged c.15

I have head and shoulders out of the window, and as I see the loom of the country station I feel the brakes. Yes, there is a little group there. I wave my hat, and the next second five brothers followed by my father are running alongside my door. They look very tall, and are all in flannels, four older than me, one younger …

Luggage brings one to earth again. It is put in the carriage, and I drive slowly away with my father, the others hanging on behind. Half-way up the hill I see figures in white in the dusk, and the next moment I am out of the carriage and surrounded by sisters. Sisters let themselves go in a way that brothers don't, and I shall never forget those soft, yet excited, voices, nor the sudden realisation of what I had been banished from so long …

I am home again – no longer alone.[3]

The Royal Naval College, Osborne

H.M.S. *Britannia,* where both Reggie Tyrwhitt and William Fisher had received their early training, was eventually replaced by shore-based establishments at Dartmouth and Osborne House. After the death of Queen Victoria, Edward VII donated the Osborne House estate on the Isle of Wight to the nation. New facilities were built and it duly opened as a naval college in 1903. The cadets, aged 12, undertook two years' training there before moving on for two further years at Dartmouth. They thus gained an education not dissimilar to that of a public school, but with rather more practical science and engineering – and everything, of course, was done 'at the double'.

With an intake limited to about 75, competition for places at Osborne was great. Medical and written tests had to be passed and an all-important interview was added, in which it would not be unusual for a boy to be confronted by a panel of admirals and headmasters. As if that was not enough, while waiting your turn with them a 10-minute essay on a given topic had to be completed.

One candidate was given the question 'Do you think war is necessary?' He thought for 8½ minutes before writing, 'Yes, war is necessary because if there was no war there would be no need to have a Navy and I want to join the Navy, so war is necessary'.[4] Faultless logic, if nothing else.

A candidate would also need the support of his previous headmaster, who would be asked, 'Does [the candidate] tend to lead other boys? If so, is his influence on them good?'[5]

Much as Skipper Lynam was a man of the sea, he would not have liked two things about the new arrangements. First, the navy were asking for the boys to enter at only 12, and so miss their final prep school year. Second, there was also the matter of the written examination, which invited competition and therefore 'cramming' for it. There were institutions to which parents could send their sons for this purpose, but this was not what Skipper, or indeed the navy, wanted.

In a letter sent to prep schools in November 1910, the Admiralty emphasised that they were 'strongly opposed to all special preparation'. They preferred that 'candidates should receive the usual education which preparatory schools give to boys who are about to pass on to public schools; we even deprecate special Navy Classes in Preparatory Schools'. Music, no doubt, to the Skipper's ears.

Finally, in 1913, the navy very sensibly fell in line with the normal time boys moved on to their public schools, aged between 13 and 14. Skipper was delighted at this news.

> *The Admiralty have this year, wisely as we think, raised the age-limit of admission to Osborne by a year … and we are glad to celebrate it by a record contribution of five cadets to the school.*

That these boys' names were listed alongside those who had won scholarships to their public schools shows how highly Skipper rated their achievement.

* * * * * *

Martin Collier, aged c.12

The first Dragon to go to Osborne was Martin Collier. At the O.P.S. he was a typical Dragon schoolboy, as Skipper remembered:

> *He used to arrive at school in the morning – hands in pockets, a battered old cap a little to the back of his head, passing jauntily through the gate leading to the asphalt, and on frosty mornings, rushing to the top of the slide to take his place in the queue.*

Despite his dislike of 'cramming', Skipper realised that Martin would need help if he was to be successful at the interview. He arranged to take him with two other young Dragons on a cruise off the South Coast during the Easter holidays. Skipper had heard that the best way to tackle the interview was for the candidates to have something to talk about.

On returning to school he taught Martin to draw a detailed picture of the yacht and made him spend hours copying the chart from the Isle of Wight to Dartmouth, with the lights, ports, five-fathom line, etc. It did the trick.

> *After the Interview* [Martin] *came dashing up to me with a splendid grin. 'The Admiral said, "I hear you have been doing some yachting. What was the yacht like? How rigged? Her tonnage?" and then told me to sit down and draw a map of our cruise. I was rather a long time over it, and he came and looked at it and carried it off and showed it to the other interviewers – I was just putting in the five-fathom line, and they seemed very pleased with it!'*
>
> *Of course to a boy a cruise is just a holiday with plenty of fun and amusement, but he does not naturally get into his head much about the rig of boats or the intricacies of a chart, and what a terrible loss it would have been if Martin had not been 'passed' by the Interviewers! I have no repentance for that bit of 'cram'.*

Two happy years at Osborne followed. A fellow cadet, Sidney Herbert, remembered stories of Martin roaming the island, 'sometimes within bounds, sometimes with long chases that brought him in contact with authorities in a way which made the less daring among us hold our breath'.

The German Threat

The years leading up to the First World War saw much Anglo-German naval rivalry. The arms race, including the development of the Dreadnaught battleships, ensured that the Royal Navy was well prepared for the war when it came.

During this period William Fisher was busy passing the examinations at the Royal Naval College at Greenwich to ensure promotion to the rank of Lieutenant. Here he narrowly missed a 'First Class', but he found his niche: gunnery. William was to build a formidable reputation at a time of great advances in the effectiveness of gunnery at sea. He served on the Atlantic Fleet flagship H.M.S. *King Edward VII* and met with great success in the annual competitions.

Fisher was aboard this ship in Gibraltar when Kaiser Wilhelm made a dramatic arrival in port. Although there was increasing rivalry between their nations, it must be remembered that the Kaiser was a grandson of Queen Victoria. His close relationship to the British royal family meant that he had to be treated courteously. It was a complex situation, as Fisher observed.

> [The] *Kaiser's advent was sensational. He came in the* Hamburg *with thunders of gun salutes all round him and, in the meanwhile, his attendant cruiser, the* Friedrich Carl, *quietly rammed the* Prince George, *one of our battleships. The* Prince George *had to be put into dry-dock hurriedly … The whole thing is rather humorous really –*
>
> 1. *Arrival of Bill.*
> 2. *Half sinks a Battleship.*
> 3. *Dashes on board* King Edward VII *to find out all he can about our latest ship.*
> 4. *Inspects the Rock and sees all the gun positions.*
> 5. *Leaves – having done us a good deal of harm and put us to a lot of expense.*
>
> *With regard to Item 3, I carefully covered with canvas all the fire control instruments and locked the conning tower. They looked awfully sick, but when they asked in broken English why, I said, 'No savvy de Lingo'.*[6]

When war did come in the summer of 1914, a test mobilisation of the navy had by chance just taken place. George V had reviewed the combined fleets of the Atlantic, Home and Reserve Fleets off Spithead in early July.

Heligoland Bight

Reggie Tyrwhitt, now a Commodore in command of the two Destroyer flotillas, was stationed at Harwich with the job of patrolling the east coast. As with the armies of Europe, the navies had done their fair share of planning for war. On the outbreak of war the German High Seas Fleet was mainly in harbour, but their ships were making forays out. Tyrwhitt, together with Commodore Roger Keyes, in charge of a flotilla of submarines, persuaded the Admiralty to allow them to attack these German patrols in what was to become the first naval battle of the war, the Battle of Heligoland Bight, on 28 August 1914. Although not everything went entirely to plan (they were to a degree 'bailed out' by the arrival of reinforcements under Admiral Beatty), it was a clear victory in terms of losses inflicted versus losses incurred. It was thus a cause for great rejoicing. On returning to port in the severely damaged H.M.S. *Arethusa*, Tyrwhitt was welcomed by Winston Churchill, then the First Lord of the Admiralty, who came aboard to congratulate Reggie on his forthright actions and 'fairly slobbered' over him.[7]

The *Arethusa* had only been released from the shipyard that built it 48 hours before the battle, and so had not been fully checked for faults. As a result guns jammed, and at various times in the battle a number were out of action. A direct hit set fire to the deck and this, although quickly extinguished, added to Reggie's problems. On return to port he advised his wife as to the extent of his ship's damage.

> *We had fifteen direct hits on the side and waterline and many in board, besides hundreds of shrapnel holes.*[8]

He enlarged on this a few days later, in a letter to his sister.

Reggie Tyrwhitt

> *I can only wonder that everyone on the upper deck was not killed. The air seemed thick with bursting shells and the sea alive with splashes from shell and splinters ... My signal officer was the only man killed on the bridge, such a nice boy. He was talking to me at the time and had just pointed out that we were on fire ...*
>
> *I could not say exactly what my feelings were all the time, but I don't think I ever thought of the danger nor do I think anyone on board did. I was very agreeably surprised as I was under the impression that the first time everyone bobbed their heads when the shells flew over them etc, but it was not the case.*[9]

This victory, which dissuaded the German navy from ever leaving port again (with the notable exception of Jutland two years later), led to Tyrwhitt being made a Companion of the Order of the Bath.

Battle of the Falkland Islands

During the remaining months of 1914 the British navy chased down the German ships that were not already bottled up in port, particularly Admiral Spee's East Asiatic squadron. A British fleet under Vice Admiral Sturdee was dispatched to intercept the squadron. They made their way to Port Stanley in the Falkland Islands to refuel – which just happened to be the next target for Spee's fleet.

The action that ensued, on 8 December, was recounted by an Old Dragon, Desmond Stride. He was serving as a Royal Naval Lieutenant on H.M.S. *Cornwall.*

> *A flag-lieutenant in his pyjamas hurried off to tell Admiral Sturdee that they had sighted the enemy and he found the Admiral shaving. 'You had better get into your clothes, and I will finish what I am doing,' was the calm comment, 'then we will have breakfast'.*

Thus fortified, the British ships, having now been observed by the German fleet, gave chase. The speed of the British battlecruisers proved too much and the armoured cruisers *Scharnhorst* and *Gneisenau* turned to give battle. Both were sunk. Stride's ship was responsible for the sinking of the *Leipzig*. Others in the squadron were sunk by the Germans themselves, ammunition expended, when they opened up their torpedo tubes.

Stride had been in charge of a 6-inch gun; he was in action for about four hours. Although the ship sustained a number of hits, damage was slight and there was only one casualty aboard.

> *I asked my servant how things had gone. The man looked very grave. 'Well, what is it?' I asked. 'It's my poor canary; he's dead. All the feathers were blown off, and the cage, for which I paid 2s 9d at Plymouth, is smashed to pieces. It was a beautiful cage, sir.'*

It was indeed a clear victory. Only one German ship escaped and while over 2,000 Germans were killed, there were only ten British casualties.

No further major naval action took place until May 1916, when the German High Seas Fleet ventured out of harbour to make an attack on the east coast of England. As (more famously) in the Second World War, the German codes had been cracked by the British and they were ready for them.

'Hell, but an intensely interesting hell'

Seven Old Dragons were present at the Battle of Jutland, the only major sea battle of the entire war. This version of what occurred on 31 May 1916 was submitted anonymously, but clues point to the author being on board H.M.S. *Valiant*. This (censored) account must therefore be the work of Royal Naval Commander Geoffrey Freyberg, whose brother Lance had been killed on H.M.S. *Russell* on his way back from Gallipoli (see pp. 152–53).

> *4 June 1916*
> *By all the laws of the game I ought to be dead at the bottom of the North Sea, but some Divine Providence watched over us throughout the fury of the long battle. I really thought at the time that death was on the threshold. Well, I was not touched in any way throughout the long day and following night. Many friends are dead, but it was a fine finish as we drove the Huns after the arrival of Sir John Jellicoe, but it was Admiral Beatty and his friends who bore the heat and burden of the day until he came. One was far too excited to be afraid, as the panorama was simply stupendous; the dead and dying in the water; ships vanishing close by; the lame ducks on both sides being polished off. It was hell, but an intensely interesting hell.*

According to the Captain of H.M.S. *Valiant*, they were almost the only ship to keep any real record of 'the show' at the time. That they did so was thanks to Geoffrey, who 'dictated notes throughout to a Midshipman with a note-book squatting down at my feet'. He subsequently produced a 16-page (foolscap) report with two diagrams. This clearly took him some time, as it was five days after the battle that this entry was written.

> *5 June 1916*
> *I've been at work on a plan of the scrap all day ... I must have seen as much of the fight as any man in the fleet. Beatty got hell to start with, as, to his surprise, the Huns accepted action with the utmost alacrity at 3.30 p.m. on the 31st. At 4.01 we came into action; at 4.02* Indefatigable *blew up; at 4.15* Queen Mary *ditto. Not an encouraging start, as I saw both go. At 4.30 our Battle Cruisers legged it at 28 knots, and we were left to fight a rear-guard action; our four against eleven Huns, with the light in their favour. From 4.30–6.15 p.m. we drew them on towards* [Admiral] *Sir John Jellicoe ...*
>
> Defence *and* Black Prince *were sunk at 6.15 as they came up and Sir John Jellicoe arrived. Then the Huns got hell till 7.25, when they broke off the action and fled.*

By 6 June it sounds as if the author is done with the minutiae and has reached the conclusion that he cannot ever expect to do full justice to the events of that day:

> *One can only liken it all to some of the pictures of Hell by Gustav Doré. No artist could ever reproduce the scene on canvas, and no pen except that of a master of prose could help people to realise what it was like.*

However, Geoffrey obviously felt that one final story, probably that of H.M.S. *Onslaught*, needed recording:

> *There were some weird happenings: we picked up a W.T. signal from one of our destroyers from the Sub-Lieut., worded as follows:- 'My Captain is dying, the 1st Lieut., Surgeon and gunners are all dead, my bridge has been shot away so I do not know my position as I am isolated. Request instructions.' That boy got his ship back safely as I saw her here two days later, and if any boy deserves a D.S.C., he does.*

H.M.S. *Valiant*, on which Geoffrey Freyberg served at the Battle of Jutland

Prior to the battle William Fisher, now Captain of H.M.S. *St Vincent,* had been able to spend some time with his brother Charles, who was serving on H.M.S. *Invincible*.

William Fisher

Charles and I were on shore together having the greatest fun when recalled, as we have been recalled dozens of times before. Exactly twenty-four hours later the St Vincent *steamed past the wreck of a ship which we took to be a German. We were, with other ships near us in the line, engaging four German Dreadnaughts at the time, but I looked to see if there was anyone in the water near this ship and saw nothing – not even floating wreckage. All round was still calm water. The wreck might have been there for weeks – and yet we know now she went down only about a quarter of an hour before our arrival. Her bow was high in the air and so was her stern, the centre having been split in two and apparently resting on the bottom.*[10]

The *St Vincent* was not the only British ship to mistake this ship's identity – some on H.M.S. *Tiger* let out a large cheer as they went past. But on the starboard side at the stern the name of the ship was clear to see: H.M.S. *Invincible* – Charles Fisher's ship. It cannot have been long before William realised that he had lost his brother.

Commander Dannreuther, who by chance had served with William Fisher before the war on H.M.S. *Albemarle*, was one of the six survivors. He described Charles's final moments.

> *We hit the* Derffinger *with our first salvo and continued to hit her entirely owing to the perfect rate Charles gave us. It was all over in a few minutes and death came suddenly and painlessly. Everything was going splendidly at the time, and it was entirely due to Charles's cool head and excellent judgement that our firing was so effective. I saw him only a few minutes before the end – a smile on his face and his eyes sparkling. He was by my side and in the highest spirits when there was a great explosion and shock, and when I recovered consciousness I found myself in the water. Ship and crew had disappeared.*

Although William Fisher had been late on the scene of the Battle of Jutland, he was to play an important role on the committee set up in the aftermath by Sir John Jellicoe. There were a number of unsatisfactory aspects to be accounted for.

Invincible – one of the navy's most prestigious ships – had gone down with the loss of 1,032 lives in about 15 seconds. Its light armour had proved inadequate and the flash from the explosions was able to penetrate down to the magazines below deck. As British shelling of the German ships had not been so effective, there were also questions asked about their manufacture.

In matters of gunnery William was an expert, and many improvements were made on the basis of his recommendations.

Submarine Warfare

Even if the Royal Navy had won a far from convincing victory (if that is what it was), the German navy did not venture out of port again until the end of the war. After Jutland the Royal Navy's main concern was the German submarine force, which sank an enormous tonnage of shipping and threatened Britain with starvation; as Jellicoe exclaimed, 'The submarines are bleeding us to death'. William Fisher was appointed Director of the Anti-submarine Division in May 1917. His role in the instigation of a convoy system, the speeding up of building replacement ships and the intensification of the war against U-boats was considerable. When Sir Henry Newbolt wrote his *Naval History of the War* in 1920, he was to dedicate it to 'William Wordsworth Fisher. In the crisis of our fate from June 1917 to November 1918, Director of the Anti-submarine Division of the Admiralty'.[11]

* * * * * *

Martin Collier (Lieutenant, R.N.)

One Old Dragon who decided on the submarine service was Martin Collier. From Osborne Martin had gone on to Dartmouth, where his sport flourished. He was a talented rugby player who played for the United Services and was described as 'the hardest working forward in perhaps the best club pack in England'. In 1913/14 he played for the South and could well have gone on to make the England team. Martin was also a boxer of note, winning the Navy & Marines' middle weight boxing championship of 1910. His combative edge meant that when war came he was more than keen to be involved. However, the work required of him is largely unrecorded and certainly lacked the drama he may well have craved. Even his final trip, from which he never returned, is shrouded in mystery.

In January 1918 Martin Collier received orders to go on a patrol of a given sector. His submarine, H10, set off from Yarmouth with a crew of 26 on 6 January and was expected to return on 14 January. It did not. H.M.S. *Lurcher* and H.M.S. *Melampus* spent two days (15–16 January) looking for the submarine, but they found no trace. On 19 January H10 was formally declared lost in the North Sea.

In *The Draconian* of April 1918 Martin's old friend from Osborne days, Sidney Herbert, made a poignant observation.

> *Martin Collier was captain of one of those of our submarines which go out and are no more heard of, and had I any official knowledge of how they were lost I might not reveal it.*

For Skipper this was another deeply upsetting blow. 'The war continues to take toll of our very best and best-loved Old Boys,' he wrote, adding simply, 'Martin Collier loved the School as the School loved him'.

Martin Collier was one of six naval Old Dragons to appear on the O.P.S. Roll of Honour. Only three of them died in any sort of action: Charles Fisher at Jutland, Lance Freyberg's ship was mined and Martin was 'lost at sea'. Of the remaining three Dragons, one died in an accidental collision of two British ships and the remaining two succumbed to war-related illness after the end of hostilities.

BATTLE OF THE SOMME, 1916

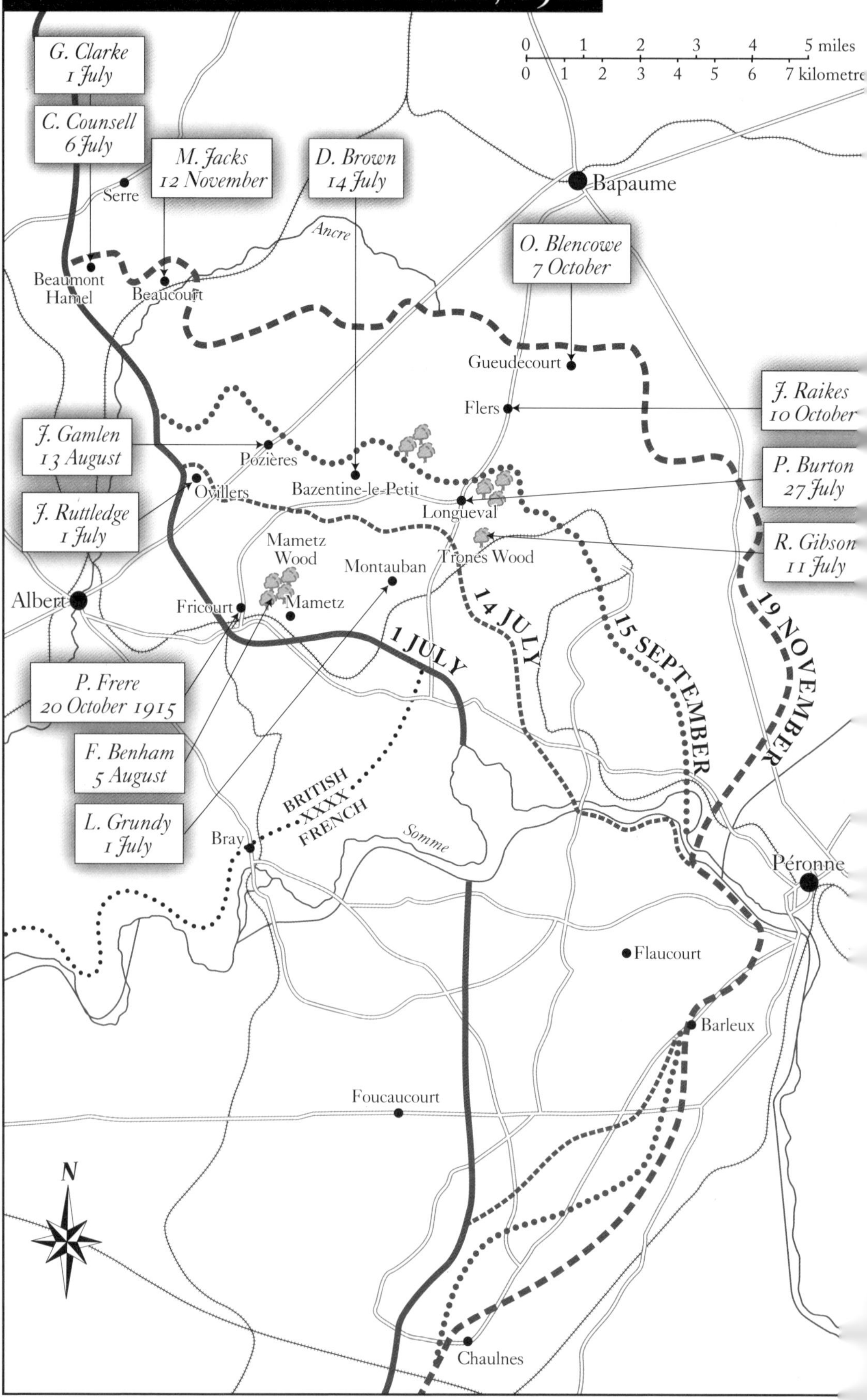

Chapter 11

The Battle of the Somme

Preparing for the 'Push'

While it was the Battle of Jutland that dominated the early summer headlines in 1916, troops serving on the Western Front knew it would soon be their turn. Like many, David Brown, serving as a Captain in the Royal Leicestershire Regiment, realised that the summer would see the launching of a new offensive. It was time to prepare himself – and his family – for what lay ahead.

David Brown

I am writing like this because summer is here, and I don't think our present peacefulness can go on much longer. People at home are beginning to wonder what they pay us for; and I think Death must come to many of us, if not to most (I am talking of officers now) before very long: and, if it does come to me, I don't want you to feel it as a shock, and I don't want you or anyone to grieve.

You know it is rather an honour to die now, to die for all that we hold precious, for our country, to die that we may live, and to die with so many better men.

I don't want to die. I want to live and tell how I was in the War, how I was a fighter in it, not merely a server; but, if I do get killed, I want you and everyone to know that I knew of the possibility, that I was ready for it, and facing it, and not shirking and dodging the thought of it. It seems to me that for a man who is, if not ready or willing to die, at least aware of the presence of death, and looking it in the face not caring or wondering what lies beyond, Death has lost its power. When you cease to fear Death you have conquered it, and Death has become only a gate, no harder to pass through than the door of a room.

Am I just being morbid? I hope not; because I feel somewhat that should the worst happen it may help Mother and Dad to know that I was not caught by surprise, not realising what I was in for.

* * * * * *

An offensive was indeed 'on the cards'. The French, experiencing enormous casualties at Verdun, were imploring the British to launch an attack to take the pressure off them.

The Somme had been an area where the French and Germans had left each other in comparative peace. The British, on the other hand, felt that they should be a lot more active. They wished to dominate no man's land and raid enemy lines. Unfortunately this encouraged the Germans to build better defences. Certain areas such as the Tambour du Clos at Fricourt became hotly contested and dangerous as a result.

During late 1915 the 8th Battalion, East Surrey Regiment did several tours of duty in the trenches occupying the Tambour. In reality these were not so much trenches as a series of mine craters. The British line jutted out into the enemy line on a piece of high ground that made a valuable observation point. A bitter struggle for supremacy took place, resulting in constant mining and counter-mining. The nerves of those occupying this front-line trench must have been stretched to breaking point at times by the constant threat of being blown up.

Philip Frere was with the East Surreys in the Tambour in October. He swiftly realised that there was a lot more to worry about than the rats (see p. 120). In the early hours of one morning he was thrown out of bed by a violent explosion. The Germans had detonated a mine under some 30 yards (c.27 m) of trench for which he was responsible. This explosion was followed by a bombardment of the communication trenches, suggesting that an infantry attack might be imminent.

Philip Frere

When I got up there, I went round to the front and started with parties of men clearing away the wreckage, trying to get out some unfortunate fellows buried underneath. It was a sad sight. A mass of earth and sandbags, broken down mine-heads and the awful smell of gas. Some unfortunate sappers were down in the mines. We pulled away stuff like maniacs, flinging it over the parapet, and succeeded in getting five men out by the efforts of some very plucky fellows of ours who went down into the broken saps and handed them out. The sappers were all badly gassed and so were the men who went down, but the latter will recover in a few days. We got some stretcher bearers up and sorted the living from the dead. It was a nasty job. The moans and contortions of the dying, the delirious shrieks of those half-gassed, the pale and sallow faces of those already gone.

The gas, carbon monoxide, also affected Philip and his fellow rescuers, fortunately not too badly. A serious dose would have been fatal, as Philip explained:

It either gets you slightly, when you have a splitting headache and feel bilious, or medium, when you kick and struggle and are delirious, or badly, when you are unconscious and die at once or a little later.

In April 1916 Philip was summoned to G.H.Q. As a German speaker, it was decided that he would be of greater use as an Intelligence Officer interviewing German prisoners and translating captured documents. So he was not with the 8th East Surreys when, under Captain Billie Nevill, they attacked Montauban on

1 July, famously kicking footballs ahead of them. Eight officers were killed and four wounded, together with 142 other ranks killed and 272 wounded that day.

* * * * * *

Robert Gibson, a Lieutenant in the Bedfordshire Regiment, returned from visiting the O.P.S. on his leave to find his regiment gearing up for this new offensive.

Robert Gibson

29 June 1916
It is many weeks ago since I pinched the Skipper's pencil to write you this letter in the train from Oxford to Paddington. Unfortunately 7 more candidates for the 6 seats got on at Didcot, and writing became impossible. Perhaps it is for the best, as you would hardly be interested in a description of the 'Reading flower-beds' or 'Trafalgar Square on a wet Friday in war time'.

Leave was a very pleasant interlude and preparation for future efforts; for this front is a very noisy one these days and I think the staff fondly hopes it is to become a mobile one. The gunners are having gala days, and the sins of the batteries are visited on the men in the line by the discriminating Teuton. The men, however, are quite willing to put up with occasional retaliation, provided they can spend most of the day lounging over the parapet watching Fritz's hearth and home going up in a cloud of smoke and barbed wire.

The week-long artillery barrage pumped over one million shells into the German lines in advance of the massed infantry attack at Z hour on 1 July. Robert clearly felt that their experience with raids meant that the troops were well prepared for what lay ahead. It was true that these raids, intended to annoy the enemy, may also have prepared the Germans for what was to come. However, he felt that they taught the British troops that the forthcoming offensive could be successful if carefully planned – and if luck was on your side.

We have got bigger fish to fry now; and I think from the spirit of our own men and the French on our right, that something will be done. Still, when we have done our best and the Boche his worst, you come back to the old saying of men who fought with their hands at close quarters, not in lead and steel at 1,000 yards and more:

Θεῶν ἐνι γούνασι κεῖται.

'It lies in the lap of the Gods.'

Best love and luck to all Dragons, militant and expectant.

* * * * * *

The British Expeditionary Force of 1914 was by this time a spent force. Any major offensive in 1916 would have to be undertaken by the new volunteer force dubbed 'Kitchener's Army'. The training of these new recruits had been rushed and they did not match up to the capabilities of the regulars. Battle tactics had to bear this in mind.

General Haig appointed General Sir Henry Rawlinson to make plans for the attack. What emerged was a strategy entirely dependent on the artillery's ability to destroy all the barbed wire, trenches and German soldiers on the front, 13 miles (21 km) in length, that was to be attacked. Once that was achieved, all the infantry would have to do was to walk across no man's land and take up the virtually deserted German positions.

1 July 1916 – Zero Hour

On 1 July 1916 the barrage lifted and 'Kitchener's Army' rose from their trenches to take possession of the German trenches opposite – only to find that the bombardment had not destroyed the German troops in them (often secure in the deep dug-outs constructed out of the chalk prevalent in this area) nor even the barbed wire in front.

By the end of the day there had been 57,000 British casualties, 20,000 of whom were killed. Among them were two Old Dragons, Geoff Clarke and John Ruttledge, both of whom were attacking the northern end of the front, which experienced the greatest casualties.

Geoffrey Clarke (2nd Lieutenant, Rifle Brigade)

Geoff Clarke was the son of Mr. A.E. Clarke, the first headmaster of the O.P.S. (see p. 23). He was only aged three when his father died and the Skipper had known Geoff all his life. He boarded at the O.P.S., in the house run by his mother, and won scholarships first to Winchester and then to New College, Oxford. He spent five years as an assistant master at the Royal Naval College at Osborne followed by two years in Bethnal Green, where he helped to found Boys' Clubs and studied social and economic conditions.

In 1914 Geoff had attempted to enlist, but was rejected on medical grounds. He therefore undertook a course of physical training, first for Home Service and shortly after for General Service in the Royal Fusiliers (Public School Brigade). He obtained promotion to non-commission rank and later received a commission in the Special Reserve 5th Rifle Brigade.

In July 1916 the Redan Ridge, north of Beaumont Hamel, was the objective of the 4th Division, which included Geoff Clarke's Rifle Brigade. Although here the bombardment had been reasonably effective on both the German trenches and barbed wire, many of the deep dug-outs were not affected. It did not take long for the Germans to come out and set up machine guns to train on the advancing British soldiers. The Rifle Brigade was repulsed with heavy losses. Geoff was one of the few to reach the second line of German trenches, though twice wounded on the way. Afterwards his sergeant described what had happened.

> *Lieut. Clarke, our Battalion Bombing Officer, had a rather a tough job and it was while going over to the German 3rd line that I came across him. He was then slightly wounded, but refused all assistance, and would insist on keeping going. He was again wounded, rather badly this time, but still refused all help and insisted on us getting along. That was the last I ever saw of him, he was then lying in a trench hole. During the fighting and the excitement that followed I lost touch with him, but was told by a man who has since been killed that he saw a shell pitch into the hole Lieut. Clarke lay in, and he saw a body blown into the air.*

* * * * * *

John Ruttledge
(Captain, Prince of Wales's Own West Yorkshire Regiment)

At 7.30 a.m. on 1 July the first wave of the attack was launched on the German-held village of Ovillers. It was virtually wiped out. At 8.25 a.m. the 2nd Battalion of the West Yorkshire Regiment moved forward in support and lost 250 men passing through the German artillery barrage. They were also fired on from their flanks, resulting in only a few isolated groups reaching the German front line.

John's commanding officer explained what then took place.

> [John] *led his men with great gallantry right up to the enemy trench, where he was killed by a shell ... I personally noted the fine leading of his company at the commencement of this action under heavy fire. The battalion maintained its splendid reputation; 702 went over and only 192 were left unwounded.*

John was from a military family – his father was a Lieutenant Colonel. From the O.P.S. he had gone via Clifton to Sandhurst to follow a career in the army, and had joined the West Yorkshire Regiment in 1914. He had been awarded the M.C. the same year and was twice mentioned in dispatches. His commanding officer wrote to John's father in glowing terms.

> *I cannot adequately express my grief at the loss of your gallant son. He was my best company commander ... Had your son survived I would have recommended him for the D.S.O.*

* * * * * *

When Captain Nevill and the East Surreys attacked Montauban on 1 July, Leslie Grundy, a veteran of the Gallipoli campaign, who had transferred to the Machine Gun Corps and had been promoted to the rank of captain, was not far behind. Once Jack Haldane's tormentor in the O.P.S. playground with his water pistol (see p. 16), he was to be the only Old Dragon to provide an account of the events of 1 July.

The bombardment of the German positions was gaining in intensity. Only 150 yards (137 m) behind Leslie's position, in what was coincidentally called Oxford Copse, some 18 pounders were making a deafening noise. They guessed the time was approaching for the infantry to 'go over the top' and ordered the issue of rum to all the men – two large jars to be shared between 150. This was at 5 a.m. Shortly afterwards came confirmation: 7.30 was to be Zero Hour.

When the time approached there was a heavy mist, but not enough to cause delay. Leslie, standing on a small rise in the ground, watched as the first wave went over. He noted only one casualty and little hostile rifle fire. It augured well for when his turn came.

At 8.30 he made his way forward just as the enemy decided to bombard no man's land, causing numerous casualties. Leslie's group made a dash through it. When they reached the German trenches, they discovered these had been so badly damaged by the artillery fire that it was difficult to tell the line of the trench.

It was a hot day and the men's packs were weighing them down, so they took a short rest before continuing the advance.

> *As it looked as if the Boches were shortening their range, we thought it best not to make too long a stay at this spot and therefore pushed on as far as the Glatz Redoubt. In a few minutes No.2 section came up; so far they had only lost three men. At this point a party of about 30 Boche prisoners were marched past; all of them apparently in great fear of their lives! They had all, seemingly, been very much shaken by our bombardment,*

and in the trench we were occupying there were many of them lying badly wounded. After a few minutes we mounted our guns and opened fire on the Boches to the left of Montauban as the Brigade there did not seem to have attained its objective.

The heavy artillery was bombarding Montauban and when it lifted the British troops moved forwards, all in line, as if on parade, and at walking pace. There was no sign of any hostile fire, so Leslie decided the time was right for him to move his machine guns into Montauban. He found the place to have been 'literally blown to pieces'; even finding where the roads had been caused considerable difficulty.

Just before dusk there seemed to be a small attack, but it was easily dispersed by rifle and machine-gun fire. All that night we fired at all small parties of Boches who could be plainly seen, and as it grew light we heard the sound of bombs exploding, and found the Boches were bombing Montauban Alley from the other end. About 7 o'clock the bursting bombs seemed to be very close to one another, and from behind between the two groups about 30 of our men jumped out of the trench and started to retire towards us in Montauban. Immediately on seeing this, the Boches jumped out of their trenches and started firing on them. We turned two machine guns on the Boches and wiped the party completely out, but not before they had accounted for all our men.

6 July – Beaumont Hamel

Despite the blowing of an enormous mine on the Hawthorne Ridge on 1 July, British troops failed to take the nearby village of Beaumont Hamel – indeed, it did not fall to the British until November. Throughout this time it remained a dangerous place to be; even when not involved in an actual attack, you were likely to come under fire. The Skipper's *War Memorials* recorded one death in such circumstances. It occurred when Christopher Counsell was involved in relatively trivial day-to-day work.

He was killed in action near to Beaumont Hamel on 6th July 1916. He was engaged in placing some advanced outposts. A machine gun opened fire, and Chris was so severely wounded that he died on the way to the dressing station. He was buried at Gezaincourt.

Christopher Counsell (Lieutenant, Royal Hampshire Regiment)

Chris Counsell was the son of Dr Counsell, who practised in Broad Street, Oxford. He had won a scholarship to Lancing College before going up to Trinity College, Oxford, where he had been awarded a first class degree in Law. In 1914 he had joined up as a private in a Public School Battalion before gaining a commission as Lieutenant in the Royal Hampshire Regiment.

11 July – Trones Wood

Robert Gibson (Lieutenant, Bedfordshire Regiment)

Robert Gibson's turn came when the Bedfordshire Regiment was involved in an attack on Trones Wood on 11 July. Lieutenant Colonel H.S. Poyntz informed Robert's father of what took place.

> *15 July 1916*
>
> *On July 11th at 3.27 a.m. we were ordered to attack Trones Wood where very heavy fighting has been going on. It had been taken by us and re-taken by the Germans, so we were ordered to re-take it again.*

Another informant was a fellow subaltern, 2nd Lieutenant J.B. Primrose-Wells:

> *We estimate that there were 300 Huns in the wood when we attacked. Your son was on my left and he and his platoon were to enter the wood a little way up on the west side. The Germans had a trench all down the west side of the wood, which we did not know about, and just where your son wanted to enter was one of their strong points. He and his platoon opened fire and he fired several shots himself with his revolver, but the Huns had the advantage from the trenches besides being excellent shots.*
>
> *Your son was shot and died instantaneously, not making a sound. I had to advance over the same ground and tried twice to get his body in, but lost men both times, so we left it until we could finally capture the whole wood. We were relieved after 48 hours of very hard fighting – hand-to-hand – and very nerve-wracking.*

Two days after, when the wood was finally taken by the British, I asked the Colonel if I might go up again and get your son's body and bury it, but he refused to let me go and our Chaplain with four volunteers went up and found the body and buried him in Maricourt Cemetery.

Robert's father was the Rector of Cranham, and Robert was another Dragon who had won scholarships to both Winchester and New College, Oxford. The following tribute was written by a great friend from his time at both the O.P.S. and Winchester.

When he came to Oxford he looked round for some kind of service into which he might throw himself and so discover something about a stratum of society widely separated from that which he knew. This he found in the boys' club which had lately been started by New College in St. Ebbe's; and if he was anything like as successful in winning the confidence of his men as he was with these boys, he must have been one of the most popular officers that ever entered the army.

M.J. Rendall, Robert's headmaster at Winchester, wrote a moving letter of condolence to the Rev. Gibson.

Your one consolation will be that he takes a very white soul to the other world, that he lived a keen, joyous, wholesome, and honourable life, very free from any sort of stain.

To this Skipper made a simple addition.

No tribute could be higher, and it comes from one who loved him, and knew him through and through.

14 July – Bazentin-le-Petit

David Brown (Captain, Royal Leicestershire Regiment)

It was not until 14 July that David Brown and the 6th Battalion Royal Leicestershire Regiment saw action.

Despite the High Command's initial distrust of the untried troops they were throwing into this battle, the events of 1 July demanded that they try more imaginative methods of attack. The situation of Bazentin Ridge was tricky, requiring an advance across 1,500 yards (c.1,370 m) of rising ground in no man's land. A night attack was proposed, allowing the battalions to edge forward under the cover of darkness to within striking distance of the German front line. David had to get his men out of their trenches and then they had to make their way across no man's land silently, to avoid the notice of German sentries. Detection would have led to heavy casualties from shell and machine-gun fire.

All went well and the infantry settled down to await not the lengthy bombardment that preceded the first day of the battle, but a hurricane bombardment of a mere 5 minutes' duration.

At 3.25 a.m. the bombardment turned into a creeping barrage, lifting 50 yards (c.46 m) every 90 seconds; this allowed the infantry to move forward. The gamble paid off. British forces arrived in the German front-line trenches to find the barrage had successfully dealt with German trenches and troops alike.

However, as the advance continued into the Bazentin villages, German resistance stiffened and some British battalions suffered heavily. The 6th Leicesters did gain possession of Bazentin-le Petit, but David was reported first to have been wounded, then to be missing in the fighting. His body was never recovered. Overall the 6th Leicesters suffered over 600 casualties, including eight officers killed and 19 wounded.

David was a cousin of Percy Campbell, one of the first O.D. casualties in 1914 (see p. 98). He was also godfather to Per Mallalieu, still a pupil at the O.P.S.

27 July – Longueval

Patrick Burton (Temporary Captain, Bedfordshire Regiment)

The attack of 14 July 1916 took the British troops through the Germans' second defensive positions of the Bazentin Ridge. However, the opportunities to exploit these gains were missed. Now the British faced the strengthened defences of Guillemont, Delville Wood, Longueval and High Wood.

Paddy Burton was a Temporary Captain in the 4th Battalion of the Bedfordshire Regiment. He reconnoitred the approaches to the village of Longueval, together with another officer; the latter recalled what had taken place.

It was a very trying job, as our guide lost himself and we sent him back. We were under incessant shellfire and we knew that a great part of the ground was exposed to snipers, and we had to find out absolutely everything for ourselves. I don't think I could have done it without Paddy ... He must have been at least as tired and depressed as I was, but he wouldn't allow it to show.

On 27 July Paddy took part in the attack on Longueval by the 4th Bedfordshires. This was a success, but isolated pockets of resistance remained. Paddy and another officer discussed how they could dislodge the Germans from a house in which a machine gun was located, sweeping over the British position. Paddy decided on an attack with hand grenades, during which he fell wounded in the leg. Company Sergeant Major Afford went to his assistance, dressing his wound before attempting to carry him to a place of safety. During this time Paddy received a second wound which proved to be fatal; a bullet penetrated the lower part of his head.

In a moving letter Afford described Paddy's last moments.

[He] *remained conscious for a few hours, during which time I stayed with him and comforted him. His last words were to me, requesting me to carry on with the task he had so nobly set out to do ... At day-break I supervised his body being laid to rest close by the spot where he met his end.*

Despite this burial, the location of the grave was never established. All soldiers carried two identity discs, one to be left with the body and the other to be handed to military authorities to confirm the soldier's death. A number of bodies were found in the 1920s and interred in the Longueval Cemetery. As the identity discs, which were made of leather, would have rotted by then, it is impossible to know whether one of them was Paddy Burton.

In his tribute to Paddy, Skipper recalled him as a young Dragon.

Paddy was one of those boys who make life ceaselessly interesting to a schoolmaster. It may be said that he was a strange compound of liberal and conservative, but what characterised him most was his independence of judgement and his pluck.

He had won the top scholarship to Repton and from there an Exhibition to Wadham College, Oxford.

Paddy was due to be married during his next leave.

5 August – Mametz Wood

Frank Benham was a professional soldier; he joined the R.F.A. in 1906 after attending Marlborough and the Royal Military Academy, Woolwich. He fought at both Mons and Le Cateau.

On 5 August 1916 Frank was in command of his battery at Mametz Wood when he was severely wounded by the explosion of a German shell in his dug-out. He received wounds to the right side of the head, neck and shoulder and was sent for treatment. On 8 August Frank arrived at the No. 2 Stationary Hospital at Abbeville,

Frank Benham (Captain, Royal Field Artillery)

from where he was able to write three short communications to his wife Margaret. He was expected to be transferred back to England on 11 August. Silence and confusion over his whereabouts followed, however, until he sent a telegram to Margaret to tell her he had arrived in Southampton on 20 August. The following day Frank was transferred to Queen Alexandra's Hospital in Millbank, London.

Gradually more details emerged. Frank had in fact spent the week following 11 August at the No. 2 General Hospital at Le Havre, the medical staff having decided that he was too exhausted to continue the journey. On 14 August he suffered a minor haemorrhage from the neck wound. It stopped quite quickly, but the cause remained unexplained.

On 22 August, having endured a painful return back to England, Frank suffered another haemorrhage and underwent an unsuccessful operation to save his life. Margaret was at his side when he died.

13 August – Pozières

Following the attacks in July there was a process of wearing down the enemy prior to the next set-piece battle in mid-September. Jack Gamlen, serving as Lieutenant in the Oxfordshire and Buckinghamshire Light Infantry, joined 'the Push' on 13 August, as the advance continued from Ovillers towards Pozières. His first impressions were very vivid, even after the censor's interventions.

> *I shall never forget it. Less than three hours' march had carried us from corn-fields and unruined villages to an obscure desert which looked like nothing but the surface of the moon … passing streams of wounded and weary men who were returning from the front line …*
>
> *A week later we were back again, further to the left, and in full sight of Thiepval, which looks so harmless and so near in the strong sunlight of a hot morning. In all this part of the line, the trenches were really not trenches at all. They had been blown to bits, weeks before, and gave scarcely any shelter to my men, several of whom were under fire for the first time.*

> *On the afternoon of our first day up, an attack was to be made by the <******> on our left against the enemy line some 200 yards in front. I was in charge of a bombing section, with orders to push on to the enemy trench at Point <******> as soon as the <******> went over, and to join up with them.*
>
> *From a shell-hole I watched our wonderful preliminary bombardment of the enemy's lines. It was terrifying, but extraordinarily interesting. I say 'terrifying', because some of our shells burst very close to us; far too close to be pleasant. Then the barrage suddenly stopped, and the <******> went over, alas, only to come back (what was left of them) in a very few minutes, for they were mown down by machine-gun fire which started the moment our own barrage lifted.*

Jack was ordered to push on with his men if he could. They were in a communications trench (which ran at 90 degrees to the fighting lines) and his two scouts reported that there were about 20 of the enemy behind the next traverse but one. Not believing them, he went forward himself and found 10 German soldiers behind the next traverse but two. They looked at each other before Jack beat a hasty retreat. The attitude of the enemy, he felt, was 'expectant, but not very menacing'. After half an hour 'to allow the Huns to recover from the sight of me', he ordered his party to advance.

> *We all expected death, but there was no time to think about it. When we reached the point at which I had sighted the enemy, I found a German, three yards in front of me, who was just about to descend into a dug-out. His head was already out of sight. I had a beautiful revolver shot at him, and his body and legs followed his head. It was a good moment. Immediately afterwards the enemy woke up, and there was bombing at close quarters. We conjugated the verb 'to bomb' in all its moods and tenses, and my party had wonderful escapes and only two slight casualties. The enemy then retired round the corner of the communicator into their own trench and, as I did not feel equal to attacking their whole first line with one section, I 'consolidated my position' and remained where I was until I was relieved …*
>
> *This is all I will tell you this time. The Somme trenches are very horrible; shells are very horrible; and fighting is* tiring *beyond anything which can be conceived at home. What most impresses me is the speed with which one forgets the horrors as soon as one leaves them behind.*
>
> *I shall not be able to criticise the* Midsummer Night's Dream *next term, but instead, I shall dream mid-winter nights' dreams about you all.*

7 October – Guedecourt

The son of a Banbury vicar, Oswald Blencowe, like 22 other Old Dragons, served with the Ox. & Bucks. – the local regiment for many O.P.S. Old Boys. He was killed at Guedecourt on 7 October 1916, while temporarily attached to the Rifle Brigade.

Oswald Blencowe
(2nd Lieutenant, Oxfordshire and Buckinghamshire Light Infantry)

Oswald Blencowe was hit by a shell when leading his men, about 10 yards (9 m) from the enemy's line. He was buried close to where he fell, but the location of his grave was subsequently lost. Today his name is one of the 70,000 on the Thiepval Memorial that records Somme casualties with no known grave.

A fellow officer in the Ox. & Bucks. wrote to express the loss they felt:

> *In the line he was of immense value to us, and in the most trying hours, when things were as bad as shells and foul weather could make them, he showed that rare kind of cheerfulness which does not offend nor depress by its artificiality. He set a high value on music and poetry. He sang well, and was strongly heard in a dug-out – carols, songs and choruses, old English songs, and Gilbert and Sullivan. One day he pulled out the books he always carried with him – Omar Khayyam, and two volumes of the hundred best poems.*

10 October – Flers

Another Old Dragon with a father in the church was Johnnie Raikes. He had won a scholarship to Radley and then a Mathematical Exhibition to Corpus Christi College, Cambridge – the first Radleian to have done so for many years.

Johnnie had joined the Essex Regiment as a 2nd Lieutenant and on 10 October 1916 he was killed by a shell near Flers. A 'brother-officer' present at his death wrote:

> *He had gone to his dug-out to get some rest; we were being heavily bombarded, and a high explosive shell burst right on the top, destroying the place and killing him instantaneously.*

John Raikes (2nd Lieutenant, Essex Regiment)

Skipper recorded in his *War Memorials* this one of many tributes that he had received.

> *John's servant, also aged 20, was killed by the same shell. This lad, writing home to his mother a few days before, had said, 'You needn't worry about me. I am with a* proper gentleman'.

12 November – Beaucourt

In November 1916 the decision was taken to launch a final attack north and south of the River Ancre against the German strongholds of Serre, Beaumont Hamel, Beaucourt and St Pierre Divion. This was a daunting task: previous attacks on these positions in good weather with fresh troops had ended in disaster. Since then the German positions had been strengthened and the weather conditions had deteriorated appallingly. This was the final throw of the dice before winter made further action impossible.

All objectives were taken. Maurice Jacks, a Lieutenant in the King's Royal Rifle Corps, described his experience of the bitter struggle for Beaucourt. Here the K.R.R.C. joined with the remnants of the Royal Naval Division led by Lieutenant Colonel Bernard Freyberg, whose heroic leadership in this action earned him the V.C.

Maurice Jacks

> *The preliminary bombardment was in full swing, and our guns were giving the Germans beans; we were in the middle of them, so the noise was pretty terrific …*
>
> *It was the night of 12 November when we swam into our tents; we had to be up early the next morning ready to support the Division who were attacking. At 5.40 a.m. the guns loosed off 'five minutes intense', and at 5.45 the infantry went over the top.*
>
> *Shortly afterwards we moved up close behind them and halted in a valley to await orders. Bunches of 'Kamerads' were coming in, many*

> *of them wounded and all more or less sullen; even our witticisms failed to cheer them up. Absurdly exaggerated reports of the success of the attack were current.*
>
> *It was not until late in the afternoon that our orders arrived; and it was dark when heavily laden with every conceivable form of tool and weapon, we went over the top. The guns showed amazing excitement, and their flashes were even more brilliant and alarming than Skipper's lighting in* Macbeth.

Maurice was then given the job of clearing the German lines of any remaining resistance. There was little 'with the exception of a few rash Prussians'. All night long they continued to come across dug-outs full of prisoners.

Maurice and his men also had to reverse the good work of the artillery, which had reduced the German trench to about one foot (0.3 m) deep. By morning they had dug down to a level of 4 feet (1.2 m). They were only 70 yards (64 m) from Beaucourt, which they were due to attack at 7 a.m. However, about half an hour before this attack was due to go in, 'the Boches clearly "got the wind up", and bombarded us vigorously'.

From this point on Maurice was in the thick of it: first a large chunk of shell hit him in the shoulder, then he was buried on five successive occasions. The fifth, as he noted, was total and 'finally laid me out – leaving me with nine bits of shell in the head and face'.

> *Somebody dug me out and bandaged me; and for the next half-hour I was busy digging out my Company Commander, who had been buried by the same shell, and tying up badly wounded men. Then, feeling rather 'groggy', I decided to try to get out; by this time the trench had been nearly filled in, and the Germans were active with their M.G's; so the journey was not altogether a safe one.*

On his way he came across a wounded German who had difficulty walking. Helping him along, the men got talking about the state of the war.

> *He thought that we would win the war but 'would not need many ships to take our men home'. This, I must say, is a very prevalent idea among the German privates.*

Finally Maurice reached a dressing station, after which his 'progress to Blighty was slow and painful, but sure'.

Counting the Cost

The Battle of the Somme officially came to an end on 18 November. The British army had advanced a maximum of 9 miles (14.5 km) on a front 13 miles (21 km) in length – at the cost of over 400,000 killed and wounded.

Back home, it had been possible by the end of August to see the film *The Battle of the Somme*. Within six weeks of its first screening, the film had been viewed by some 20 million people. Most of it showed the lead-up to the battle, but the last part certainly portrayed some of the devastation. Even more telling were the enormous casualty lists, printed daily in the newspapers, which made it clear things had not gone according to plan.

Nine more names were added to the Skipper's list of Old Dragons who had lost their lives. They were all very talented Old Boys. Six of them had won scholarships to their public schools. All came from typical O.P.S. families; four of them had fathers in the Church.

These families suffered tragic losses. Claude Burton, father of Paddy and a regular contributor of verse to the *Daily Mail* under the pseudonym of 'Touchstone', put into words most poignantly the feelings of sacrifice and pain experienced by the bereaved.

Killed in Action

The world seems full of you, now you are gone.
You were, of all these dear familiar things,
Part of our daily life that still drags on
And still around small, trivial objects clings
The sweet and subtle fragrance that is you,
Half balm, half torture to the stricken heart
That knows high courage is a hero's due –
That we, like you, must strive to bear our part.

Though the blood drip unseen from wounds within
That even length of years must leave unhealed –
You bid us conquer pain that we may win
To that high goal your passing has revealed.
You gave your life, and if we too must give
Our very flesh and blood – a sacrifice
That that great cause that claimed you still might live;
Surely the gift is fitting in God's eyes.

Somewhere beyond the range of mortal sight
We know you strive as nobly as of yore,
A soldier still amidst the Hosts of Light;
Though we may see your well-loved face no more.
Oh! Pity us if from these realms unknown
Your eyes look down upon our mortal pain
And plead for us before your Captain's throne
That we may reach those heights you died to gain.

Chapter 12
'The School-house afar …'

The school song, written in 1900 with words by Frank Sidgwick, anticipated that there would be 'Dragons in lands far apart' whose thoughts would drift back to their old school, 'the School-house afar, on the banks of the Cher'. He did not think that the reverse could be true – but of course it was.

A 'Prince among his Fellows'

The pain suffered at home by the families of those lost at Jutland and on the Somme, so vividly expressed by Claude Burton, bore down on the Skipper too. Charles Fisher's death at Jutland was felt deeply, not only by the Skipper but by the whole academic community of Oxford. The Fisher family came from the heart of both the O.P.S. and the University. Herbert Fisher, a former Christ Church student himself, had been tutor to the future Edward VII in 1859, subsequently becoming his private secretary. Together with his wife Mary, Fisher brought up seven sons and four daughters – a considerable family for even the largest of north Oxford residences.

Undoubtedly Charles could be regarded as another 'particular favourite' of the Skipper's. He had been one of the most faithful of his Old Boys and regularly visited the school. The Skipper had always been delighted to see him.

Charles Fisher (Lieutenant, Royal Naval Volunteer Reserve)

Left: Dragons ice skating on Long Meadow, February 1917

Charles frequently used to stroll up to the School to encourage and criticise our games, to chaff Lindsay Wallace, to hit the Skipper on the back (he once told me that he and I had been classed together as the two worst dressed men in Oxford – a great honour to me!). And he would laugh his glorious laugh and pull out a dirty pipe, and tell us some undergraduate story or some anecdote of his many travels; and always a shadow seemed to fall as he strolled away and the sun seemed to come out when he came back to us. Two such splendid men as Charles and his brother William would be [hard] *to find. It is strange to think (and yet perhaps not so very strange) that the great Oxford Don should after such short training be found to be one of the best range-and-rate-finders in the whole fleet.*

His brother H.A.L. Fisher, shortly to become Lloyd George's President of the Board of Education, wrote a moving tribute.

Though his manhood was passed for the most part in a college, nobody can ever have thought of Charles as a scholar or a don, or indeed as belonging to an established class or category. He was too big a man to be classed, and whatever profession or calling one might think of as specially suitable to him seemed, on second thoughts, to be like a suit of clothes at least a size too small … He was full of merriment and vigour, broad in his sympathies, quick and subtle in his moods, a poet and a scholar no doubt, but primarily designed for action and to lead men. It was good to hear his great laugh or see him stride to the wicket with bared head.

But though he played for Oxford and Sussex, he never lost his balance about games, and after two seasons of first-class cricket, which he did not greatly enjoy, he gave up three-day matches and contented himself with an occasional game in term time, a cricket week at a friend's house or a fortnight's tour with the Authentics in the summer. Games were made to be enjoyed, and Charles did not much care how he played them so long as they were enjoyable. His capacity for enjoyment was like a mountain spring. All the simple things of nature – the wind, the sun, the scent of the grass, the many graces of the valley and the wide, air-washed solitude of the hills – filled him with unspeakable delight. He seemed made for a life in the open.[1]

The *Morning Post* sang his praises too.

Charles Fisher towered a very prince among his fellows … Joyous friendships, many, various and intimate were his. His likings were strong, his admiration generous, his hate and scorn severe.

One of Charles's most joyous Old Dragon friendships had been with Lionel Smith. The two men were regular walking companions, going on tours of Italy every Easter. They wore black bowler hats and carried umbrellas, claiming that thus attired they were ready for anything from the heaviest rain to the politest of society.

George Lyttelton, in a piece in Charles's memory, recalled his friend telling him that all he wished to do after the war was to go to bed for five years, only getting up for meals – before adding that this was not to be considered incompatible with an earlier wish to end his days in a Worcestershire vicarage, having helped to settle the date of Deuteronomy.

The Poet Laureate Robert Bridges dedicated 'The Chivalry of the Sea' 'to the memory of Charles Fisher, late Student [Fellow] of Ch.Ch., Oxford'. The poem appeared in *The Times* on 14 August 1916 and was written, by request, for a musical setting. Sir Hubert Parry took up the challenge; the work was to be one of the last choral pieces he wrote before his own death in 1918.

Summer Term 1916

When the Skipper rose to address the parents on Prizegiving Day in July 1916, he was able to list an impressive number of decorations won by Old Dragons: 1 V.C., 1 C.B., 8 D.S.O., 14 M.C., 3 Special Promotions, 4 Legion of Honour, 1 Croix de Guerre and 1 Order of St. George, while 34 Old Dragons had been 'Mentioned in Dispatches'. However, the only list that really mattered to him would have been that of the 30 Old Dragons who had died over the previous year, many of whom he would have thought of as 'an old familiar friend and companion'.

It seems a terrible grim Fate which has robbed us of these our friends in their youth and manhood, and yet if the veil were lifted we might understand that it is not all sheer waste, that the life and death and memory of each one of them is a stone upon the Altar of holy doing and deserving which will raise us and all who have known them nearer to a heaven of love and peace. Let us look to a happy day, in no distant future, when the blast of war's great organ shall be hushed in peace, and victory shall have crowned our great sacrifice.

The Skipper, like everyone else, struggled to make sense of the slaughter – not only for himself, but also for his boys. If it was difficult to understand, it was not so difficult to keep busy and do practical things that would help. He was proud to announce that the O.P.S. was second only to Charterhouse School on the list of subscribers to the Fresh Air Fund. Founded in 1890, this fund provided days out for over 3 million underprivileged children and a two-week holiday for over 30,000 sick children. In addition Dr Barnardo's, Star & Garter, the Red Cross Society and Pearson's Blind Soldiers Fund also received support from the Dragons.

The Skipper discovered too that the school Ford, which had replaced his beloved L.M. cycle car earlier in the war, could be put to a better use. It was sent to Rochdale where a 'Scott' ambulance body was fitted on to the Ford chassis. Thereafter the vehicle was in constant use, taking wounded soldiers to and from Oxford station and various hospitals, and taking the men out for country drives. It could accommodate two stretcher cases or six or seven sitting patients. They might also enjoy bunches of grapes, purchased with money kindly raised by O.P.S. boys and their families.

One highlight of the Summer Term was the school production of *The Gondoliers*. A lucky group of 112 wounded soldiers (presumably from the 3rd Southern General Hospital in Oxford) were invited to attend.

> [They] *came limping in, some on sticks, some on crutches, some in chairs and some on stretchers, but one and all meant to have a good time, and the Dragons in charge saw to it that they had it. What the doctors said the next day about the effects of too many cigarettes and too many other good things does not concern us here.*

One thing that confused the soldiers was that the female parts were being played by boys.

> *In short nothing would persuade* [Tommy] *that black was white, and when he saw 3 or 4 girls, and very pretty ones too, girls they were and he did not believe for one moment they were boys. The actors themselves got a little mixed sometimes, and once one of them earnestly assured us that he would make a 'dutiful husband, I mean wife'. This made Tommy think a little, and one of the staff had the great idea of getting the 'boy-girls' amongst the wounded, and parting the golden and raven locks to show the unbelievers the unmistakable hairy heads of Dragons beneath. On the way from the green room one of the damsels tripped, and what he (she) said, made the soldier … remark, 'Well, that one's a boy anyhow'.*

Conscription

Old Dragons would also attend school performances, if they were able to. Following the introduction of conscription for single men aged between 18 and 41 in January 1916, however, Treffry Thompson, a Captain in the Royal Army Medical Corps, had to attend performances of a different kind. He was sent to work on a Medical Board in Cowley, where he assessed those who were less than enthusiastic about joining up.

Treffry Thompson

> *Two gypsies were presented. The entire room is suddenly disturbed by loud groans from No. 2 of the above pair who is in the hands of the 2nd Inquisitor.*
>
> *Watch the performance. He groans loudly while his arms and legs are gently moved; swears he cannot move his right shoulder; forgets this a minute later and says it is his left. Says he has violent pains in the right knee and cannot bend it. Limps badly on trial, but unfortunately on the wrong leg.*
>
> *The 4th Inquisitor arrives with another victim: a hard, burly looking man, obviously very reluctant to be passed.*
>
> *'This man says he cannot work and never has.'*
>
> *'How old are you?' '32.'*
>
> *'What's your work?' 'Labourer.'*
>
> *'When did you do any labouring?' 'I can't do none.'*
>
> *'What do you live on?' 'On me wages.'*

'Well you can work then?' 'Yes.'

'What do you complain of?' 'Pains.'

'Where?' 'In me 'ead.'

'Do you get any pains in your chest?' 'Yes, awful pains.'

'Do you get any in your stomach?' 'Yes, they does fair double me up.'

'Do you get any in your back?' 'Yes, something cruel.'

'Do you ever drink any beer?' 'What me? No never. Well perhaps I does have a drop occasionally.'

'Do you get any trembling fits?' 'Yes, I goes all of a tremble at times.'

'Especially when you see work?' 'Yes – er no.'

'Do your feet get cold?' 'My feet gets terribly cold.'

'Well, when you are in the army you can find out what "Cold Feet" means.'

The Hardman Family

During the winter of 1916, although the focus of most people's thoughts was still on the Somme, numerous Old Dragons were fighting in other theatres of what was by now very much a world war.

Wallace Hardman (2nd Lieutenant, Manchester Regiment)

In late January came news that Wallace Hardman had been killed. He had died in an engagement on 9 January 1917 at Mahammed Abdul Hassan, north of Kut in modern-day Iraq.

His young Hardman and Mallalieu cousins must have received the news just as they were settling into a new term at the O.P.S. Per Mallalieu (then aged eight) remembered in later life that the previous autumn he had been out with his Aunt Minnie (Wallace's mother) on a walk that took them past her local Post Office.

Someone had come out to them with a telegram. She must have feared the worst, but it transpired that it was only to give her the news that Laurie (her third son) had arrived safely back at Bedford School.

'Auntie Minnie held the message so that we could see it; but her hand was shaking so much that we could not read it,' Per recalled.[2]

The telegram his aunt so feared at that moment was the one she received on 13 January 1917.

Of the ten grandchildren in this picture (right) with their grandmother, three had given their lives by 1917. Four others were serving officers.

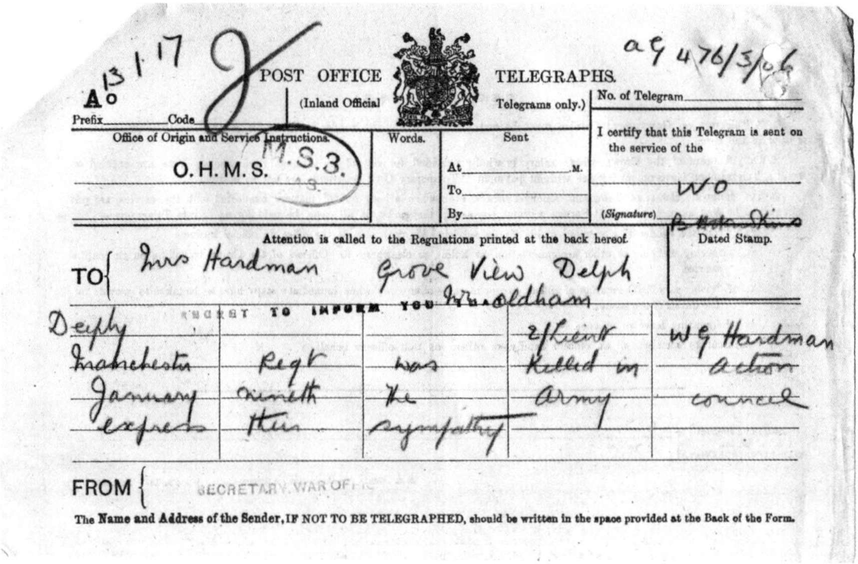

13.1.17 ag 476/3/06

POST OFFICE TELEGRAPHS.

(Inland Official Telegrams only.)

A O

Prefix Code

No. of Telegram

Office of Origin and Service Instructions. Words. Sent

O. H. M. S. M.S.3.

At M.

To

By

I certify that this Telegram is sent on the service of the WO

(Signature)

Attention is called to the Regulations printed at the back hereof.

Dated Stamp.

TO Mrs Hardman Grove View Delph Nr Oldham

REGRET TO INFORM YOU

Delph 2/Lieut W G Hardman Manchester Regt was killed in action January ninth the Army council express their sympathy

FROM SECRETARY, WAR OFFICE

The Name and Address of the Sender, IF NOT TO BE TELEGRAPHED, should be written in the space provided at the Back of the Form.

Above: '2nd Lieut. W.G. Hardman Manchester Regt was killed in action January ninth The Army Council express their sympathy'

Right: A family photograph of 1902. Top row: David Brown (killed), Maurice Campbell (Lieut., R.A.M.C.) and Percy Campbell (killed). Middle row: Pat Campbell (2nd Lieut., R.F.A.), Hugh Brown (Capt., Bedfordshires and recently wounded) and Geoffrey Brown. Front row (with their grandmother and babies): Donald Hardman (Artists Rifles/ R.F.C.) and Wallace Hardman (killed)

Easter Term 1917

As was the tradition, the top form had spent the second half of the autumn term getting to know a Shakespeare play – in this case *A Midsummer Night's Dream*. Skipper, announcing the cast list in *The Draconian*, demanded that the parts 'must be known absolutely pat. Boys should get their sisters etc to improve their acting in the holidays'.

Normally Jack Gamlen would have been at a performance to review it. Now he was otherwise engaged on the Western Front (see pp. 180–81) and some words of encouragement to the cast in the form of this poem would have to suffice.

Dear Players, take from one who used,
Each year, to be your faithful critic –
A task he'd never have refused,
Though deaf, or blind, or paralytic –

A tribute to your former skill,
Good wishes for your next excursion
In plays which universal Will
Devised for his and your diversion.

I mind the day, in 'ninety-eight,
When I myself appeared as Theseus,
(At two days' notice, let me state,)
Expecting hisses loud as geese use,

And, I can tell you from my heart,
To have such memories to remember,
Helps me to play the harder part
Of fighting Germans in December.

When performed in the first week of the Easter Term of 1917, the play received its usual plaudits from an (anonymous) reviewer.

It was indeed a welcome boon that the Dragons gave us this year to transport us for three hours' space away from the sorrows and difficulties of this unintelligible war to the flowers and forest glades of Shakespeare's Warwickshire …

Many of the O.D.s now in the trenches were doubtless present with us in spirit that night.

* * * * * *

Towards the end of January the weather took a turn for the worse. Skipper characteristically determined that the best should be made of it, giving up on lesson time and over £1,000 (in today's money).

A popular alternative to morning lessons, January 1917

> *We will remember this term particularly for the ice-skating. In the end, we had glorious skating for three weeks on the University Skating Club flooded meadow. The authorities were good enough to admit us at half fees (3d a time) and, even so, got about £15 from the School!*
>
> *The morning was quite the best time to go and we took off one of the morning hours of work. Often the caravan-ambulance* [the converted Ford] *made three or four journeys, packed with small boys and provisions for picnic lunch on the ice.*

* * * * * *

The financial outlay was not insignificant. The O.P.S., like other prep schools, had to contend with rising prices and increased rationing, voluntary to begin with and later compulsory. War Rations for schools became a topic for letters to *The Times*, to which the Skipper contributed his views. Following this, the Skipper reported a further development.

The Food Controller has declared that in the case of growing boys and girls the Ration order is not expected to be strictly complied with. In meat I find that we are within the mark, but I cannot bring myself to believe that a restricted bread supply is good for young people.

Although sugar was not formally rationed until January 1918, Skipper felt compelled to cut back.

Each boy and grown-up had a cardboard box containing 10 oz. of sugar for the week – it being considered that 2 oz. per week per head should be used in cooking. By the end of the week most boys had a good deal left. Some had not touched their rations; they proposed to take or send it home, or to have a good toffee-making at the end of the week. My lady housekeeper, seeing the boxes were not empty, thought the boys had been practising economy, and merely filled up each box to 10 oz. In the morning there were cries of dismay.

Many a prep school headmaster would have had no truck with such demanding behaviour. Indeed, in many schools boys would have been unlikely to dare to question any adult decisions. But this was the O.P.S. and it operated under different rules, as Skipper explained.

The boys naturally thought that the amount saved was their own property, and I could but declare that 'a ration's a ration' and that it is the property of the rationee! So each boy had to estimate the amount of sugar left in his box and it was weighed out to him. At the end of term I bought back a good many pounds of sugar. Well, either they previously had too much or else now they were having too little!

* * * * * *

For those freezing in wartime Oxford, the following news from Macedonia must have brought welcome warmth. Rev. Robin Laffan, who had been elected a Fellow and Chaplain of Queens' College, Cambridge, in 1912, had been appointed padre to the Mechanical Transport Companies, supplying the Serbs in the mountains of Western Macedonia. He had recently received his copy of *The Draconian*; it had also impressed his colleagues, who were surprised to learn that they were reading a preparatory school magazine. Robin felt compelled to contribute an article, 'if it be thought worthy', illustrating the amusing consequences of language difficulties encountered in dealing with the Serbs.

Robin Laffan

For instance, a doctor in one of our hospitals for Serbs, thinking that he was beginning to get on well with the language, went round his ward asking each patient 'Imate li jenu?' (which means, though he was after something quite different: 'Have you a wife?') Those who replied 'yes' were left in peace. When any patient replied 'no', the doctor told the nurse to give him a dose of castor oil.

The next day all the patients asserted they were married. As they did so again the third day, the doctor asked a further question. 'Koliko imate jene?' ('How many wives have you?') At this they thought he was being insulting and an unpleasant situation was only saved by calling in an interpreter. He explained that the 'gospodin doktor' was really inquiring after bowel movements, not families.

* * * * * *

Hugh Sidgwick

A letter from Hugh Sidgwick must also have been a welcome tonic. He had been summoned back to England in January 1917 by the Board of Education to assist the minister, H.A.L. Fisher, with a new Education Act. Important work no doubt, and certainly more worthy of Hugh's extraordinary intellectual capabilities than the Royal Garrison Artillery. Yet in this contribution for *The Draconian*, he depicted himself as a 'shirker' in a 'funk-hole' in London.

From a Funk-hole

1.
This is the song of a shirker in a funk-hole.
He has alternated, and will continue to alternate, between
being a shirker in a funk-hole, and an over-fed hero
intrepidly sitting at a telephone in France.
But for the time being he is a shirker in a funk-hole again.

2.
The men in funk-holes are acute, over-worked, and tired.
They get no leave and no potatoes.
They are insulted in the press.
They are assisted temporarily in their labours by dons,
women, and business men.
But they stick it.

3.
The warmth and cleanliness of the funk-holes are pleasant after France.
The shirker is glad to have interesting work to do again
Until it comes to doing it.
In France the work is not so hard.

4.
London is a good place compared with France.
But it involves being taken to revues.
Revues are better than violent shelling,
But moderate shelling is better than revues.

5.
Of course there is the moral aspect.
But moral aspects don't worry the shirkers much.

6.
If you consider who are really enduring the hardships of war,
There are eleven classes in order of endurance.
The first six all consist of people who go into the
front line and get shelled, or who go about in ships, or fly.
The seventh consists of people in this country who work.
The eighth consists of Staffs, Base Censors and others,
who sit behind the line
And have a high old time.
The ninth consists of a Railway Transport Officer, whom I know.
The tenth consists of journalists.
The eleventh consists of people who appear in the Sketch
in full evening dress as interested in War Work.

7.
The shirker has belonged to Classes Four, Seven and Eight.
So he knows.
At the moment he belongs to Class Ten
If you consider The Draconian *a journal.*

8.
Having concluded his song the shirker returns to his funk-hole
In the hope of persuading someone else to do the work.
Unfortunately there are no N.C.O.s there.

In April 1917, before returning to the Front, Hugh went to hear H.A.L. Fisher speaking about the Education Act.

> *Last night I sat in the H*[ouse] *of C*[ommons] *listening to all my dreams coming true. Fisher spoke admirably: he is really a bit too good for that mediocre assembly.*

Passed the following year, the Act was to raise the school leaving age from 12 to 14.

A Warrior's Return

Even more appreciated than letters were the visits of Old Dragons back from the conflict (often recovering from wounds). Some 50 of them visited the school in the Easter and Summer Terms of 1917, one of whom was Rupert Lee, who had been serving as Lieutenant in the Worcestershire Regiment. He had been wounded in the retreat from Mons in 1914 (see pp. 71–72) and was subsequently sent to the Persian Gulf. In April 1916 he was home on sick leave and was a most welcome visitor to the school. The boys much enjoyed his exhibition of conjuring, which included producing two doves from a hat – a trick learned in India. Rupert was no doubt persuaded at the time to write this article describing his time in Mesopotamia. It appeared in the April 1917 edition of *The Draconian.*

Rupert Lee

An extraordinary affair occurred in our Mess in Busra [Basra] *just before I left; we all had native servants and it was customary to put the most reliable in charge of the whole; this man incurred the lasting hatred of one of the other servants (of another religion) through accusing him of the theft of a tin of stewed fruit.*

So one day, when the butler went out to the town to see some of his friends, this other man came to me and asked to be allowed out. On my giving him permission, he proceeded to steal a bottle of whisky: and fortified by it, took one of our revolvers and sallied forth intent on the slaughter of his enemy. He explained to me afterwards that a natural delicacy forbade him carrying out this business in our quarters, where he could have met him any day.

We captured him after all his ammunition (about 20 rounds) was expended and he was locked up. His subsequent examination was really very amusing, if one could forget the tragic side; he explained the whole thing in detail, regretting that these men were killed, but of course that was their fault for getting in the way.

What he was really most sorry about was that he failed to kill the butler and made a petition that he might be allowed to do so before being hanged.

I tried to get a plea of insanity brought forward, but the man himself would not hear of it and from his behaviour after the event it would never have gone through.

Entente Cordiale

One of the most regular of correspondents was Jack Gamlen (Lieutenant, Ox. & Bucks.). He wrote to *The Draconian* to sing the praises of 'our French allies' and convince young Dragons that they must all visit France at the first opportunity after the war.

Jack's article described his experience of taking over a section of the trenches from the French. He was acting as Brigade interpreter, and was impressed by the French Colonel's insistence that business could wait as lunch should come first. There followed a five-course meal, described by Jack 'as one of the best lunches I ever came across'. There was red wine and champagne, 'yet everything was simple and the meal was short'. Initial shyness was soon overcome, and by the end of the meal 'everyone was talking some sort of French'.

After lunch we got to business at once. The Colonel was wonderful. He had every detail that we wanted at his finger tips and scarcely ever referred to his Adjutant. After an hour in looking at maps and discussing dispositions, he took us some way forward to an O.P., from which we had a wonderful view of the German front …

The next day Jack returned with the Brigade Major. He called upon the French Brigadier, in order to arrange the final details of the forthcoming relief.

> *He spoke the most exquisite French and had the most exquisitely simple manners. I am sure that he is descended from one of those French Officers of the old days, who used to call out to their men 'Messieurs les gendarmes de la maison du Roi, veuillez assurer vos chapeaux. Nous allons avoir l'honneur de charger ...'*
>
> *The French fighting man is a glorious creature and the sight of him should convince any armchair pessimist that nothing can ever kill France, however full her cemeteries may be (and they are terribly full round here) ...*
>
> *Let there be no misunderstanding about what France is. She is, and has been for a thousand years, the most civilised country in the world and her salvation is the first and greatest object of the war, for the presence of a single German soldier on French soil is an obscene thing.*
>
> *My dear Dragons, educate yourselves to love France. Learn to read and speak French well, NOW, and, after the war, get your parents, whether they can afford it or not, to take you often to France ...*
>
> *There is nothing un-British or decadent in this love of France; and there is something very stupid and ugly in the want of it. Every civilised being ought to write on his heart the fine old motto,*
>
> *'Chacun a deux pays: le sien et La France.'*

Clearly Skipper needed to organise more French lessons!

Historically, France had been England's traditional enemy rather than Germany (a new nation created only 43 years before the outbreak of the First World War). Early in the twentieth century, however, Germany's emergence as a military power had certainly drawn England and France closer together. As far as the O.P.S. was concerned, they had happily taken on a number of French children before 1914. Following the outbreak of war, ten Old Dragons fought under the French flag.

Somerville

Somerville College was situated beside the Radcliffe Infirmary, so it was not surprising that the War Office requisitioned it to be a recovery hospital for wounded officers. The Maitland Buildings that they used were the work of Old Dragon Edmund Fisher, the architect brother of Charles, William and H.A.L. Fisher. The war was to cost Edmund his life too; he succumbed to appendicitis while on active service in 1918.

The Hall was used for a time as a medical ward, before being converted into an Officers' Mess. On the outbreak of war Maud Wilkinson, the O.P.S. nurse, had left to work at the Infirmary (see p. 66). She ensured there was a regular flow of visitors to the O.P.S. from Somerville, whether to see the plays and concerts or to take part, as best they could, in cricket matches against the boys. The time spent with young enthusiastic Dragons was a tonic in itself, as one of the patients testified.

The Maitland Buildings, Somerville College, 1913

> *During the Summer Term, some of us who are at present in Somerville have been trying, we hope more or less successfully, to fill the shoes of the school cricket sides, and have played several matches against the School ... One can imagine no surroundings in the world more fitted for the healing and comforting of the scars of life, than among the boys at Lynam's.*

Wounded soldiers with Skipper's brother Hum Lynam (far right, top row) and the young pupils of the O.P.S., 1917

The games were greatly enjoyed by young Dragons. With mild mumps and some German measles prevalent at the O.P.S., it had not been possible to arrange cricket matches against other schools that term.

Francis Wylie, a Dragon boy at the time, remembered:

An experimental match was played against 'Sister Wilkinson's XI', who was in charge of Dragon boarders before the war. Some of the visiting batsmen needed a runner, some of their bowlers had to dispense with a run-up, and they were suitably handicapped in the field – and the game was so much enjoyed by both sides that it was repeated each week for the rest of the term, with the visitors bringing, wheeling and even carrying more and more supporters with them each time.

In the evening bathe that followed each match, we were joined by those of our opponents who had Sister Wilkinson's permission, and by one or two more who had arranged for her attention to be distracted. [3]

Popular as the cricket matches were, the teas were perhaps even more enjoyed – particularly by the Skipper and his macaws.

The Skipper and his macaws

Bath-chair cases were very grateful to Mrs Vassall and her lady helpers. Instead of being wheeled along dusty streets, obtaining in the process parched throats and having to swallow mouthfuls of 'petrofine', several have been able to sit in comfortable surroundings, watch the cricket and enjoy themselves thoroughly.

Skipper was in agreement.

I think that the matches have been at least as good for the boys, and in many ways more enjoyable, than the usual matches with other schools.

Nor was this the end of the soldiers' presence at the school.

Our friends from Somerville muscled in on the Tug of War competition, until they managed to break the rope! One of the most exciting races of the afternoon was the 100 yards race for officers – a pair of crutches won by inches from a bath chair, and the prize-winners received a stirring reception at yesterday's prize-giving.

Per Mallalieu holding the Somerville Cup, 1922

The prizes included a Challenge Cup inscribed 'From the Officers now in Somerville. July 1917' which they presented to the School. It was to be awarded each year, by the vote of the whole school, to the boy who had 'the most gentlemanly bearing and best influence on other boys'.

In 1922 the Cup was to be awarded to Per Mallalieu, later to feature in John Betjeman's *Summoned By Bells.*

Percival Mandeville, the perfect boy,
Was all a schoolmaster could wish to see –
Upright and honourable, good at games,
Well-built, blue-eyed, a sense of leadership
Lifted him head and shoulders from the crowd.[4]

Just how much the young Dragons helped to reinvigorate these battle-scarred soldiers can be seen in an appreciation received from one of the Somerville officers.

To us it has been unalloyed pleasure and no words could express our gratitude in being privileged to enjoy so many happy afternoons among the boys ... The golden days of youth came back to us this summer, those glorious days when enthusiasms are fresh and alive, when one never sickens of effort and when the game we play is everything to us ...

You have given us many happy days and have helped us once again to re-discover the springs of youthful joyousness and love of life. May the memory of those happy days, spent with you on the banks of the Cher., ever live with us, go with us when we return to duty.

Sunday Sermons

A mumps epidemic in the Easter Term had obliged the Skipper to quarantine his boys, meaning that Sunday services in the local church were no longer possible. So started a tradition for services held at the school, which survives to this day.

Who would preach the sermon, many wondered. The Skipper had a ready answer.

> *We have therefore had Old Boys on leave preaching – or rather talking (the word preaching, except in the case of a minister of religion, has an annoying meaning).*

During the Easter and Summer Terms of 1917, three such talks stood out. The first was that of Stuart Taylor, still known as 'Fluff' and now a Lieutenant Colonel in the West Yorkshire Regiment. His theme was the importance of discipline to ensure a person did the right, rather than the natural, thing.

Stuart Taylor

> *You see, in the Parks, the Drill Sergeant drilling the soldiers. Perhaps you wonder why it is necessary to be so particular that the soldiers should turn their heads and eyes to the right on the words 'eyes right', why they should spring smartly to attention at the word of command or why they must stand absolutely still and steady in the ranks. Why is it?*
>
> *Why shouldn't 1,000,000 men each be given a rifle, taught how to fire it and be sent out to kill Germans? Simply because they will have, in the course of their work, to face unusual situations, sudden dangers, where steadiness, coolness and level-headedness are necessary.*
>
> *You cannot trust a man's or boy's instinct to prompt him to do the right thing. It will make him do the natural thing. The natural thing is to avoid danger, to run away from it. Instinct will prompt this. But habit, which is the child of discipline, will make a man or boy face the danger and act rightly in an emergency …*
>
> *The soldier is taught to keep his buttons bright, his hair brushed and short, his clothes clean and smart, not because these things in themselves are of great importance, but because they all tend to make him punctual, clean, smart, cheerful and tidy in mind and body throughout his life.*
>
> *A smart, well turned out, well-disciplined regiment always fights much better than a dirty, ill-disciplined one. There is no doubt whatever about that …*
>
> *If a bomb dropped in the street and damaged some people, the natural inclination of a man or boy is to avoid the danger and ugliness of pain and suffering. But the habit of your training, to command yourself and your natural instinct, will teach you to go and succour those who are injured and prevent others coming into danger.*

The second talk was given by Ernest Baker, a friend of Skipper's and an O.P.S. parent. While he besought the boys to 'play fair' and 'seek the truth', they were also to 'serve the brethren'. This he meant in its widest context, as he explained.

What I would have you try to believe is that elementary school boys are your brothers. I say this because I am anxious that when you are men, practising, as most of you will, what are called the liberal professions, you should realise that the working men side by side with whom you will live are your brothers, members of the same society, equally vital with you to its life.

He went on to remind them that, given the advantages they had in life, they had correspondingly greater responsibilities.

We are all, when it comes to the ultimate test, equal in the sight of our Maker; and we have all to live together as brothers in the society in which He has ordained us to live.

However, the most striking sermon recorded in *The Draconian* is that delivered by C.R.L. Fletcher. He was the father of Regie and George, both of whom had lost their lives in 1914/15 (see pp. 82 and pp. 99–100). Rather than keeping the war distant from the O.P.S. boys, he wanted them to understand that it might become their lot too.

We old ones have to learn to give up what is far dearer to us than life, the lives of our children; I wonder if you boys realise what the sight of a telegram, or even of a telegraph boy going down a road, means to half the parents in Oxford? It may mean 'Hurrah, I am coming home on leave'; it may mean we shall never see him on earth again. Really the chances, which of these two things it means, are about even …

Then the full-grown fighters are learning to give up their own lives, often not nearly such a cruel prospect as that of living on maimed or in constant pain, which may only too probably be their lot.

Lastly, you boys are learning to give up a hundred things to which you have been accustomed; I don't in the least underrate the difficulty of giving up favourite things to eat … but you are also learning better and greater sacrifices than this, you are learning to 'put away childish things', to grow old and thoughtful before your due time, to help fathers and mothers to bear their unforgettable griefs, to harden yourselves to face a sterner life, in a poorer England, than any of which your fathers and mothers dreamed when you were born.

For the course of time has 'swerved and crooked backwards' in our days – probably just because we were all too comfortable and happy (and therefore growing selfish and lazy). The ship – I like to compare Britain to a ship – is scudding before a fearful hurricane, with half her sails blown away, and with jury masts very imperfectly rigged. The best and bravest of her crew have been washed away and swallowed up. Whether she will right herself in your time depends very much upon you – upon your grasping now the meaning of the words 'duty' and 'sacrifice', and keeping them steadily in view as the only worthy ends of your lives.

You will one day have to rebuild not merely the material city of Ypres, and a few hundred of other ruined places, but the whole fabric of European civilisation, and you must take care to lay its foundations so well and truly that such desolation as that of the last three years shall never occur again. And, even before you come to rebuild, it may very well happen to you, yes even to the youngest of you, to be called on to defend the last relics of that civilisation. The real end of this war is yet a very long way off, and, if an inconclusive peace is now patched up, the flame will burst up again (all history is a clear proof of this) and that rekindled flame may very probably burn up your own lives.

How true this proved to be, for a large number of those listening were to risk (and some to lose) their lives in the Second World War. At the time, however, Skipper may well have felt that Fletcher had 'laid it on a bit thick' for the boys and he needed to redress the balance. His instincts told him he should keep on as much as possible 'as normal', and the boys should not worry themselves about the more distant future and its possibilities. As was his habit, he spoke to the boys at the last Sunday service of the term.

I do not know whether it is right, but I have tried all through to let the war make as little difference as possible to the lives of you, my boys. We older people feel it intensely; it has turned our world upside down. We have lost some of our best and dearest, and we are always full of anxiety. But we try to keep our anxiety and suffering from you and to save you from all this as far as we can.

You have done your work and played your games and eaten and slept as far from the strain and stress of this terrible struggle as has been possible. You who have relations and friends in danger on sea or land must be always in dread that the news of wounds or death may come, but it is the nature of the young to hope for the best, and I do not wish you to think too much of the dread possibilities that are always present to your elders.

But I want you to feel that the war is very largely being carried on for your sakes. It is in the hope and belief that the world will be better for the generation that is growing up and for future generations – for us, it can bring little but sorrow and loss, however victorious we may be in the end.

But for you we hope for a brighter and happier and better world – a world where you will prepare for peace rather than for war, where love, not hate, shall be the motto of the nations, where helping others, not beating others will be the ideal and aim of life. And for this future do try to make yourselves ready.

He finished with two favourite quotations, the first from 'The Invitation. To Tom Hughes' by Charles Kingsley and the second 'Be kind to each other' by Charles Swain.

Do the thing that's nearest though it's dull at whiles,
Helping, when you meet them, lame dogs over stiles.

and

Be kind to each other; the night cometh on
When friend and when brother perchance may be gone.

Chapter 13
War in the Air

Aerial Ambitions

Growing up during the First World War, particularly for boys of public-school age and background, focused thoughts on what must have seemed an inevitable future in one of the armed forces. In the past this would have been a choice between the army and the navy – but by 1916 many were attracted to a new possibility.

Nevil Norway had moved on from the O.P.S. to Shrewsbury School in 1913. He remembered the beginning of the war as being 'still romantic in those days'.[1] Then his older brother Fred joined up and in the summer of 1915 was badly wounded. His trench was undermined and, although he survived the explosion, he was hit by shellfire as he tried to dig out his sergeant. After ten days in hospital gangrene set in and, with his mother at his side, Fred died. It was a turning point for Nevil:

Nevil Norway

For the remainder of my time at Shrewsbury I don't think I had the slightest interest in a career or any adult life; I was born to one end, which was to go into the army and do the best I could before being killed. The time at school was a time for contemplation of the realities that were coming and for spiritual preparation for death, and in this atmosphere the masculine, restrained services in the school chapel under Alington played an enormous part. The list of the school casualties grew every day.

Older boys that we knew intimately, one who had perhaps been monitor in one's own bedroom, left, appeared once or twice resplendent in new uniforms, and were dead. We remembered them as we had known them less than a year before as we knelt praying for their souls in chapel, knowing as we did so that in a year or so the little boys in our own house would be kneeling for us.[2]

While many of those for whom Nevil prayed were victims of trench warfare, he noted a group whose lives were clearly even more dangerous.

Most moving of these casualties, perhaps, were those of the Royal Flying Corps, whose joy in their vocation was so great, whose lives so short. With the love of aircraft that I

Left: A sketch by Jack Slessor showing his encounter with enemy cavalry and the resulting 'most perfect chaos' **(see p. 214)**

was developing I envied them so greatly, though it was well known at the time that the average life of a pilot on the Western Front was three weeks. What I did not know until the war was over was that they were being sent to France as fully trained fighter pilots flying Sopwith Pups and Camels with as little as twenty hours total solo flying experience. And in that war pilots went on till they were killed; there was no relief after a fixed number of missions.[3]

* * * * * *

Nevil had arrived at the O.P.S. in 1909, the year following the first successful flight over the English Channel by Louis Blériot. A contemporary of Nevil's at the O.P.S., although nearly two years older, was Jack Slessor; and while Nevil was clearly inspired by this event, Jack was not. His father was in the army and that was where his ambition lay, despite the fact he was lame in both legs due to childhood polio and was unable even to play rugby. This was to put him in the same boat (literally) as Jack Haldane's sister Naomi.

Instead of 'Games' – and I really would have liked playing rugger – I used to go rowing on the Cherwell with Jack Slessor ... Jack and I were good friends and talked a lot between rowing; I am sure the British Empire came into it. Both of us read Kipling. Jack desperately wanted to go into the Army, following his father, but this ambition was thought to be hopeless.[4]

Jack left Haileybury in December 1914, even more desperate to join up. Given his infirmities, this was not going to be easy. He explored every avenue, eventually discovering that the officer in charge of the branch of the War Office responsible for the selection of officers for the Royal Flying Corps (R.F.C.) was one Lieutenant Colonel W.W. Warner. He had by chance served with Jack's uncle in the Indian Cavalry. This connection did the trick: Jack got an interview with Warner and another officer by the name of Ferdy Waldron. Having seen Jack walk across the room, both officers agreed that Jack could fly and sent him off to complete his application form (with both his father's and headmaster's signatures) and to attend a Medical Board at the War Office at 5 p.m. the same day. This was something of a logistical challenge.

Taking the train to Broxbourne, near Haileybury, Jack found his father, at this time commanding a company of recruits, riding behind a column of marching soldiers.

A quick two minutes work and I was galloping up the road to Haileybury on the commanding officer's charger, umbrella in hand, bowler crammed down to my ears and my application form, bearing my father's signature, in the pocket of my blue London overcoat, leaving a somewhat dazed parent to watch (a) his horse, and (b) his battalion disappearing up the road.[5]

Jack's three-mile journey concluded with his clattering into the Quad at Haileybury. He handed the reins to a bemused porter, then 'bolted down to the Master's Lodge, got Mr. Malim's signature and was away again at a smart canter just in time to catch a train back to London'. He arrived in time for his medical, only to be summarily declared 'totally unfit for any form of military service'. Jack's efforts, it seemed, had been in vain.

> *But* [the medical results] *meant nothing to Willie Warner. Within a few weeks I received a nice eighteenth birthday present in the shape of orders to join 1 (Reserve) Squadron R.F.C. at Brooklands for flying instruction. And that is how I got into the Air Service.*[6]

The experience gave Jack 'a life-long conviction that one of the best methods of selection of officers is by selective and controlled nepotism'.[7] Yet the results could seem arbitrary. Towards the end of the war Nevil Norway, with no such contacts, was considered unfit and dismissed from Woolwich for nothing more than his stammer.

Training

If aerial warfare was dangerous, so was the training British pilots received. Many a trainee met his death without ever getting near the enemy. The flying schools, both military and civilian, saw many casualties – some 15 aircrew based on Oxford's Port Meadow were killed.

Some of the recruits for training came from the ranks of the army. Geoffrey Buck, who had joined the Royal Fusiliers in 1914, aged 17, won the M.C. 'for gallantry in the field' before switching to the R.F.C. in 1916, intent on becoming a pilot. At this point, trainee pilots were receiving between 3 and 4 hours of flying tuition with an instructor, followed by just 8 hours of solo flying. Geoff's diary entries reveal his love of flying and the nature of his training.

Geoffrey Buck

> *5 August 1916*
> *This is absolutely* the *life. I have done one hour's dual control and can fly the bus by myself, but have never been up alone yet; they won't send us up alone till we have done three hours dual. I simply love it! Better than skating, rugger, or even ski-ing. I want to be in the air the whole day long, but of course we have to do a lot of technical work too. Engines, motors, signalling, construction, theory, photography – and all is most interesting.*

> *16 August 1916*
> *I did my first solo tonight in rather bad weather, made a perfect landing, and went to 700 ft. It was too perfect for words …*

> *23 August 1916*
> *I flew to Norwich on Sunday, stopped the night, and flew back on Monday. Two machines crashed under me as I was starting to land (it was awfully windy and bumpy), and one pilot was killed, but I landed perfectly. Some game.*

* * * * * *

Donald Hardman was one of the two boys to have so impressed C.S. Lewis when they both arrived at Malvern College in 1913 (see p. 32). Donald left school at the age of 16, however, and started his military training the following year to become a 2nd Lieutenant in the R.F.C. As with Geoff Buck, this training was hardly extensive: four or five hours of 'dual' were all that was required before his instructor considered this 17-year-old ready for his first 'solo'.

Donald Hardman

> *A first solo is an unforgettable experience because never before and never afterwards in your life will you have felt so utterly lonely as that first time, when you find yourself in the air by yourself. The painstaking circuit with one eye glued to the airspeed indicator and the other never for a moment letting the airfield out of sight, the judgement of the approach and the unbelievable relief of the touch-down.*[8]

Donald might never even have got to the Front, had it not been for a remarkable piece of luck.

> *I remember walking down for breakfast one morning with a friend called Cobb and we both had to fly B.E.s that morning and we tossed up as to who was to have the 2E and he won the toss and I was horrified to learn when I landed that his* [wing] *extensions had come off during a manoeuvre and he was killed.*[9]

The Zeppelin Menace

The Germans brought the war to England on 19 January 1915, with the first attack over East Anglia by one of its airships. A further 20 raids, leading to the death of some 200 civilians, were to follow before the end of the year. On 13 October 1915, less than a year after joining the R.F.C. Jack Slessor found himself in pursuit of a Zeppelin, located by chance over his old school, Haileybury. But the Zeppelin was easily able to outclimb his plane and disappeared into cloud. Having lost his target, Jack returned to his base, where he landed in fog.

> *My first operational sortie came to an ignominious but painless end in the turnips by the edge of the stubble … – one of three out of the five aircraft that went up that night to crash in the fog, all without hurting their pilots. I suppose I can claim the distinction of being the first pilot ever to have intercepted an enemy aircraft over Great Britain.*[10]

Even if Jack had managed to get above the airship, the chances of his having brought it down were small, given his limited weaponry.

> [He had only] *a small oblong bomb full of petrol, of which three or four were carried in the cockpit. They were pushed by hand through a tube in the floor. In the tube an electrical contact ignited the fuse, whereupon the bomb burst into flames and a bunch of large fish-hooks came out at the top. These, theoretically, would catch in the Zeppelin's envelope and allow the burning bomb to do the rest. It was a weapon worthy of Mr.*

Heath Robinson at his best, and never succeeded in destroying anything more than the odd haystack or two.[11]

* * * * * *

William Leefe Robinson

William Leefe Robinson was born in 1895 in Coorg, in the south of India, where his father was a coffee planter. The family came over to England for the year in 1901, during which time William and his brother Harold attended the O.P.S. A couple of years later he returned to England to complete his education at St Bees School in Cumbria. He was no academic, but excelled in sport. When war was declared William entered Sandhurst, intent on a career in the army. He did not find this to his liking, however, so in March 1915 he transferred to the Royal Flying Corps as an observer.

The principal role of the R.F.C. at that stage was very much one of observation, spotting enemy positions and directing fire upon them. In May Robbie, as he was known to his fellows, was wounded by some shrapnel and invalided back to England. Once he had recovered, he set about becoming a pilot.

By the end of the year 'Billy the Birdman', as he signed himself off in another letter to his mother, found himself seconded to help with the defence of London against the menace of the Zeppelin. With these airships often attacking at night, the British pilots had to master the art of flying at night themselves. Their planes – particularly the instruments – needed to be adapted. Landing flares, or rather paraffin-soaked rags in barrels, often proved inadequate. Many pilots were killed landing from night operations.

Airship raids continued throughout 1916, causing many casualties across the Midlands and South. Improvements in aircraft and ammunition were needed before the airship, which usually flew at comparatively high altitude, could be attacked effectively. However, when Robbie took to the air on 3 September 1916, he had three drums of the newly invented explosive bullets, combined with incendiary bullets, for his Lewis machine gun. He spotted a German airship, which was caught by two searchlights over Woolwich, and gave chase. He managed to hit the underside, but with no obvious effect. A further burst of fire along the length of the airship was similarly ineffective and so he aimed his final drum into the rear from about 500 ft (c.150 m) below the airship. Within seconds it became a blazing inferno.

Robbie's account of his exploits appeared in the December 1916 edition of *The Draconian.*

Soon she appeared to catch fire in her forward petrol tank. The flames spread rapidly along her body. She made off eastwards on fire. In several minutes she dipped by the nose and dived slowly in flames to the earth. I was so pleased, that in my excitement I pulled the 'joystick' and looped the loop several times.

The destruction of the airship was witnessed by thousands of Londoners. They were prepared to risk injury to watch Robbie do battle with a German airship whose bombs had already killed 16 people on the ground.

There were immediate celebrations and large numbers headed for the site where the airship eventually crashed down with the bodies of its crew of 16. It continued to burn for two days and over 10,000 people came to see the wreckage.

Robbie became an instant hero and his feat was quickly recognised. Within a couple of days it was announced that His Majesty the King had been graciously pleased to award the Victoria Cross to Lieutenant William Leefe Robinson.

Gifts of money poured in from the general public – over £4,000 – in addition to the reward for being the first to shoot down an airship. Invitations to numerous official engagements followed, leading Robbie to complain that 'Babies, flowers and hats have been named after me, also poems and prose have been dedicated to me – oh, it's all too much!'[12] Only ten days later he was brought sharply down to earth. He crashed on take-off when his plane was caught by a gust of wind and was fortunate to get out before the plane caught fire.

Wounded in Action

Although *The Draconian* recorded no aircrew deaths throughout 1914–17, there were a number who sustained injuries. Jack Slessor, now a fully-fledged Lieutenant in the R.F.C., had hoped to see action at Gallipoli. No sooner had he arrived at Mudros, the campaign base, however, than it was coming to an end. Instead he was transferred to Egypt.

C Flight, 17th Squadron Base, M.E.F., Egypt.

We have been having a most exciting time of it since we arrived here (Suez). I have been on about half-a-dozen reconnaissances, it is most awful mountainous country to fly over, but it is great fun as a rule.

Jack Slessor mid-air in his cockpit

The enclosed is a sort of picture [see p. 208] *of an incident that happened to me when I was on a patrol job in the desert, with an observer. We came upon quite a large reconnoitring patrol of the enemy's cavalry, come down from the hills to have a look round. We had a machine gun with us and promptly came down to four or five hundred feet to make sure of them. They behaved in the most idiotic manner and seemed to lose their heads, for instead of scattering, they most of them dismounted and gathered in a bunch, offering an ideal target; so we circled round and attacked them with the machine gun from about 400–500 feet. It really was the funniest thing to watch, for as soon as I opened fire the horses took fright and bolted full speed to the mountains, leaving those who had dismounted running about in the sand, and the whole scene was the most perfect chaos.*

The Draconian of August 1916 reported a change in Jack Slessor's luck.

> *During the Sudan revolt, when the Sultan of Darbur's capital was taken and 1,000 of the enemy killed, a valuable air reconnaissance was carried out (so the Secretary of the War Office announced) by Lieut. J.C. Slessor of the R.F.C. He succeeded by means of bombs and machine-gun fire in forcing first a large body of hostile cavalry and then a body of some 2,000 infantry to retire in disorder. He was wounded by a bullet in the thigh, but returned safely to Abiad, a flight of 90 miles.*

This journey was not without difficulty. In order to make a right turn, Jack had either to press down on the rudder bar with his right leg or lift it with his left leg. Unfortunately it was his right leg that was wounded and his left leg was pretty useless, due to his childhood polio. The only way out of this dilemma was to lean out of the cockpit and grab the wires that led from the rudder bar to the rudder pylon.

The turbulence caused Jack to be airsick, but after a flight of over five hours he landed back at his base. Here he had the bullet removed from his leg – something he endured with bravery and good humour.

> *They took the bullet out with a large knife. There was no anaesthetic. A couple of bottles of hot champagne and a swig of brandy had to do instead. The operation was bad enough, but the hangover … that was really awful.*[13]

* * * * * *

Sydney Carline

Sydney Carline was both a war photographer/artist and an airman. He was attacked and injured during the Battle of the Somme (during which 800 planes were lost in action). As he returned from a mission, Sydney got separated from the rest of his squadron and came under attack by four German planes. They followed their usual tactics of diving down on their prey, firing at close range before veering off and continuing their dive to their aerodrome and safety.

Sydney's older brother George visited him in hospital. He took care to extract an account of events for *The Draconian*.

> *My brother was apparently unconscious of any enemy machines about, until he heard the firing of the gun behind him. He says that owing to the noise of the engine it is impossible to hear anything except a gun at close range or the explosions of anti-aircraft shells.*
>
> *The first German machine damaged his engine slightly and wounded him in the leg. He says there were eight holes in the petrol tank, and other shots hit the back of the seat he was sitting on. With his damaged engine he had to put his nose down to keep up speed and consequently could not bring his gun into play. His machine was a single-seated Scout, with a Vickers gun timed off the engine to fire through the propeller, and to aim the gun the whole machine had to be directed towards the object, as the gun is*

> *a fixed one. Not being able to turn and fly upwards at the German machines and so use the gun, he had to continue his course and keep turning about trying to escape the Germans or at least make their firing harmless, and at the same time firing a Lewis gun fitted behind him. But this gun, he says, is very difficult to aim with success and fly a machine at the same time.*

The four German planes dived on him in turn, but when Sydney had descended to 5,000 ft (1,524 m) they headed off – leaving Sydney wounded and facing the none-too-easy task of getting his machine safely home.

> *His leg was numbed by the wound, so that it did not pain him, and by using his heel on the rudder instead of his toe, he was able to manage his machine all right and get back to the aerodrome. The petrol pouring from his tank was very useful, he said, as it kept his leg cool and he was able to drive his engine off his spare tank.*

Sydney made a good recovery. In February 1918 he was posted to the 28th Squadron in Italy. By now a fully fledged war artist, he nonetheless flew his Sopwith Camel (a notoriously difficult aircraft to fly) with a machine gun mounted, just in case a tempting target presented itself. It was surely superfluous, as he had his hands full enough making watercolour, pencil or charcoal sketches while flying the plane with his knees.

> [Sydney] *remarked at the time to* [his brother] *Richard that it was no fun at all trying to defrost a watercolour at 15,000 or 20,000 feet by breathing on the surface of the paper while dodging minute yet wickedly sharp particles of ice flying off the paper, which kept threatening to be torn from his drawing board by the sheer force of the slipstream.*[14]

* * * * * *

In April 1917 Jack Slessor reported that he had been in further trouble.

> *I have just been mixed up in a difference of opinion between an aeroplane, a telegraph pole, and a ditch, so just at present I am convinced that flying is an over-rated pastime. My engine played me foul getting out of a field, and the machine, as the papers say, was seen to descend steeply, with the result that the telegraphic communication between two towns was seriously impaired and one telegraph pole and a formerly perfectly good machine badly bent. Now I must depart to make supplication to my commanding officer for 48 hours leave, to rest my shattered nerves and throbbing brain.*
>
> *J.C. Slessor*
>
> *P.S. Just returned from the aforesaid interview with the C.O. Nothing doing. He says it has been tried before.*

Bombing

As the war progressed, the role of the Royal Flying Corps changed. While observation of enemy positions remained important, better armed aircraft allowed the R.F.C. to take the war to the enemy and attack these positions with increasingly effective bombs.

By September 1916 Geoff Buck, now a Lieutenant in the R.F.C, was in France. Here he undertook his first bombing raids. Geoff's diary entries reveal a strange, adrenaline-fuelled world, driven by excitement and fear.

27 September 1916
I took a machine and eight bombs and went off with 16 other machines to raid Bocheland. Flying close together with 16 others is 'anellofajob'. But anyhow we all came back, and it was quite pleasant – no Hun machines and very few Archies. You can't think how queer a big battle looks from upstairs – frightfully interesting, but I simply hate to think of the poor blighters on the ground …

2 October 1916
Flying high in formation we got slightly 'Archied' over the lines (I disliked this because a little bit of iron on one of my eight bombs means that I go simply to swell the Roll of Honour). We dropped our bombs, and they all fell on their objective, and probably strafed some French peasants, mice and woodpeckers. But I hope we killed more Boches. Then the fun began, pop-pop, bang, fizz-whizz, hiss, pop, bang, little black puffs all around us, and each explosion shook our little machines as if they had been kicked. This was most dangerous and unpleasant (so I thought), and after waving to my nearest fellow-sufferer to keep clear, I performed a memorable series of switchback vertical turns at an average speed of 150 m.p.h. This upset Archibald's calculations some, I guess, and anyhow I lost control and was much too frightened trying to get control of the machine again to be frightened about Archie. It really is a sporting kind of life, and I laughed till I could hardly see the instruments.

11 November 1916
About a fortnight ago we met eleven Hun machines over the lines, which was exciting. The difficulty is to avoid running into someone in the excitement. We brought one Hun down, but it looks rather nasty to see a machine brought down from the air (at least I think so). We don't often fight, though, as our machines aren't meant for it.

The Flying Circus

It became important that the enemy was denied the opportunity of observing any build-up and positioning of forces in advance of a battle. In consequence more and more the rival air forces fought for domination of the skies in their increasingly powerful fighter aircraft.

April 1917 was a time of German air superiority, deservedly known as 'Bloody April'. Numerous British pilots were brought down by the 'Red Baron', Manfred von Richthofen, and his 'Flying Circus'. Three of them were Old Dragons.

Peter Warren was up at Magdalen College in 1914 (where his uncle, Sir Herbert Warren, was President). He was then only 17 years old, so was not eligible for military service, although he did join the University O.T.C. He eventually received his commission in July 1916 and trained as an Observer with 57 Squadron.

He transferred to 34 Squadron in November that year to train as a pilot, graduating in early February 1917. At the end of the month Peter was sent to the front to join 43 Squadron as a Lieutenant in the R.F.C.

On 2 April 1917 C Flight 43 Squadron was sent on a mission to photograph a section of the Hindenburg Line near Vimy Ridge (just before an offensive). In the process they had the misfortune to run into Werner Voss, Manfred von Richthofen and his brother Lothar – three of the enemy's most feared pilots.

It was not until after the war that Peter was able to tell his story. He was flying at the apex of a 'V' formation when his gunner Sergeant Dunn, seated behind him, shouted a warning just as a spray of bullets splintered the dashboard in front of him. He dived and glimpsed von Richthofen's red plane passing under him to the rear.

Looking over his shoulder, he could not see Dunn and feared that he had either been thrown out of the plane in the emergency dive or was dead on the floor. Peter, now defenceless to the rear, tried to engage von Richthofen with his forward machine gun, but found 'Richthofen was too wise a pilot, and his machine was too speedy for mine'.[15]

> *He zoomed up again and was on my tail in less than half a minute. Another burst of lead came over my shoulder, and the glass faces of the instruments on the dashboard popped up in my face. I dived again, but he followed my every move. I had lost several thousand feet, but still below me was a layer of clouds. I dove for it, hoping to pull him in it and shake him off …*
>
> *I found that the red Albatross with those two sputtering machine guns had come through with me. Another burst of lead from behind and the bullets spattered on the breech of my own machine gun, cutting the cartridge belt. At the same time, my engine stopped and I knew that the fuel tanks had been hit. There were more clouds below me. I dove for them and tried to pull up in them as soon as I reached them. No luck! My elevators didn't answer the stick. The control wires had been shot away.*[16]

Peter put his plane into a dive, but he lost control and the plane went into a spiral. Von Richthofen continued to fire on him and Peter later found bullets had gone through both of his sleeves and boots. Somehow he managed to regain control before landing heavily, noting that 'the red machine swooped over me, but I don't remember him firing on me when I was on the ground'.[17]

Interestingly, this does not match with Manfred von Richthofen's account.

> *My adversary would not surrender and even as his machine was on the ground,* [he] *kept shooting at me, thereby hitting my machine very severely when I was only five*

yards off the ground. Consequently, I once more attacked him … and killed one of the occupants.[18]

The historian Peter Hart reckons von Richthofen was confused by machine-gun fire from another Sopwith. Either way, this was von Richthofen's 33rd victory. Sergeant Dunn was killed and Peter spent the rest of the war in captivity.

* * * * * *

William Leefe Robinson

William Leefe Robinson, somewhat bored by inactivity after his V.C. triumph, returned to active service having been promoted in October 1916 to the rank of Flight Commander and temporary Captain. He was posted to France in March 1917 – not a good time to be there. The 'Flying Circus' was causing carnage among young British pilots, many of whom had minimal combat experience. They were indeed lucky to survive more than a few weeks.

On 5 April, over Douai, Robbie and his flight of six untried Bristol F2a planes were intercepted by von Richthofen's Albatross fighters. Four of them, including Robbie himself, were shot down. After the war a 'brother officer' provided *The Draconian* with this description of what had happened.

I well remember the morning he set off on his last flight; it was the first day of the April offensive, and his flight was detailed for the first offensive patrol. The Army Corps General was on the aerodrome, and shook hands with him and wished him success.

I was shot down a week later and was fortunate in being able to share a room with him at Karlsruhe, where he told me that he led his flight over Douai, as ordered, and was attacked by Richthofen's squadron of Albatrosses, but owing to the wrong quality of oil having been used in his guns they failed to fire, and being outnumbered he was forced to land quite near Douai with three other machines of his flight. It was one of those horrible mistakes that so often happened with new squadrons.

Robbie, like Peter Warren, spent the rest of the war a prisoner.

* * * * * *

Aubrey de Sélincourt had won a scholarship to University College, Oxford, in 1913; he had just enough time to win a 'Half-Blue' for Athletics before war was declared. He joined up, serving first in the North Staffordshire Regiment and then the Royal Flying Corps. He joined 25 Squadron in France on 11 April 1917.

On 28 May Aubrey went on a mission, flying over a German aerodrome with three other machines to take some photographs of it. He came under fire from the ground, but managed to swing his machine around to make it a more difficult target. By so doing he came through this zone without being hit.

Having taken his photographs, Aubrey was looking for the point at which to turn for home when he came under attack.

Aubrey de Sélincourt

> *Suddenly my Observer began to gesticulate, and to shoot off red lights out of his Very pistol. I could see him shouting, and behind the absurd goggles his prominent grey eyes bulged at me in intense excitement. Over my shoulder he pointed, at an angle, downwards. 'Look, look!' he seemed to yell, 'they're coming – do something!' I turned, but the mass of the engine blocked my view. Leaving for a moment the controls to look after themselves, I half struggled up in my seat, and peered. There they were, a long way off as yet, but gaining on us very fast – with twice our speed and climb. Three German machines coming from behind and under. An F.E. is a heavy machine; we used to rely in a fight upon mutual support and well-kept formation.*

Unfortunately Aubrey had become separated from the three other planes coming through the shelling, and they failed to see his distress signals. He was alone.

> *Meanwhile our pursuers were overtaking us. I couldn't see them; I could only measure their approach by my Observer's signs and by the expression in his eyes … Now the leading German machine was very close, almost within range. It was the critical moment. We couldn't defend ourselves with the guns; for they cannot be trained below and behind. Should I turn, and try our fortune alone? One more moment, and my friend ahead will surely see our signals and come … one more moment.*
>
> *'Turn!' said my Observer's eyes, 'Turn and let me shoot!' A few streaks of light flashed past us – the German's first attempt to hit at long range. We could see the tracer bullets …*
>
> *Now! Just as we heeled over and swung upwards and round, came a long burst of fire from the German. Our engine stopped dead, hit. Down we come, writhing, spinning, doing all we can to make ourselves a hard mark for our pursuer's gun. The bullets flick past our ears. Swiftly the earth sweeps up to meet us. It is time to check the headlong descent. I get the machine level; throw a quick glance for somewhere to land. Roofs, trees, fences – no aerodrome landing this! The rudder control is partially gone – and still that gun spitting at us from behind … Leave it to luck then.*
>
> *Bump! There is a crash as the undercarriage goes to splinters, and I find myself lying face downwards on the ground with a throbbing pain in my eye.*

Aubrey found himself being taken prisoner by German soldiers, who provided field dressings and 'with genuine solicitude set about tying up our bleeding heads'.

Aubrey de Sélincourt had become the 31st victim claimed by flying ace Werner Voss (said by von Richthofen to be his 'most redoubtable competitor'). He spent the next 18 months in Germany as a prisoner of war.

Casualties of 1918

Cyril Emmett (Flight Sub-Lieutenant, Royal Naval Air Service)

The first Dragon airman to be killed was, like so many, not a victim of aerial combat. He was another tragic example of an inexperienced and under-trained pilot having an accident.

Cyril Emmett left Repton and joined the R.N.A.S in May 1917. He trained to be a pilot, although in hindsight evidence suggests this may not have been the right career for him. In July 1917 he met with a serious accident.

> [He was] *accidentally slightly injured in aeroplane and admitted to hospital ... report of total wreck of aeroplane through failure to flatten out when landing.*[19]

Although it appears that Cyril graduated from Cranwell in November, an entry in his record dated 1 January 1918 states that he 'failed in theoretical subjects'. Nonetheless, he was 'recommend[ed] to be considered as graduated', with the result that on 17 January he was off to France. He was killed barely 8 weeks later.

> *He appears to have choked his engine. He tried to regain the Aerodrome, but crashed to the ground from a height of about 200 feet.*[20]

* * * * * *

Ronald Stonehouse (Lieutenant, R.A.F.)

Ronald first joined the Army Service Corps, as he had injured an ankle in his early training and could not march. In August 1917 he joined the R.F.C. and, after his training in aerial gunnery and as an Observer, went out to France. Here he was to work on a night-bombing aeroplane with 101st Squadron.

His pilot revealed the unfortunate circumstances of Ronald's death.

> *On the night of March 31st he and I had made two trips together over the lines. Just as daylight was breaking we had landed and were walking together to report to the Major. He turned back to get something he had forgotten. Half a minute later 6 or 7 bombs fell on the aerodrome and we found him lying under the machine. He was killed instantaneously.*

Ronald had taken off on the evening of 31 March as a member of the Royal Flying Corps, but landed in the early hours of 1 April as a member of the newly formed Royal Air Force (an amalgamation of the R.F.C. and the R.N.A.S.). It is very possible that he was the first member of the R.A.F. to be killed in action.

* * * * * *

Geoffrey Buck (Flight Commander and Captain, R.A.F.)

By 1918 Geoff Buck was flying Handley Page bombers, capable of long flights into Germany.

Geoff Buck in his Handley Page bomber, 1918

Skipper's *War Memorials* tells of two very similar scenarios involving Geoff, but with completely opposite results.

> *His worst journey was on 25th August when the flight started in clear weather, but met an awful storm of hail and thunder. All the machines turned back except his. He went through it somehow, dropped his bombs from only 500 ft up, and came back safely through the storm, though everyone had given him up for lost. Both he and his Observer were awarded the D.F.C.*

Just over a week later, on 3 September 1918, Geoff's luck ran out. He was returning home from another night raid over Germany.

> *He crashed his plane into the high petrol tank building in the black darkness, and that was the end. He once said that very few people knew how hard it was to keep every nerve strained and the brain working its utmost for five hours on end.*

Geoff Buck had had no fear of death. Earlier in 1918 he had written from France saying that 'Life has been so topping that I don't mind how short it is'.

Skipper was not the only one on whom Geoff had made an impression. His Winchester housemaster paid similar tribute.

He stood out as something very different from the ordinary boy. In the first place he always knew his mind; he knew where he was moving to and what he wanted. Whether by reading in books, thinking for himself, or talking with his friends, he had formed an idea of what life should mean for him and how he should train himself for it.

He never accepted conventional standards or ideas because they were conventional; yet, unlike many who have tastes and interests of their own, he never shirked the ordinary routine of work or neglected his Latin and Greek for excursions into other fields ...

None who knew him could be blind to the strong stamp of his individuality.

No doubt his early years at the O.P.S. had played their part.

Flying Aces

In the last year of the war, two Old Dragons gained the distinction of being recognised as 'flying aces'.

Jim MacLean

Jim MacLean, who had attained the rank of Captain in the R.A.F., had added a Bar to his Military Cross 'for conspicuous gallantry and devotion to duty', which the citation described:

While leading a patrol he attacked and drove down an enemy two-seater machine and destroyed an enemy scout. He showed the greatest determination in leading patrols and splendid coolness and courage, most of his work being done under very difficult weather conditions.[21]

Whilst in 41st Squadron Jim was accredited with the five aerial victories required to enter this elite group.

However, the top Dragon 'ace' was Donald Hardman. He was the brother of Wallace Hardman, killed in 1917 (see pp. 191–92) and cousin to both Percy Campbell, killed in 1914 (see p. 98) and David Brown, killed in 1916 (see pp. 177–78).

Donald had joined 19th Squadron at Baillieu, flying a Sopwith Dolphin – just in time for the German Spring Offensive of 1918. In the final eight months of the war he shot down nine enemy aircraft. Two of his total were achieved on the flight for which he was awarded the D.F.C. The citation highly praised his technical skill and temperament.

A bold and courageous officer who has shown most praiseworthy devotion to duty, both in the March retreat and during the more recent operations. On 30th October, while escorting a bombing raid, he, with his flight, encountered some 40 enemy machines. In the combat that ensued he shot down two, and it was mainly due to his cool judgement and skill in leading that the flight inflicted heavy casualties on the enemy, destroying five machines and driving down another out

> *of control. In all, this officer has seven hostile aircraft to his credit – destroyed or driven down out of control.*[22]

At the time of the Armistice, Donald was taken ill with 'flying sickness'. This condition was thought to be the result of differences in air pressure and temperature, causing headaches, pounding ears and breathing difficulties. It was often a precursor to a mental breakdown. He was admitted into hospital in Boulogne before being transferred to a London hospital to complete his recovery.

* * * * * *

In total, 28 Old Dragons served with the R.F.C., R.N.A.S. and R.A.F. Six of them (over 20 per cent) were killed, all in the year 1918. Of the survivors, Nevil Norway went on to become an aeronautical engineer; he worked on the development of airships, including the R100 airship under Sir Barnes Wallis. However, Nevil achieved greater fame as the author of 24 novels, using his middle name, Shute, to protect his engineering career from any adverse publicity. Jack Slessor and Donald Hardman continued to serve in the R.A.F. after the war, ending their military careers as Marshal of the R.A.F. and Air Chief Marshal respectively.

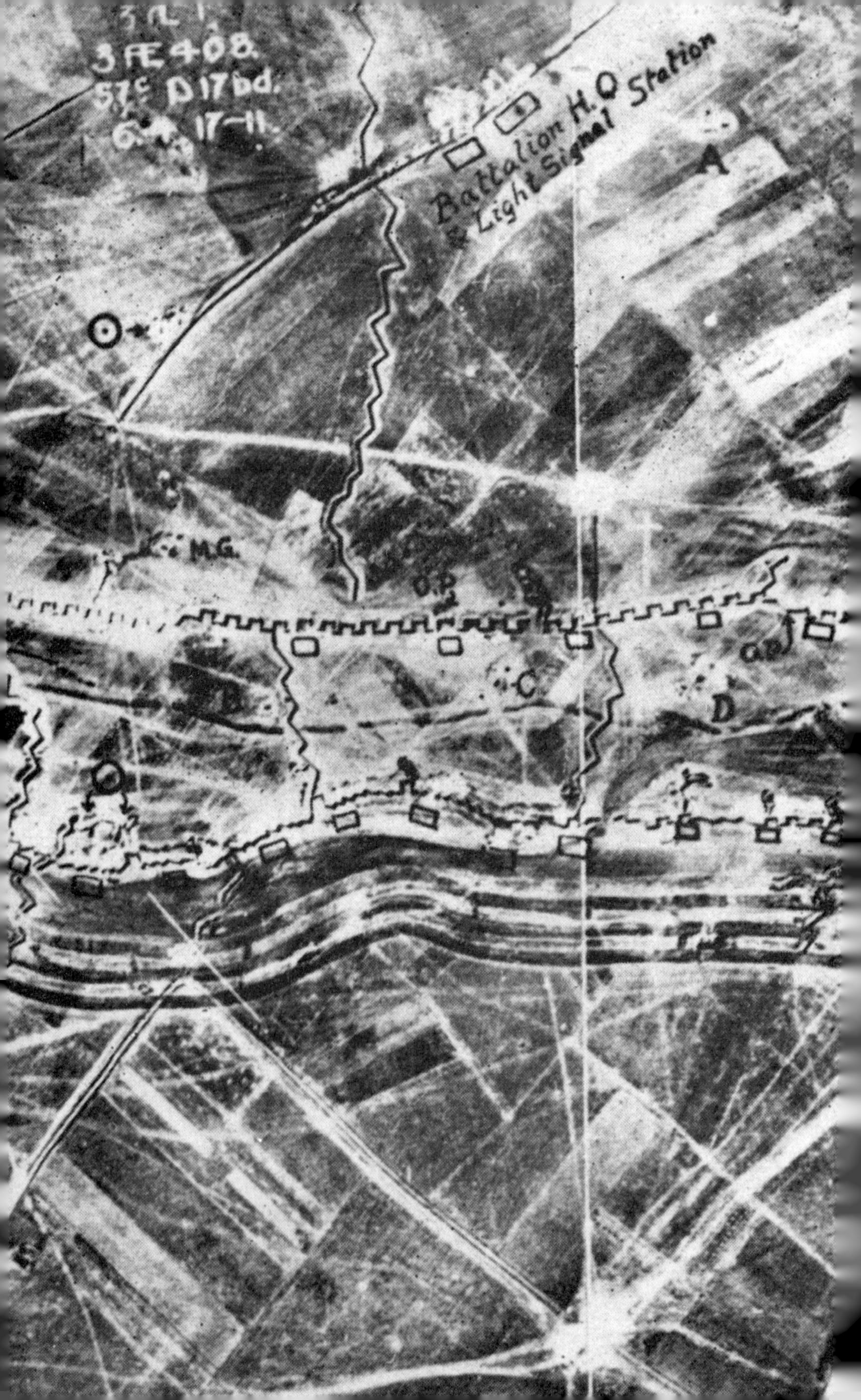
3 FE 408.
Battalion H.Q
& Light Signal Station
A
M.G.
O.P.
C
D
O.P.

Chapter 14

1917/18 – The Losses Mount

The Hindenburg Line

The Battle of the Somme had been costly to both sides. The Allies suffered over 600,000 casualties and the Germans around 500,000. With nearly half the number of troops available to the Germans being on the Eastern Front fighting the Russians, it became evident to German military commanders that shortening the line on the Western Front would save both on men and munitions.

This strategy was decided upon by Field Marshal Hindenburg, whose name the British gave to the line to which the German forces retreated. To the Germans it was known as the 'Siegfriedstellung', and work on it commenced in September 1916. However, it was not until 14 March 1917 that the withdrawal was fully apparent to the British troops, among them Humphrey Arden, serving as 2nd Lieutenant in the Royal Garrison Artillery.

Humphrey Arden

So it has happened at last! What a hopeless wish it seemed a year ago that in twelve months the Hun would be deliberately retreating, and that after shooting on a point one day at a range of 8,000 or 9,000 yards, we could go on the morrow and examine the very spot, and see the craters made by our own shells.

Even the battle-hardened Humphrey was shocked at the scene he saw.

Dead men, dead horses, shattered gun emplacements, broken limbers and wagons, rifles, bombs, equipment, and all the ghastly filth of carnage. How the Hun has stood the hammering so long is a marvel. He says he goes willingly and I don't doubt it. There is a valley leading down to a famous ravine which is enough to make one sick if one hadn't become hardened gradually to such things. In one spot evidently our guns caught a Boche battery taking in ammunition. The teams and their drivers had been blown to pieces, the wagons are pitiable wrecks, and the whole place stinks of death.

Nonetheless Humphrey took professional pride in the accuracy of his work. He was most gratified to find the heads to his shrapnel shells right in the middle of the gun emplacement at which he had been aiming a few days before.

Left: Aerial view of part of the Hindenburg Line, submitted for the August 1917 edition of *The Draconian*

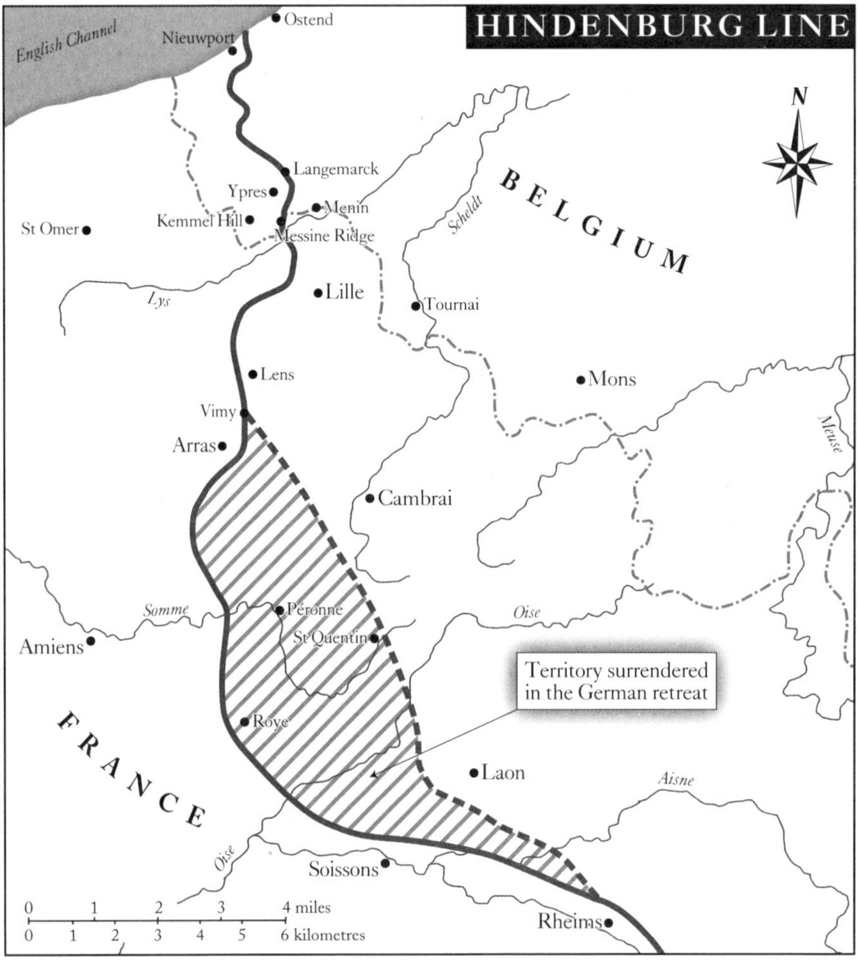

In the days before the German retreat, a thick fog had masked their movements and they had been able to get their guns away, destroy dug-outs and retreat behind their new line of defence. Despite following up as quickly as they could, the British infantry were held up by the barbed wire, which needed artillery shells to destroy it. However, the terrain was almost impossible for the guns to traverse. As Humphrey explained, there were no serviceable roads.

> *Oh yes, they are marked on the map all right, but it would puzzle you to pick out any but the two principal ones from the desert of shell holes; and even the principal roads are swimming in mud, pitted with craters, and at vital points ruined and blown up by the Hun.*

New infrastructure had to be created without delay. The engineers worked remarkably quickly, building light railways up to within 400 yards (366 m) of the infantry within two days. Water mains were also carried right up to the front and armies of men set about creating the necessary roads to allow the guns to advance, much to Humphrey's approval.

> *Soon our guns were ready to deal with the next line of barbed wire, and having shattered it to bits and cleaned up the enemy garrison, the same thing occurred again. This time the Hun did not wait for the attack but bolted as soon as our shower of shells showed him it was imminent. And so I suppose it will go on till the vaunted concrete line or 'Hindenburg Stellung' is reached.*

That indeed proved to be the case.

The Third Battle of Ypres

In the summer of 1917, however, the British military hierarchy turned their thoughts back to the Ypres salient. The Third Battle of Ypres (commonly referred to as Passchendaele) was felt necessary by Field Marshal Sir Douglas Haig for two major reasons. The first was, as ever, to take some of the pressure off the French. With mutiny in their ranks, their troops needed respite if they were to become an effective fighting force again. The second was the belief that if a breakthrough could be achieved at Ypres it should be possible to clear the Belgian coast, where German U-boats were based. In February 1917 Germany had resumed a campaign of unrestricted submarine warfare, sinking all shipping going to or from Britain, regardless of its nationality. The aim was to starve England into seeking peace. The U-boats achieved considerable success, sinking over 3 million tons of shipping between February and June 1917.

Fresh out of Winchester College and now a 2nd Lieutenant in the Royal Field Artillery was Pat Campbell; he was the younger brother of Percy, killed in 1914 (see p. 98). Pat arrived at the front just in time to hear the detonation of some 19 mines under the Messines Ridge in the early hours of 7 June 1917. (It was said that the explosion was so loud that it could be heard by Lloyd George in Downing Street.) However, Pat was otherwise engaged.

Pat Campbell

> *I went to the latrine and I was there, sitting on the pole at Zero Hour … Books have said it was the greatest noise of the whole war … but I was so engrossed in my own concerns that I was hardly aware of the noise.*[1]

Aged only 19, he was in charge of two guns, 50 horses and 50 men. Within a month of his arrival, he found himself in the midst of the biggest battle of the war, and one in which artillery played the leading role.

The action at Messines was just the curtain-raiser for what was to follow at Ypres. The main action followed a similar plan to that seen on the Somme: a preliminary bombardment followed by infantry attacks, but this was on an even grander scale. Over 3,000 guns fired over 4 million shells before the infantry battle even started.

This time Pat Campbell was ready for Zero Hour – 3.50 a.m. on 31 July 1917 – when the infantry advanced, supported by the artillery.

* * * * * *

Alan Jenks (Major, Royal Engineers)

The first day of the battle claimed the lives of two more Old Dragons. One was Alan Jenks who, as an Engineer, was well aware of the difficulties caused by the terrain. The previous winter he had written to the O.P.S. to deliver a mock remonstrance about the geography teaching he had received.

> *I learnt at Lynam's or somewhere that water flowed downhill. France is the exception. No well-behaved water does it here. It just stays… Generally one digs a trench or ditch in peace-time in order to drain a field. Here one has to try to drain a trench into a field. That is what sappers are endeavouring to do here. Action and reaction being equal and opposite, result nil. The only feasible method is to use language so warm that the water boils and so evaporates.*

In the same letter to *The Draconian*, he had recalled skirmishes at school with Jack Haldane, when he had wisely adopted the motto of 'he who fights and runs away will live'. Alan claimed that he had pursued this motto ever since, adding, 'if I am caught, it will be through not running away fast enough'.

But there was no running away from a sniper who had Alan in his sights as he made a reconnaissance near Kemmel Hill at the southern end of the Ypres salient.

* * * * * *

The terrain and later the weather at Ypres conspired against the attack. The banks of the streams that ran across the battlefield were breeched, and to make matters worse it was a very wet August. The result was that both the infantry and artillery would find significant advances almost impossible.

Things soon ground to a halt. The advance that Pat Campbell was due to make with his guns never happened. He recalled the exasperation expressed by the major in charge of his battery:

'It's utter lunacy. We shell the place for a month till there isn't a yard of ground left that isn't a shell hole, and then they expect the infantry to be able to advance and they tell us to move our guns up there.'[2]

Chaos reigned. It was clear that no one seemed to know where their front line was, or the enemy's, or whether they were still making an attack. The next morning their officer returned from Observation Post duty to inform them:

'Of course it was a bloody failure, but I'd been expecting that, so I wasn't particularly depressed.'[3]

The nature of the battlefield was very different to that of the Somme, due to the higher water table. As a result, soldiers could not dig down more than a couple of feet (0.6 m) before they came to water. As Pat explained, this led to strengthening any house or farm building available with rubble-filled sandbags or blocks of concrete, particularly to house machine guns. He noted that the Germans were somewhat better at this than the Allies.

These were the pill-boxes, as they came to be called later. Almost indestructible by shell-fire, they were extremely difficult to capture, and time after time during the fighting … our attacking infantry overran a line of pill-boxes and advanced to the top of the ridge behind them, only to be shot at from behind and forced to retire by unwounded enemy soldiers, unaffected by our barrage fire, who had come out of the forts.[4]

For the second time in the conflict (the previous one being in 1914), Ypres saw three Old Dragon deaths in one day.

Alan Cam (2nd Lieutenant, Royal Engineers)

George Falkiner (2nd Lieutenant, Royal Dublin Fusiliers)

Hamilton Jefferson (Lieutenant, Oxfordshire and Buckinghamshire Light Infantry)

The fatal date in question was 16 August 1917. On this day Alan Cam, like Alan Jenks serving in the Royal Engineers, was killed by machine-gun fire on the Ypres–Menin road. George Falkiner died in a heavy artillery and machine-gun barrage at Frezenberg, along with nearly the whole of his company of Dublin Fusiliers. Hamilton Jefferson was killed at Langemarck. A fellow, and much older, officer expressed his high regard for him.

> *Home service quite failed to bring out his real qualities. He was just a nice, good, rather irresponsible boy. But the real thing discovered him … A capital instructor, an absolutely brave leader, and the most dear companion one could find. If ever a boy lived and died well, he did; no more need be said.*

These Old Dragons were aged just 22, 19 and 19. Their names are three of the 35,000 on the Tyne Cot Memorial commemorating those who fought at Ypres and have no known grave.

The Ox. & Bucks.

Captains G.K. Rose, W.H. Moberly and C.S.W. Marcon

Not surprisingly there were a number of O.D.s serving in the Oxfordshire & Buckinghamshire Light Infantry, the local regiment to the O.P.S. Three of them found the time to have this team picture taken for the December 1917 edition of *The Draconian*.

The 2nd/4th Ox. & Bucks. had come up to the Ypres Front on 20/21 August, nearly a month after the start of the battle, to take part in an attack near St Julien. Into this attack went another three of the Skipper's Dragons: Will Scott (D Company), Gifford Turrell (A Company) and Walter Moberly (B Company).

As was customary by this stage of the war, a battalion did not commit all its officers and men to an attack. Captain Geoffrey Rose was ordered to remain behind, where he was able to observe and record the events of the day.

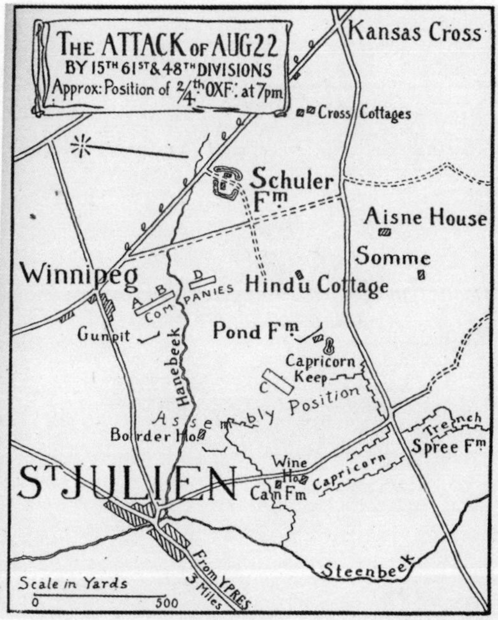

Geoffrey Rose's diagram of the events of 22 August

The attack, following a creeping barrage, designed to lift as the infantry advanced, was made from the Capricorn trench with the Winnipeg/Kansas Cross road being the objective. Within half an hour A, B and D Companies were digging in only 150 yards (137 m) short of this target. Less successful was C Company, who were held up by the concrete stronghold that was Pond Farm. It was not until the following night that they were able to capture it.

The position was not a good one for A, B and D companies. Although they had suffered few casualties in the attack, they were now becoming victims of sniping and machine-gun fire from Schuler Farm (which was being reinforced) and, of even greater concern, from an old gun-pit that lay behind their left flank.

An attempt to take the gun-pit succeeded, but only temporarily. This left Walter Moberly, whose commanding officer had been killed, in charge of these three companies in an extremely exposed position for some 50 hours before they were relieved.

Walter's conduct earned him the D.S.O. The citation described his extraordinary resourcefulness whilst under fire:

> *Communication with battalion headquarters failed, as runners were unable to get through the machine-gun and snipers' fire from the front and flanks. In these circumstances this officer determined to hold on to the advanced line at all costs. He took steps to defend his flanks, and organized an effective resistance to counter attacks. By his prompt and decisive action and complete disregard of danger he inspired his men with confidence.*[5]

Although Walter pulled through unscathed, Will Scott and Gifford Turrell were not so fortunate.

William Scott
(Lieutenant, Oxfordshire and Buckinghamshire Light Infantry)

Soldiering in general, and the Ox. & Bucks. in particular, were in Will's blood. His grandfather and his great-grandfather had both served in that regiment, the former at Waterloo.

As Will got up to lead D Company over the top at 5.30 a.m., he had Sergeant Major Edward Brooks V.C. at his side. Will was wounded in the wrist and leg in this advance, but not seriously. Consulting with Brooks, he decided a message needed to be sent back to headquarters. Will got out his map to work out the map reference, which he swiftly did. As Brooks extracted a pencil ready to write it down, a machine gun rang out. Brooks later recalled what happened:

> *We looked rather startled at each other for a few seconds and then I quickly discovered that my Commander had been hit. I placed him under cover as quickly as possible, but sorry to say he passed away in about half a minute from the time he was struck by the bullet ...*
>
> *This was the end of my brave Commander; I can tell you I have never seen or heard of a braver man.*

As Brooks himself had won the V.C., this was no mean praise.

Will was described as 'shy and retiring' at the O.P.S. and Rugby. Despite having an academic background (his father was a Fellow of Merton College), he did not excel at work, or at games. Walter Moberly wrote a moving tribute to Will for *The Draconian.*

> *Having no specially showy gifts, he might at ordinary times have made no great mark except upon a few intimates. But in the call made by war he instantly found himself and the true nature of his talent became clear ...*
>
> *His enthusiasm for military life and military work in all its details was whole-hearted and infectious ... At first he appeared – and did not mind appearing – both to his men and to his colleagues, a little fussy, rigorously and even pedantically insistent upon exactness of detail. But by degrees his men came to realise that he was making them into*

the best platoon in the battalion and so to understand and to respect him. And before long he was generally acknowledged to be one of the best officers we had.

His commanding officer and fellow Old Dragon, Geoffrey Rose, agreed, rating Will as the best officer he ever had.

Gifford Turrell
(2nd Lieutenant, Oxfordshire and Buckinghamshire Light Infantry)

Another 19-year-old, Gifford Turrell, had left the O.P.S. only three years before the outbreak of war. On leaving Sherborne School, he had joined the Ox. & Bucks. in 1916 and had gone into this attack with A Company. During the advance he received gunshot wounds to the head.

Gifford was brought back to St Thomas' Hospital in London, where an operation was performed to remove fragments from the wound, leading to hope that he might make a recovery. During his time in hospital he was barely conscious, however, and on 1 November he was assessed by a Medical Board. The Board noted that the brain had swollen to such an extent that it protruded through his skull and had become infected.

He appears to be totally blind, and consciousness is very feeble. Pupils dilated & inactive, no motor paralysis. Sensation cannot be determined. In the last two days, there has been fever and meningitis has set in with a fit. Recovery is improbable & he is failing rapidly.[6]

Gifford died the following day, 72 days after he had been wounded. His body was brought back to Oxford so that his funeral could be at Queen's, his old college. He was laid to rest in Holywell Cemetery on 5 November 1917.

The attack of 22 August was, from the perspective of a four-month-long battle at Ypres, a comparatively insignificant event. In such circumstances, the citation for Walter Moberly's D.S.O. has an ironic aspect.

If it had not been for this plucky decision and courageous determination on his part the whole of the objectives gained would have had to be abandoned.[7]

According to Geoffrey Rose, the ground won by the Ox. & Bucks. was surrendered almost at once by the troops who replaced them.

The battalion left the Ypres battlefield in mid-September 1917. Their losses had been heavy, with the casualty list numbering 14 officers and 260 men.

Old Wykehamists

Nine of the Roll of Old Dragons killed in war had gone on to Winchester College (five of them with scholarships). It was the school that had spawned *The Draconian* (see pp. 44–45) and the ties between the two schools were close. In the autumn of 1917 they were united in grief over the loss of two Old Dragon Wykehamists, whose families were also at the heart of the academic community in Oxford.

Revere Osler was a descendent of Paul Revere, who took part in the Boston Tea Party and became famous for riding through the night to warn American rebels of the approach of the British in 1775. Revere's father, Sir William Osler, was born and bred in Canada. In 1905 he was offered and accepted the Regius Chair of Medicine at Oxford. He and his wife Grace were known for their hospitality. Their home in Norham Gardens became known as 'The Open Arms'. It welcomed, among many others, Mark Twain, Walt Whitman, Rudyard Kipling, John McCrae – another eminent Canadian doctor and author of the poem 'In Flanders Fields' – and, in May 1915, an old family friend, the American neurosurgeon Harvey Cushing.

Revere Osler was wounded on 27 August 1917 on Pilkem Ridge. A shell landed among a group of officers supervising the movement of some guns, wounding him in the chest, stomach and thigh. Revere was stretchered to the nearest Advance Dressing Station, and then transferred to the Casualty Clearing Station at Dozinghem. Word was immediately sent to Harvey Cushing, now working with the U.S. Army Medical Corps at nearby Mendingham. He arrived to find Revere in extreme shock, drifting in and out of consciousness.

Revere Osler (2nd Lieutenant, Royal Field Artillery)

Other friends of Revere's father came to his aid, including George Washington Crile, the first surgeon to have succeeded with a direct blood transfusion. Revere had lost a lot of blood and Crile immediately carried out a transfusion, which enabled surgery to start.

Crile recounted the events that followed.

> *The long marquee tent was quiet and dim; the end was fast approaching. The boy's features were serene and a faint smile illuminated his face when he was told that his father's American friends were there ... Durrach and Brewer operated, Harvey held his pulse and I continued the transfusion ...*
>
> *Large rents were found in the colon, much blood in the chest and a large wound in the thigh... Obviously all was lost.*[8]

Despite such expert attention, there was nothing they could do for him.

* * * * * *

Hugh Sidgwick (Captain, Royal Garrison Artillery)

There was little time to mourn Revere Osler's death. Just over two weeks later, the Battle of Passchendaele claimed another Dragon Wykehamist life. It belonged to one of the O.P.S.'s most regular correspondents and another of Skipper's 'particular favourites'. Hugh Sidgwick was not one to share the full horrors of war. As his sister Rose wrote, 'he conceived it a primary social duty to amuse his company'.[9] In one letter, published in the Summer Term 1917 edition of *The Draconian*, he suggested a novel reader's test as a profitable way to while away the time.

> *Write down the full names of 12 characters in each of 24 novels. Most people can do 8 or 9 names in about 20 novels without difficulty: it is the last few names and books that cause the trouble, unless, like myself, you have a mis-spent youth behind you.*

By nature Hugh was one to worry. Was he doing a useful job? Could the job be done better? But, as the saying went, 'What's the use of worrying?' and he recognised the sense of this.

> *I have long since ceased worrying. As my late O.C. remarked in a moment of pardonable irritation, the Heavy Artillery only exist in order to be badgered about (that was not exactly the word he used) and the main thing is to take life calmly.*
>
> *Since war broke out I have belonged to six batteries, a Group and a Headquarters, have been a Civil Servant, a shirker, an indispensable, a Derby recruit, a special constable, an unrecognised volunteer, a temporarily recalled indispensable, a returned dispensed with, and several other things.*

He treated his promotion to Captain with his usual humour, merely commenting, 'I have spent money heavily on new spots to cover myself with', and added some interesting suggestions on how people back home might spend the summer holidays:

> *30 August 1917*
> *For a purely restful and irresponsible holiday I can recommend active service, provided you choose your front carefully. Charming scenery, cheerful company, unlimited food and drink, corps intelligence supplied daily and shelling on alternate Tuesdays.*

Regarding his own personal safety, Hugh had weighed up and rationalised his need to worry (or not) in one of the letters to his family.

> *If you are sent to an area that is shelled, there is a choice of two things. The shells either burst at a safe distance from you or they do not. If the former, you need not worry.*
>
> *If the shells burst near you, there is a choice of two things. You are either killed or wounded. If the former, you need not worry.*
>
> *If you are wounded, there is a choice of two things. You are either seriously wounded and invalided home, or you are lightly wounded. If the former, you need not worry.*
>
> *If you are lightly wounded you are sent to the depot. There is then a choice of two things. You are either kept at the depot, or sent to the front line. If the former, you need not worry.*
>
> *I think this is a fair summary of the usual effects of the chance of death in modern warfare. It may happen at any moment, when you are sleeping or shaving or eating or heading a charge or rescuing wounded, or reporting on the telephone to headquarters. So you need not worry.*[10]

Hugh Sidgwick

Somehow Hugh's eventual fate did not quite fall into any of these categories. He was leaving the front in a car when he was seriously wounded by a shell on 16 September. He died the following day, hopefully having had no time for worry. The war had taken its toll on him, as this final picture of him clearly indicates. In a letter of 15 September the previous year, Hugh had revealed to his sister Ethel the props on which he leant

– copious amounts of whisky and tobacco – and commented, 'If I get back, I shall have to look out in this matter and make quite an effort to revert to normal'.[11]

The tributes received by his family were many and some were published in the December edition of *The Draconian*. His former boss Amherst Selby-Bigge, Permanent Secretary to the Board of Education, for which Hugh Sidgwick worked, reflected on his loss.

> *He was not only a perfect Private Secretary, but a very dear friend who could be trusted with anything. His loyalty, sincerity and candour were perfect and I never found in him the slightest touch of vanity or self-seeking ...*
>
> *His mind was singularly cool and well balanced and his exposition of intricate problems admirably clear and logical. His knowledge of Mathematics and power of handling figures was invaluable ... He had the gift of writing straight ahead in good proportion and with clear expression and articulation of argument almost as quickly as another man could dictate ...*
>
> *When he was in doubt about coherence and lucidity of an important paper for publication he used to test it by turning it into Greek, and I have in my possession an admirable Greek version of a letter addressed by the President of the Board (H.A.L. Fisher) to teachers concerning their duties in regard to military service.*

The Skipper also wrote to Hugh's mother.

> *My dear Mrs Sidgwick,*
>
> *No words can express my sorrow and feeling of personal loss – it is too, too cruel a fate – such a glorious intellect and so noble a character, with so splendid a future before him. There must be some future reunion with these noble souls – or we are all in the hands of a fiendish force which drives us and jibes at our hopes.*
>
> *I have just told the boys of the severest loss we have yet suffered. With the exception of Frank (& that possibly because I have seen more of him) Hugh was of all my old boys the best beloved and most proudly looked upon by me – and this does not express my very deep feeling of sympathy with you & Frank & his sisters. His father is I hope spared the full knowledge of the loss he has suffered, but I do mourn with you all and sympathise most deeply.*
>
> *Yours ever*
>
> *His old Skipper*[12]

* * * * * *

The Third Battle of Ypres eventually petered out at the end of December. For an advance of about 5 miles (8 km), the British had suffered nearly 250,000 casualties. In a battlefield that had absorbed some 100 million shells, it is no surprise to learn that 75,000 of these soldiers have no known grave.

The Battle of Cambrai

Whilst the Battle of Ypres was raging in Flanders, an attack on the Hindenburg Line at Cambrai was prepared in great secrecy. It was reckoned that the German forces were weaker there and could be overcome in a surprise attack. Although it became famous for the involvement of over 400 tanks, infantry, artillery and indeed cavalry played important parts.

Geoffrey Rose described a raid undertaken by his 2/4th Ox. & Bucks. near Arras. Its aim was to draw the attention of the Germans away from Cambrai the day before the attack was launched there. Walter Moberly and his company were chosen to carry out this diversionary attack.

The attack was preceded by a gas attack using a mixture of non-lethal and lethal gas, intermingled with high-explosive shells. If you began to sneeze from the effect of non-lethal gas, you could not wear a gas helmet to resist the lethal type. The high-explosive shells had the effect of disguising the different types.

Lethal gas was fired at the enemy for several nights in advance of the raid, but non-lethal gas was what was used during the raid. As the two gases smelled alike, it was hoped the Germans would be inconvenienced by still wearing their gas masks. Geoffrey described Walter's progress.

Geoffrey Rose

B Company, though they missed the gap through the enemy's wire, entered the trenches without opposition and captured a machine gun which was pointing directly at their approach but never fired ...

As often, there was difficulty in finding the way back to our lines; in fact, Moberly ... after some wandering in No-Man's-Land, entered the trenches of a Scotch division upon our right. His appearance and comparative inability to speak their language made him a suspicious visitor to our kilted neighbours. Moberly rejoined his countrymen under escort.[13]

At Cambrai there was no preliminary bombardment, not even ranging shots. The approaches to the German lines were therefore devoid of shell holes that would hinder the advance of either tanks or infantry.

On 20 November 1917 the artillery opened up, and under the cover of a creeping barrage the tanks and infantry attacked. The tanks were very effective against the barbed wire and an advance of over 3 miles (4.8 km) was made with under 5,000 casualties being sustained. This success was short lived, however. Of the 476 tanks involved, 179 had been put out of action, and the narrowness of the front had created another salient. In addition, the Hindenburg Line's provision of in-depth defence allowed for such events; it enabled reinforcements to gather and launch a very effective counterattack to recapture lost ground.

The counterattack came on 30 November. Reggie Carr-White, serving as Captain in the Indian Army, was in reserve with Hodson's Horse; he found his breakfast being rudely interrupted. The optimists among his group (including Reggie) thought this signified that the German line had been broken; the pessimists feared the reverse.

'Tank Dump', a sketch made by Geoffrey Rose before the Battle of Cambrai, autumn 1917

The closer they got to the action, the clearer it became that the pessimists were right, as Reggie explained in a specially written article for *The Draconian.*

> *We trotted about another six miles and then halted again, and watched a fine but very sad spectacle. We were in a valley, and about 500 yards in front of us was a low ridge. Along the top of this a British Cavalry regiment was galloping, with German crumps bursting in amongst them. Many of the troops got direct hits on them, and one could see a troop galloping along and suddenly it would practically disappear as a shell burst in it, then a second or two later one would see a few of them straggling forward and a small mound left behind. It made me feel sick. But not a man checked, and all galloped steadily on ...*

Reggie's squadron was at the rear of the regiment. He noticed another squadron 100 yards (c.90 m) ahead of him, trotting through a gap in the wire before disappearing over a ridge.

> *As I came to the gap and topped the ridge, an extraordinary sight met my eyes: galloping horses everywhere, many of them riderless, and there were many dead horses and men on the ground. Into this medley the Germans were putting crump after crump. B squadron was retiring at a slow gallop and in perfect formation.*

Reggie was told to retire with his squadron and find another way round, to avoid the artillery fire. It was a very confused situation, under shellfire, with troops from numerous regiments and 'tanks barging about'.

They came back to a British-held trench. Reggie was possibly understating the case when he remarked that 'It must have surprised them to have two squadrons of cavalry jumping over their heads'. An alternative route was found and taken. Eventually the squadron found their way to the top of a low ridge where the rest of the regiment were digging in, alongside the Guards who successfully attacked and took Gouzancourt.

Digging in meant it was time to send the horses back and for the cavalry to become infantry, ready for another German attack. Just then, some British tanks appeared. Not surprisingly for a cavalryman, Reggie viewed them with suspicion; he described them as 'nosing about like puzzled rhinoceroses' for whom he felt rather sorry. Then, he noted, they 'seemed to become inspired and waddled off one after the other towards the Germans'.

But there was no doubt in Reggie's mind that those who operated tanks were 'the bravest fellows on earth'. He witnessed shell after shell bursting around them, with several receiving direct hits.

> *Before long four of them were burning like great bonfires. Later in the day I met one of the officers, who had been in one. He told me all the crew in his had been killed and he was very cut about himself.*

With the German attack aimed at the neck of the salient, the British troops in the salient were in danger were of being cut off. On 3 December 1917 Haig ordered a withdrawal.

Net gain of this offensive? Very little.

Missing in Action

At the end of 1917 four Old Dragons serving on the Western Front were in a column headed 'missing'. All of them had been killed on the days they disappeared, but their families had to endure months of uncertainty before their deaths were officially confirmed.

One of them was 20-year-old John Dowson, a Captain with the Berkshire Regiment. He had been notified as 'missing' following the attacks on 3 May 1917 in the Arras district. Nearly a year later, on 10 March 1918, his family finally received this notification.

> *No further information has been received, and in the view of the lapse of time since he was reported missing, his death has now been accepted for official purposes as having occurred on or since the 3rd May 1917.*

Skipper may have noticed this entry in the 'In Memoriam' column of *The Times* of 3 May 1918: 'in proud memory of our dear son … missing near Oppy Wood'.[14] Although the wording still held out the faintest of hopes, the entry indicated that John's family now accepted that he was dead.

John Dowson (Captain, Royal Berkshire Regiment)

The August 1918 edition of *The Draconian*, while still not including John on their formal Roll of Honour in deference to the family's hopes, printed this touching tribute from Mr H.C. Bradby, his old housemaster at Rugby School.

> *His intellectual abilities were curiously uneven. He was backward at most of the work which is done at schools and he became the 'doyen' of the Lower Middles. It was always a toss-up in his Latin exercises whether Caesar would mount his horse or the horse mount Caesar, but when Shakespeare's Caesar went out to his death on the Ides of March, no one could be more keenly alive than John to the situation; for he was a born actor, and was never so much himself as when imitating somebody else.*
>
> *He was in short no reasoner, but an artist with a real love of beauty: and he showed it in his writing, for he could write with freshness and humour, as the pages of* The Draconian *can testify; in his music too, for he was a most promising cellist, and sang as a boy with admirable taste; more recently he had shown it as well in some models for statuettes, which are remarkable for their suggestiveness and originality.*
>
> *How far he could have gone as a musician or sculptor no one can say: undoubtedly there was in him a touch of genius struggling all the time for expression, and with more and more success.*

The Skipper later wrote warmly of John in his *War Memorials*.

> *John was one of our most faithful and loving and beloved of Old Boys. It cheered us up to see his fine face and gloriously radiant smile, and indeed few boys have been so much loved by his comrades and masters and all who had dealings with him.*

* * * * * *

Autumn Term 1917

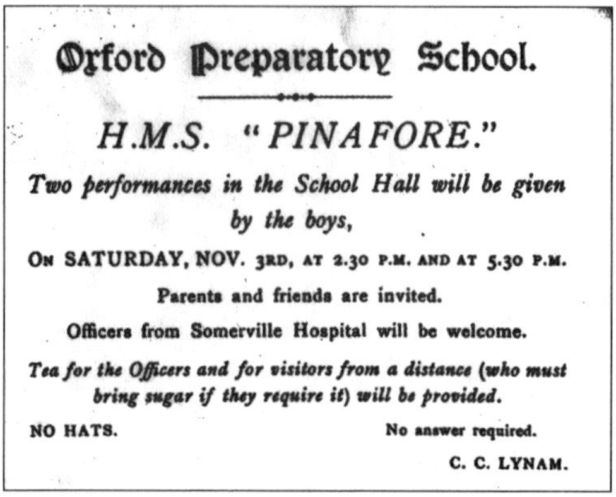

Oxford Preparatory School.

H.M.S. "PINAFORE."

Two performances in the School Hall will be given by the boys,

On SATURDAY, NOV. 3RD, AT 2.30 P.M. AND AT 5.30 P.M.

Parents and friends are invited.

Officers from Somerville Hospital will be welcome.

Tea for the Officers and for visitors from a distance (who must bring sugar if they require it) will be provided.

NO HATS. **No answer required.**

C. C. LYNAM.

Invitation to the O.P.S. performance of *H.M.S. Pinafore*, 3 November 1917

At the O.P.S. Autumn Term 1917 was drawing to a close with another Gilbert and Sullivan production, this time *H.M.S. Pinafore*. One performance was seen by about 100 wounded soldiers. At the request of Sister Wilkinson, it was performed a fortnight later at the Somerville Hospital before a large audience of wounded officers resident there. The production was a great success. Certainly one of the critics attending an earlier performance described the chorus in very positive terms, noting the infectious enthusiasm engendered by their dancing and acting. Both John Betjeman and Per Mallalieu featured in the chorus of 'sisters, cousins and aunts', while Hugh Gaitskell joined in the chorus of sailors.

The cast of *H.M.S. Pinafore*, November 1917

* * * * * *

In the Christmas 1917 edition of *The Draconian*, the Skipper shared with his readership his continuing concerns regarding the school's financial situation. He had been relying as much as he could on donations, rather than putting his fees up, but this was no longer enough.

May I thank those parents who, in response to the bursarial appeal accompanying the last School accounts, have added various sums to those accounts? I am afraid I must add that those additions, which amount in all to about £100 for the term, were far from enough to meet the vastly increased expenditure. It is inevitable that all the salaries of the masters, mistresses and other workers have had to be raised considerably, in addition to the great increase in housekeeping expenses. I only ask those whose means enable them to do so, to increase their payments for their sons. Many schools have raised their fees all round, but I know that that would hit some of the parents of my boys very hard, and I will not do it.

However many sleepless nights he may have had over the school's finances, there were much deeper sources of grief. Most importantly for the Skipper, 1917 had seen the deaths of 21 of his Old Dragons, making it the worst year of the war for the school. Of these, nine had been victims of the fighting at Ypres.

For the O.P.S. there then followed a welcome break from this stream of bad news. Apart from the death of Martin Collier at sea (see pp. 166–67), there were no O.D. casualties in either January or February 1918. This brief window was not enjoyed by Skipper's own family, however. In the space of five months he was to mourn the death of two of his nephews.

Greville Thomas

By this stage of the war, worrying about family members and friends engaged in the conflict had become a way of life. As well as his daughter Kit (Marshall) and his son Garner, a Lieutenant in the Royal Naval Volunteer Reserve, the Skipper had a number of other close relatives in uniform. His younger sister Helen, who had married Rev. Thomas, had three sons – Eric, Greville and Lynam Thomas. Two of them had been drawn into the conflict. Eric (who, unlike his brothers, did not attend the O.P.S.) had been killed in action in December 1917. Even as the family grieved for him, there must have been a collective intake of breath when it became apparent that Greville was about to go into action for the first time in far-off Palestine.

A great writer of letters since his youth, Greville wrote to the family on 26 March to warn them that 'pretty stiff opposition' was expected.

If I get through all right you'll know. I'll write as often as I can; if I don't, you'll know I have done my best from the day I entered the Service and you needn't worry about anything else ...

I'm looking forward to tomorrow night and the following weeks. I shall see my first real fighting then. I'm enjoying every minute of the life now and wouldn't miss it for anything.

His family were encouraged by his fine words, but understandably anxious to hear that he came through all right. Fortunately, they did not have to wait long to hear that, for the time being at least, all was well. In a letter dated 29 March Greville wrote again, albeit in the midst of the battle, to say that he had come through his first engagement unscathed.

> *We captured the ridge we are on the night before last, and we have been fighting to hold it ever since. The hillock I and my Company took was defended by a machine gun, a Lewis gun and about ten men – all Germans we think ...*
>
> *My only kit now is a blanket and note books and the small photos I have of you all. Well, cheerioh, all of you, and don't worry about me. I quite enjoy the show. One has got one's job to do, and I try to do mine to completion, and yet don't take any unnecessary risks.*

Greville Thomas (Lieutenant, Gurkha Rifles)

It cannot have been long before the Skipper received from his sister the letter sent by his commanding officer, Lieutenant Colonel Shaw. It contained his account of Greville's final action, which took place near Ramleh in modern-day Israel on 10 April 1918.

> *On April 9th orders came for an advance for the 10th ...*
> *As one of the preliminary moves of the day, we were to take the hill I have marked* **6**.
>
> *Your son's Company (D Coy) was detailed for the job and, after a preliminary bombardment by our guns, he rushed the hill with practically no casualties ...*
>
> *At about 10 a.m. the real advance began ...*
>
> *The General sent me orders to rush the* **Pimple** *from the direction of Hill* **6** *with the company holding that hill. I passed on these orders to your son, and we had a long talk on the telephone, discussing the matter and arranging for artillery co-operation. He was absolutely confident about it, though he knew the attack would involve loss, across*

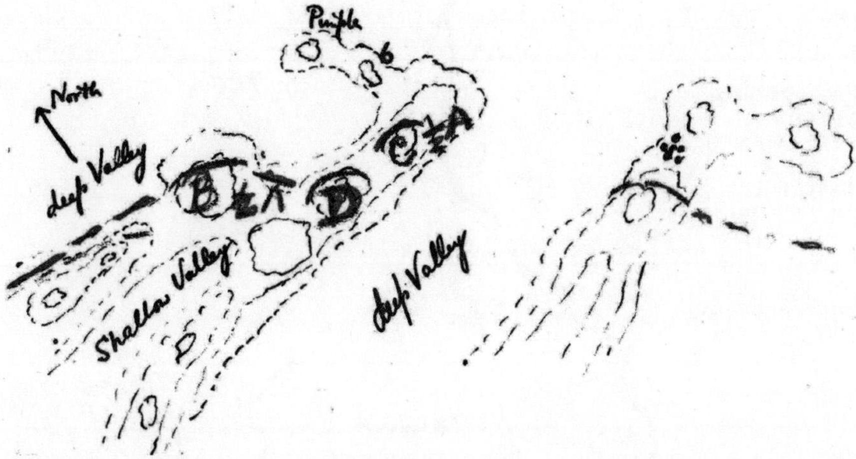

Lieutenant Colonel Shaw's sketch showing the action near Ramleh in April 1918 that led to Greville Thomas's death

> *the open as it was. His last words on the telephone were a very cheery 'Very well sir; goodbye' and I answered 'Good luck, old boy', and we shut down the telephone.*
>
> *The attack failed completely, though most gallantly made. The Pimple turned out to be the surprise of the day, and was heavily held by the enemy ... the attack was simply swept away. The two leading platoons were shot away to a man, and the support platoon practically shared the same fate.*
>
> *Greville fell while leading this platoon in its dash across the open. He died instantaneously with three machine gun bullets in his chest.*

Greville's parents had only recently received a letter from him, written two days before his death, telling them that he was to take his company into action the following day. He described it as 'not a very big show and mine is the only Company in the Battalion doing it, but one never knows what opposition there will be'.

With so many soldiers (including the Skipper's other nephew Eric) having no known grave, it must have been of some comfort to the family to hear from Lieutenant Colonel Shaw that, in Greville's case at least, his body had been recovered. He was buried by their Medical Officer on 17 April, following a negotiated truce for both sides to bury their dead.

Of Skipper's three Thomas nephews, only Lynam Thomas, too young to fight, survived the war. He was to follow the Skipper into education, eventually becoming headmaster of Jack Smyth's alma mater, Repton.

However much this family tragedy must have been in the minds of the Lynam family, by the end of March 1918 the focus was very much back on the Western Front, as the Germans made their final attempt to win the war.

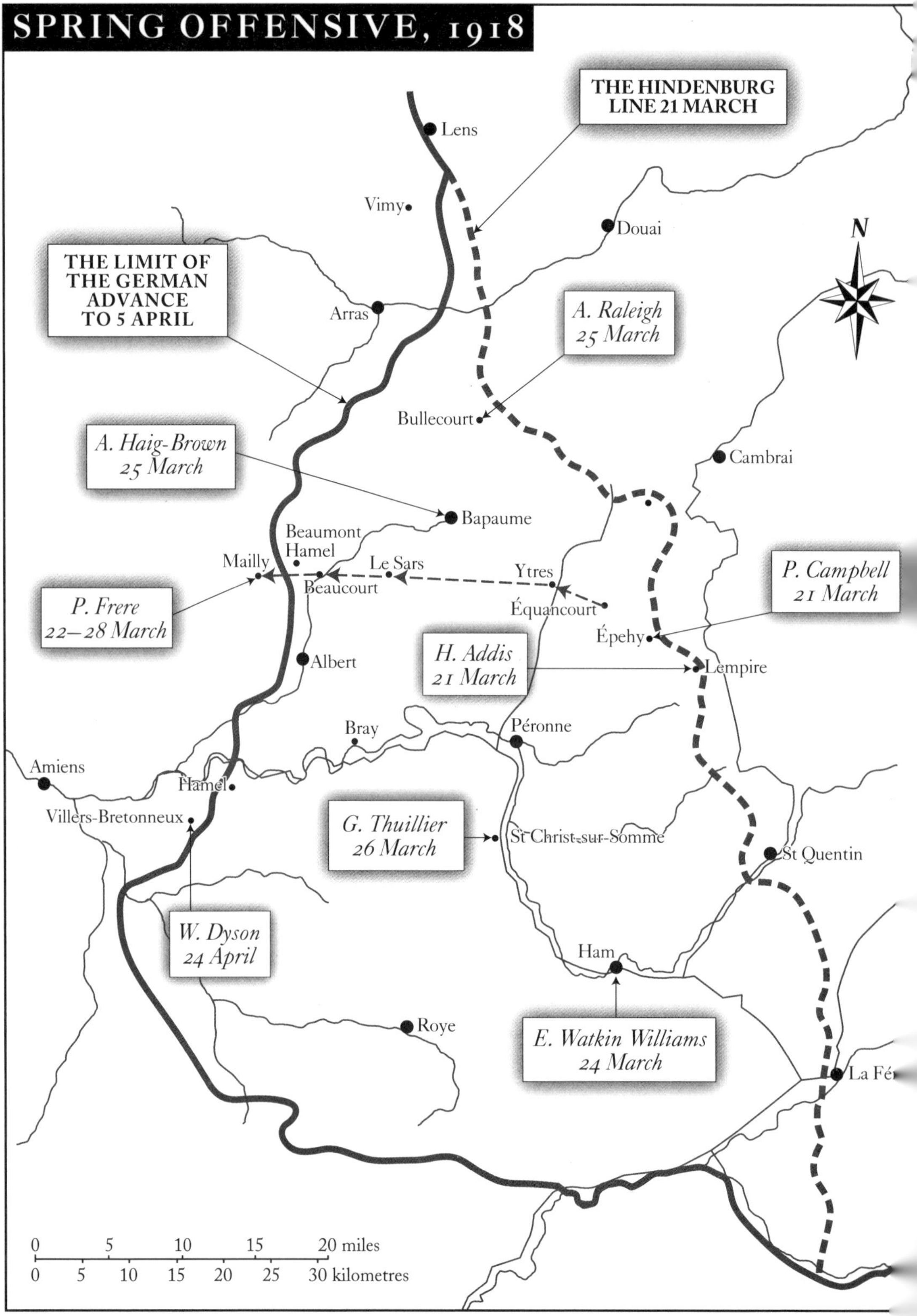

German advances from the Hindenburg Line (21 March to 18 July 1918)

Chapter 15
The Road to Victory

New Tactics

Following the Revolution in April 1917, the Russians made peace with Germany. This released a large number of German troops to fight on the Western Front. This numerical advantage would not last long, however, as in April 1917 the Americans had decided to enter the war on the Allied side. Once their forces arrived, then the position would be reversed.

For the British, a period of recovery and reflection was necessary following the six-month horror that was Passchendaele. It was inevitable that the Germans would make a concerted attempt to win the war in early 1918 before the Americans became a force to reckon with, but exactly where and when they would strike was not clear.

British defences needed improving, for this time they would have to be on the defensive. The trench system prevalent earlier in the war was no longer considered viable. So Captain Geoffrey Rose explained in the history of his regiment, the 2/4th Oxfordshire and Buckinghamshire Light Infantry, written in 1920.

Geoffrey Rose

It was acknowledged that against attack in weight, no actual line could be held intact ... Faith in lines became qualified in favour of the series of 'strong points' or redoubts, which were constructed to defend 'tactical features' ... All the redoubts constructed in the area were so well sited and so strongly wired that the faith seemed justified that they were part of one impregnable system. But against loss of one important factor no amount of industry could serve to insure. 'Strong points' must act in concert and for such mutual action 'on the day' good visibility was essential.[1]

In effect, this meant that defence in depth was required. With this in mind, a system of three zones was developed. First, the enemy would encounter the 'Forward Zone', populated relatively lightly by various patrols, snipers and machine-gun posts, whose aim would be to break up any attack in its early stages. The main body of troops would be ready in the 'Battle Zone', while reserve troops would be held at the back in the 'Rear Zone'.

There was a lot to be done and unfortunately the Rear Zone was far from complete when the Germans struck in the Somme sector on 21 March 1918.

The Spring Offensive

Pat Campbell (2nd Lieutenant, Royal Field Artillery) had spent a spell in hospital for the removal of his tonsils. Having recovered, he returned to the front near Épehy in early March 1918. There he encountered talk of a German offensive. Although he was far from convinced about this, his battery commander was sufficiently worried to sleep with a loaded revolver by his side. 'He was absurd,' Pat thought at the time. 'How could the enemy break through and overrun us before we knew what was happening?'[2]

It was not long after this that Pat found himself being roused unexpectedly at 4 o'clock one morning, to be told that he must go forward without delay to the top of the hill, survey the front and report back.

There was a very thick fog, denying the visibility that Geoffrey Rose had reckoned essential for the new system of defence to be effective. Gunfire could be heard, but that was pretty normal for that time of day. Instead of dying away as it usually would, however, it intensified. Pat then met up with retreating infantry who told him that the Germans had broken through. When he reported this back via a telephone line, the Adjutant did not believe him. 'It was in contradiction to all of the rest of his information.'[3]

The fog then lifted: there was nothing to see. That evening Pat returned to the main battery position.

The following day – another foggy one – it was clear that the Germans had broken through. What was not clear to Pat, however, was what they were supposed to do about it. There were no orders to fire. Telephone lines were down and noone knew the exact positions of friend or foe. Pat was sent back up the hill, his two signallers rolling out a telephone line as they went. He lay down and got out his field glasses.

Pat Campbell

Immediately I saw them. Germans. Thousands of them … I pulled out my map … and quickly began to work out the range and angle of fire … The Germans were coming down the hill [opposite] *in waves and in short rushes.*[4]

He signalled back, only to be told that they could not fire on them as the guns were preparing to retreat. Exaggerating slightly, Pat warned that the Germans would be on them in ten minutes. Still the battery commander refused to believe these were German troops. Surely these were retreating British infantry? Eventually he allowed the use of two of the guns to fire off a number of shrapnel shells, aimed to burst some 15 feet (4.6 m) above the advancing troops. Then came the order to stop firing and retreat without delay.

In recognition of his bravery, Pat was awarded the Military Cross. The citation applauded his conduct throughout.

He directed the fire of his battery from a most exposed position, inflicting heavy casualties on the advancing enemy. During the whole retirement he occupied most forward positions, exposing himself to great danger, and supplied much valuable information throughout.[5]

Pat was distressed by this, knowing that he had clearly failed to inflict 'heavy casualties'.

The German attack on the Somme of 21 March 1918 was on a scale comparable with the first day of the Somme battle on 1 July 1916. The Germans had assembled over 6,000 guns that delivered over 3 million shells into the battle area on the first day alone. A lot of this was aimed at the British artillery, who were hit by both high-explosive and gas shells. The subsequent German infantry attack, unlike the British effort in 1916, was entirely successful and a breakthrough was achieved. There were 38,000 British casualties, of whom 21,000 found themselves cut off and obliged to surrender.

* * * * * *

Nonetheless, the Allied armies put up stout resistance to the German attack. There were not many successful British cavalry charges in the war, but one of them took place further south, near Ham, on 24 March 1918. It was under the command of Old Dragon Evelyn Watkin Williams, a Major in the Hussars.

For three days the infantry had been in retreat and it was decided that a cavalry attack might help to restore their morale. As a consequence, Evelyn's men were ordered to attack a large body of German infantry at nearby Villeselve. It was a great success and Evelyn was awarded the D.S.O., the citation for which reveals the remarkable extent of his achievement.

> *He led a mounted charge along a hostile line, after the infantry line had broken back, taking the line in flank, and in the face of the heaviest machine-gun fire, he carried out the manoeuvre successfully, sabring nearly 100 of the enemy, and taking 100 prisoners, although his own troop was only 150. His fine action rallied the infantry, who advanced and recovered over 3,000 yards in depth of the whole line.*[6]

They had made their charge of some 600 yards (c.550 m) over open ground, some of which had been ploughed. It was not without cost, of course: although only a few were killed, nearly half of the 150 men involved were wounded.

Nor could this isolated success mask the fact that the Germans had successfully broken through, as other Old Dragons found out to their cost.

* * * * * *

Alan Haig-Brown, having run the Lancing College O.T.C. for nine years, was involved in training up the new battalions of Kitchener's Volunteer Army in 1915. He then transferred to the 23rd Battalion Middlesex Regiment, serving with them throughout 1916–18. In October 1916 Alan was promoted to the rank of Lieutenant Colonel and made their commanding officer.

Alan Haig-Brown (Lieutenant Colonel, Middlesex Regiment)

A footballer himself (see p. 55), Alan was no doubt delighted when he was joined by Lieutenant Walter Tull, another former Tottenham Hotspur player. Tull has the distinction of being not only one of the first black footballers to play in the football league, but also the first British-born black officer in the British army.

Both men found themselves under fire near Bapaume as the Germans launched the first part of their Spring Offensive, code-named Operation Michael, on 21 March. They took the full brunt of a massed infantry attack and – as was often the case – were forced into retreat when their flanks became exposed. In the confusion of battle both Tull and Haig-Brown were killed near Bienvilliers, on 25 March 1918 – quite possibly close by one another, although Tull's body was never recovered.

In times such as these, news travelled rather slowly to desperately worried families. After three weeks of hearing nothing, Alan's wife wrote to the War Office for news. Her letter crossed in the post with the official telegram informing her of his death.

* * * * * *

There followed a week of retreat before the line stabilised. Philip Frere, having transferred from his intelligence role during the Battle of the Somme to be Captain in the King's Royal Rifle Corps, was in the thick of it. He wrote up his experiences in what was a most traumatic week immediately afterwards, and his account featured in the August 1918 edition of *The Draconian*.

Philip Frere

28 March 1918
We are now at rest in a little village a few miles from what is for the moment the front line; we are under one hour's notice to move, and you could put what is left of the Battalion into a drawing room. I have had a great piece of luck in coming through, and I don't know how I managed it. As far as I know, we are the only Battalion in the Division who did not lose either the C.O. or Adjutant or both; we lost the second-in-command instead. The whole affair was most extraordinary, and I sincerely hope that I shall never have to go through anything of the sort again.

Only six days earlier Philip had been in reserve at Équancourt (see p. 248, map), a few miles west of where Pat Campbell was in Épehy, and enjoying his dinner.

> *It all started on the 22nd, as far as we were concerned. We were in Corps Reserve, and had been standing by to move at an hour's notice. We were just drinking our port after an early dinner, when we were interrupted by a burst of M.G. fire from about 500 yards, sweeping the village. It was a patrol that had pushed right through. Of course, this was rather sudden when we thought we were six miles at least from the battle. We turned out at once, got the Companies into a trench outside the village and kept off the Boche. We managed to get in touch with the people on the right and left and to form some sort of line.*

The following morning the fighting started in earnest. The Germans broke through and threatened Philip's men in the flank, necessitating a hasty withdrawal. There was the added discomfort of 'whizz-bangs' being fired at them from point-blank range. Philip had never experienced such heavy fire before.

> *All this sort of thing went on till yesterday* [27 March]*; always trudging back, across the devastated plains of the Somme, without food or water, holding on to each ridge and staying until we found our flank was turned, as it invariably was, sooner or later, and wondering how we were going to extricate ourselves. At night, throwing out a picquet or two for protection, we lay down where we were, with no covering, and froze all night.*

For the first two days Philip had nothing but a cup of cocoa and a piece of biscuit and marmalade, but it was the lack of water that affected him more. It was not until the evening of the third day that they found a water supply. Philip commented, 'I did not know what thirst was till then'.

> *But even this was not so bad as the fatigue and awful depression. What was happening? When would it all end? How long were we to continue this unending fighting? We had not the least idea where the rest of our Brigade and Division were, we had no orders what to do and were left to gloomy speculation* [as to] *how on earth we were going to subsist.*

On 23 March they were at Ytres, but were still unable to hold a line as the German advance continued. Once again Philip's men were forced to fall back. No sooner had they established a new position than they came under heavy fire from six enemy 11-inch guns.

> *I then spent the most unpleasant two hours I have known. We cowered down in the bottom of a shallow trench with these huge shells falling all about the place and four German aeroplanes flying round and round fifty feet above us; not one of ours was to be seen, and we had no more ammunition left to fire at them.*

Yet again he found the forces on his flanks giving way, leaving his position untenable. They were lucky to be able to extricate themselves and fall back on the town of Bus. Here they were able to pick up much-needed ammunition and, for Philip, a much-appreciated sandwich.

On the dawn of 24 March they were still in the same predicament, finding themselves in a salient some 3 miles (4.8 km) deep and about a mile (0.6 km) across at the base. A further retreat was necessary.

> *All that day the same thing went on, the men were absolutely done, parched with thirst, and with no spirit left at all. That evening we reached Le Sars and dropped where we stood; however, we had fallen on our feet, for we found the Transport and got food and water. That night I got a little sleep, but the cold was ghastly.*

The following morning they were involved in heavy fighting outside Le Sars. In the melée, the Assistant Adjutant was killed and Philip's second-in-command saved his life by taking a bullet right in front of him. In total, he and his men fought three actions as they retreated towards Beaucourt. Here they had a better night for, as Philip noted, 'the Boche did not molest us and we managed to get hot food from the Transport; I found a tarpaulin which kept me moderately warm, though I was too tired to sleep'.

On 26 March Philip found himself back on the old British line, held before the Germans had retreated behind the Hindenburg Line. He and his men appeared to be near their breaking point.

> *On the 27th the Boche attacked again, but got shoved off. It was a nasty day and the last straw; by the end of it I hardly knew which way up I stood. Our anxiety was increased by the state of the men who were done to a turn.*

That evening, however, they were finally relieved and were sent to Mailly. Here they could recover their strength and count the cost of the past week.

> *Of all the officers who went in, Stafford, myself and four others have come out. In the Brigade too we have suffered badly; the Brigadier General and Staff Captain killed, and of the three Battalions, two have lost both the C.O. and Adjutant killed or missing, and we our second-in-command.*
>
> *And this is the story of the retreat, more exacting than that from Mons as far as this Battalion is concerned. I have often seen us depleted in numbers, but never before in a state like this, and I shudder when I think of the task of rebuilding the Battalion …*
>
> *So much for this. It is an episode about which one could easily write a book, but I have neither the time nor the inclination. I hope to be able to sleep tonight. Last night I had nothing but nightmares.*

Philip was still a few months short of his 21st birthday when his active involvement in the war finally came to an end. In June 1918 he was badly gassed and sent back to a London hospital to recover. By August, though still suffering from photophobia,[7] he was seconded to the MI7b department at the War Office. His aforementioned efforts were recognised with the award of the M.C. The citation commended both Philip's actions and his character.

> *He covered 1,000 yards of open ground under extremely heavy fire to inform the Battalion on the left that we were about to withdraw. Again, next day he personally, under heavy machine gun fire at close range, took orders for withdrawals to two companies, and was largely responsible for the successful withdrawal of his Battalion. He exhibited great courage and cheerfulness under most trying conditions.*[8]

* * * * * *

It was a nightmare week in March. Three Old Dragons were killed trying to stem the tide – Henry Addis (21 March), Alan Haig-Brown (25 March) and George Thuillier (26 March). In addition Adrian Raleigh, the son of Oxford's first Professor of English, Sir Walter Raleigh, was wounded and taken prisoner (25 March). He was serving as 2nd Lieutenant in the Royal Leicestershire Regiment.

Only after his return at the end of the war was Adrian able to tell his story. It was duly included in the December 1918 edition of *The Draconian*.

Adrian Raleigh

> *I was surrounded and captured by a Bavarian Regiment near Bullecourt on March 25th, who charged with much shouting of 'Hoch! Hoch!' They took my whole battalion and put them on to carrying wounded to the rear. Myself and the other five officers were sent back to the Corps Headquarters to be interrogated …*
>
> *We were then given a small piece of black bread and some soup and were sent back with two Uhlans on a 15-mile march to Douai. We were practically exhausted when we arrived there, but received a hearty welcome from the civil inhabitants, who brought us food, and broke into the Marseillaise as we passed. The whole time we were in occupied France, the inhabitants were continually trying to give us food, in spite of it being 'verboten'.*

Adrian spent the remaining months of the war in a prisoner-of-war camp at Mainz.

* * * * * *

William Dyson, serving as 2nd Lieutenant in the Devonshire Regiment, was captured almost exactly a month later when the Germans launched an attack on Villers-Bretonneux, near Amiens. On 24 April, under the cover of a thick mist, the Germans had attacked with tanks and infantry using the dreaded 'Flammenwerfer'. In an account created for the military authorities after the war, William explained what happened.

> *No warning of this attack having been received at Coy H.Q., we were surprised to see a tank loom through the mist 150 yds away on the left front.*[9]

What William could not have appreciated at the time was that the tank he saw, together with two others, came up against three British tanks and engaged in the first ever tank versus tank battle. One British tank was left at the end of what must have seemed like knights jousting in slow motion. Each strove to claim what would nowadays be called 'bragging rights' in an otherwise inconsequential engagement.

This was a mere distraction, as the German infantry were now upon them. On looking towards the platoons some 20 yards (c.18 m) away to his right, he saw a line of German infantry in the act of occupying the trench. It then it became a fight for survival. The order being 'no withdrawal', he and his men resisted as long as they could – until a shell wiped out all his company. Miraculously it left William 'alone and untouched'.

> *I could not withdraw so sat down in the Coy H.Q. (a pit some 4 ft. by 6 ft. by 3 ft., partly roofed with straw) to await dusk or a counterattack. Shortly afterwards, two lines of German infantry having advanced past me, I surrendered to the third line.*[10]

Although Villers-Bretonneux was lost, it was almost immediately retaken by Australian forces. With that the Germans' Operation Michael finally came to a halt. It left the British army with over 170,000 casualties (70,000 of whom were prisoners of war) since its start on 21 March.

Further German attacks followed. Operation Georgette (9–30 April), targeting the Channel ports, cost a further 76,000 British casualties; Operation Blücher-Yorck targeted Paris. Although the Germans got to within 60 miles (96.5 km) of the French capital, no breakthrough was made.

Eventually the Spring Offensive ground to a halt. The German casualties numbered some 950,000 killed, wounded or missing, with a further 1,900,000 suffering from influenza and other illness. On 17 July the Germans pulled back across the Marne and prepared to go on the defensive.

With American troops arriving in increasing numbers, the end of the war was finally in sight.

* * * * * *

Summer Term 1918

Sister Wilkinson shows her award to Miss Williams and Miss Bagguley. Buckingham Palace, 30 April 1918

The Summer Term of 1918 at the O.P.S. started with some good news regarding their former school nurse. On 30 April Sister Wilkinson had the honour of receiving the Royal Red Cross (2nd Class) from George V at an investiture held at Buckingham Palace. The award was made in recognition of her work with the 3rd Southern Hospital in Oxford, mainly at Somerville College. She was accompanied by two members of the O.P.S. staff, Miss Bagguley and Miss Williams.

Promoted from Nurse in 1915, Maud Wilkinson served all though the war until January 1918, when she developed cellulitis (blood poisoning) through dressing septic wounds. This badly affected her arm and thumb, and she was forced to take time off from her duties. She returned to work in July 1918, however, enabling her to see out the final months of the war at Somerville.

* * * * * *

While there was no doubting that the Skipper was very much the man in charge at the O.P.S., his brother Hum, who had taken over the boarding house (School House), was becoming an increasingly strong influence. Skipper was glad to see Hum maintain what he saw as being the traditions of the boarding side.

> *Self-reliance, freedom, absence of unmeaning convention, originality of character, all these have been fostered, the almost unique (in Preparatory Schools) encouragement of parents to see as much of their children as possible during term time and so to keep the home tie strong, this tradition of our school has been carried on – hospitality to old boys and parents, another traditional feature, has been maintained as far as and even further than rations will allow.*

This was perhaps a rash promise when butter, meat and sugar were all in short supply, available only via ration books. The issue of 'war economy' must have continued to concern the Skipper, who felt compelled to part with his beloved macaws and numerous other birds. Only his two parrots, Polly and Joey, remained to entertain his visitors.

For Hum the health of his boarders was of paramount importance and Skipper could rely on him to monitor what would now be called 'health and safety'. At the end of the Easter Term Hum had noted that 'If the weighing machine is a good judge of health, it appears that the substitution of cereals and vegetables for a considerable percentage of meat food is all to the good'.

Hum insisted on taking careful note of the Dragons' heights and weights, which were regularly checked and recorded in *The Draconian*. He also believed that sleep was an important factor. When it was noted that 20 boys had lost weight over the Easter holidays, Hum wondered whether this was 'perhaps due to late hours'.

Hum was a religious man, but one who understood that preaching at children was often ineffective. He wanted Sunday services to be, as much as possible, child-centred and featuring 'nothing perfunctory or merely conventional'. Services would have a theme and the giver of the 'sermon' could choose non-religious readings if he preferred. The boys did the readings and there was no organ or choir, which Hum felt were a distraction from community worship. The service would last no more than 45 minutes – about the length of an academic lesson.

The Most Rev. Cosmo Lang

In June a Memorial Service (the first) was held for those Old Dragons who had died in the war. The Rev. Cosmo Lang, who between 1890 and 1896 had taught Divinity to a number of the Old Dragons fighting in the war, was now the Archbishop of York. He agreed to return to the scene of his early teaching efforts to lead the service. He particularly remembered Hugh Sidgwick, whom he described as 'so full of promise, with the fun and eagerness of life shining out of his bright eyes'.

Lang concluded his talk, thinking of the 64 Old Dragons then on the roll of the dead, with Abraham Lincoln's famous words: 'Let us remember these great men, and let us now highly resolve that this great sacrifice shall not be in vain'.

* * * * * *

The summer of 1918 saw the early stages of the Spanish flu epidemic. The O.P.S. had five cases during the term and seemed to be over it when – on the very last day of term, in among the Sports Day events and Prizegiving speeches – six more boys went down at midday. No more has been recorded about them, so presumably they made a reasonably swift recovery.

That day also saw an unexpected visitor, who made a dramatic entrance from the Port Meadow airfield.

Jim MacLean

We were all rather startled during the High Jump to see an aeroplane circling lower and lower over our heads, only to discover later in the day that it was Capt. Jim MacLean (R.E./R.A.F.), who had flown from Chester to look us up. It was a treat to see him again at Prizegiving.

The Prizegiving Day took place just a few weeks after Skipper had turned 60, but there was no sign of him slowing down. He commented on continuing staff difficulties, including the fact that Gerald Haynes had sadly 'broke[n] down due to overwork'. (Fortunately, 'Tortoise' – the inspiration for John Betjeman's lifelong love of architecture – went on to make a fairly swift recovery and did not retire from the school until 1944.) On the other hand the Skipper was also able to announce some good news.

We have got Captain Wallace back as energetic, though not quite so active (not his fault) as ever ... and imbued with the disciplinary spirit of the Army!

While on a training course behind the front, Pug had sleepwalked out of an upper-floor window. Following a period of recovery in the Somerville Hospital, he had been invalided out of the army.

Skipper also took the chance to refer, in rather obscure terms, to the forthcoming marriage of two members of his staff.

Two of the war staff have fallen victim to one another's charms, and contemplate the consummation of their felicity in the holidays.

One can imagine a number of the boys looking rather quizzically at their parents for some clarification (and not receiving it!).

That term 13 O.P.S. boys had been successful in scholarship exams (including three to Winchester). As always, Skipper was sad to say goodbye.

I shall miss them all, and some of them are very dear to me ... [some] *have been here so long and I have known them so well that it is a great wrench to part with them.*

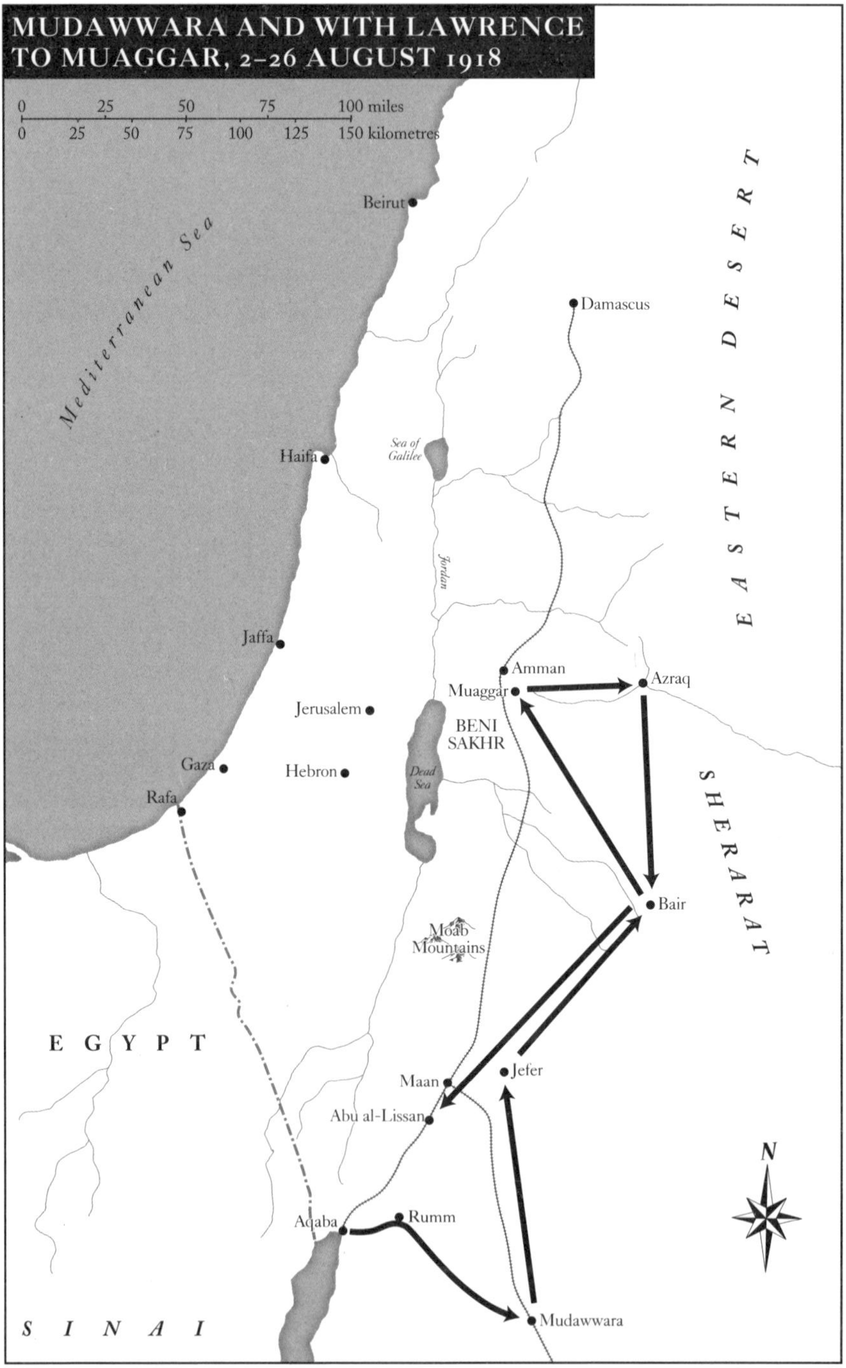

Billy Collier's expedition with the Camel Corps. The Hedjaz Railway, part of the Ottoman railway network, is shown running from Mudawwara north to Damascus.

A Middle Eastern Encounter

The summer holidays of 1918 brought news from Billy Collier, a Captain in the Royal Army Medical Corps. He was serving in Palestine, where General Allenby's forces were meeting with considerable success. Billy sent in to *The Draconian* an account of his expedition with the Camel Corps to attack the Hedjaz railway.

They set out from Aqaba on 2 August and progressed via Rumm towards their objective, the Mudawwara station. This station was protected by three redoubts, each located on a hill. Two parties were designated to attack the two southern ones from the rear, while a third went for the station itself.

Billy Collier

One of the most wonderful sights I have seen was our attack on the middle redoubt. Through my glasses, I could see a long line of men, silhouetted against the first light of dawn, as they climbed the hills, and in spite of bombs and rifle fire streamed along the crest without a halt.

Our relief was great when up went the signal for the capture of the southern redoubt, followed quickly by that from the station. From now onwards I was busy with the wounded and I did not reach the station and breakfast till about 11. Here was the Turkish garrison all captured – 6 officers and over 150 men, of whom about 30 were wounded.

The following day (9 August) they moved on, 'blowing up anything and everything of use to the Turks' as they went.

By 14 August they had reached Bair and, intent on another scheme of attack, were joined by a Political Officer – who, Billy noted, had an Oxford connection.

> *We were joined today by Colonel Lawrence as Political Officer and he remained with us, though living for the most part with his own men, practically till the end of the trip. He has a most wonderful influence throughout this country – even, I believe, throughout Arabia and Mesopotamia. In this country he always dresses and generally lives as a Bedouin and has become a sort of 'great white chief'. His home is in Oxford. His party of 50 braves or personal bodyguard arrived on camels the following day, singing and firing their rifles into the air. Firing off a rifle seems to be a popular form of amusement.*

Their plans, however, were discovered by two enemy planes that flew over them at low altitude. In addition, reports were received that their next objective was more strongly held than had been anticipated. It was decided that they could not proceed with the attack.

Their journey back to Bair was not without incident, however. Billy was summoned to tend a British officer who had been accidentally shot.

> *When we got there, we found that the bullet had gone through his heart and death must have been almost instantaneous. It appeared that one of Col. Lawrence's braves had been picking up his rifle from the ground just behind him when it went off accidentally. The rifle had a long loop of string which actually went round the trigger and*

> *was no doubt responsible for the accident; in every civilised country it would have been regarded as criminal negligence.*

Lawrence's version differs slightly, as he claimed that 'an Arab, shooting fish in the fort pool, dropped his rifle, which exploded and killed instantly Lieutenant Rowan, of the Scottish Horse'.[11] It has been suggested that it was no accident, and certainly there were tensions between the Camel Corps and the Bedouin. Billy noted earlier in their journey that water had to be obtained in competition with the local Bedouin (with whom they had strict orders not to interfere). The Bedouin resented their presence and the parties came close to violence.

> *At one point they actually drove our camels away and tore up our troughs; and peace was only restored by the political officer with the help of baksheesh (English gold).*

If Lieutenant Rowan was indeed murdered, then it is possible that Lawrence ensured that it was hushed up.

They made the journey back to Bair with no further alarms. Billy travelled in the company of Lawrence and three sick men to Aba al Lissan, the headquarters of the

Sydney Carline, *The Destruction of the Turkish Transport in the Gorge of the Wadi Fara, Palestine*, 1920.

Hedjaz northern army and the British H.Q. They were received with great excitement, for no news of the column had been received since they had left Bair eight days previously.

At this point Lawrence parted company with the Camel Corps. However, there was to be one further connection between Lawrence and Old Dragons. After the war one of Sydney Carline's pictures, *The Destruction of Turkish Transport…* (see opposite) was chosen to illustrate Lawrence's *Seven Pillars of Wisdom*, first published in 1926.

The Tables Turned

On the Western Front, once their Spring Offensive had run out of steam, the Germans found their forces depleted, exhausted and in weak defensive positions. This made them extremely vulnerable to a concerted counterattack by the Allies, who now included an American army ready and raring to prove itself.

The end on the Western Front, when it did at last happen, came relatively quickly. The Allies launched their counterattack with the Battle of Amiens on 8 August 1918. The outcome was described by General Ludendorff, the senior German commander, as a 'black day for the German Army'.

This battle seemed to provide the Allies with a blueprint for success. There was no preliminary bombardment to warn the enemy, just a rolling barrage ahead of the advancing infantry, with tanks in the lead to flatten barbed wire and machine-gun nests. However, progress slowed down when they encountered first the old Somme battlefields and then, in September, the Hindenburg Line, with its large expanses of barbed wire.

Pat Campbell (Lieutenant, R.F.A.) observed the situation near Saint Quentin, where the canal, which for a stretch was underground, formed part of the defences. Here, in particular, the artillery were expected to prepare the ground before the infantry went into action. The canal emerged from the tunnel at Bellicourt. Pat noted the deep chasm of the canal between its steep banks and the German trenches, which appeared as 'white scars against the hillside'. It was an extremely strong position.

Pat Campbell

But most of all, it was the wire in front of the trenches that was disconcerting, there was so much and wire was so hard to destroy… we had to cut it using shells that burst on percussion without making much of a hole, heavier guns could have destroyed the wire more effectively, but if they made big craters in the ground, then it was difficult for the infantry to advance.[12]

The work of the artillery was made considerably easier because the plans of the Hindenburg defences had been captured beforehand, conveniently identifying their targets. Even so, Pat had his doubts.

I could see the strength of the position; it was enough to daunt anyone. How could any troops cross that canal under heavy fire and scale the bank on the other side? An English division [the 46th] *on our right was to make the attack opposite the canal, but it looked an impossible task. And how could the Americans get through that wire! They were to make the first advance at Zero Hour, the Australians following behind.*[13]

But succeed they did – on 29 September the 46th Division forced a crossing using all sorts of improvised equipment including lifebelts commandeered from cross-Channel ferries. After a slow start the American/Australian offensive was also successful. The Hindenburg Line had been breached.

* * * * * *

Between the last week of August and 11 November, however, there was a further price for the O.P.S. to pay. By the time the armistice was signed on 11 November six more Old Dragons had been killed, the last of whom was one of Skipper's closest Old Dragon friends.

Stuart Taylor
(Brigadier General, Prince of Wales's Own West Yorkshire Regiment)

It was just before the beginning of the Autumn Term at the O.P.S. that Stuart ('Fluff') Taylor, expecting leave and the opportunity to visit the school, cabled Skipper to say he could not come. This was followed by a letter explaining why.

A special Hun-killing programme was arranged. On the day I should have come I was watching my lads kill Huns and take others prisoners, and they got a splendid haul.

On 1 October Fluff was touring the front-line trenches near Ploegsteert, south of Ypres, when a shell exploded nearby. The Brigade Major was killed and Fluff was hit by shrapnel under the helmet and down his left side. He died of these wounds ten days later, on 11 October, exactly one month before the war ended.

Fluff had been a devoted supporter of both the O.P.S. and the Skipper, although he was rather un-Dragon in many ways. His nickname among his men was 'Ticko', due to his ability to give severe tickings-off to anyone with whom he was displeased. (He once complained to Hum Lynam about a 1st XI team photo in which 'none of the boys appear to possess a brush and comb'.)

Of him it was said that there was 'no Dragon out of the whole number serving who was more intimately bound to the School … his spirit is ever with us to inspire and to cheer and to love'.

From the heart, surely, Skipper wrote this tribute:

> *Like a bright star he burnt, and is suddenly extinguished; to his friends the world is darker. How he would have loved the glory and splendour of the final triumph for which he worked and fought so hard; but he has attained the still more splendid, though more sorrowful, glory of a little white cross above his grave on the Western Front.*

* * * * * *

Once through the Hindenburg Line, the Allies engaged in all-out attack. Towns that had been in German hands since the start of the war were at last falling into their hands. Coming up hard on the heels of the retreating Germans, Leslie Grundy (Captain, Machine Gun Corps) claimed that his men were the first British troops to enter Lille, on 17 October 1918.

> *To our surprise, we found we were the first British troops to enter … The ovation we got was terrific … The men were covered with flowers and flags. The civilians were off their heads for joy and several ladies were so overcome that they kissed me on both cheeks with tears in their eyes. They must have had an awful time here with the Germans. No butter, cheese, meat or eggs for four years. Many of the women have been in prison – one case, a sentence of 15 days imprisonment for giving a cup of coffee to an English prisoner …*
>
> *When I asked at the Mairie for 'billets de logement' they went off their heads for joy, and before I could look round they had put my men into billets – everyone got a bed. I had a splendid room with real linen sheets (hidden while the Boche was in possession) and we messed in a large dining room, beautifully furnished. The people insisted on doing all the cooking and our servants had the time of their lives.*
>
> *My host was a leading brewer in the town, a M. Agache, and he was the most hospitable man I have come across for a long time. Mme Agache has been a hostage in Germany for a long time and had suffered simply horribly – thank Heaven our women have not been in a similar position. One of the minor indignities to which they were submitted was to go to their baths stark naked, escorted by soldiers.*

'The 11th hour of the 11th day of the 11th month'

Not far from Mons, the scene of the first battle fought by British troops in 1914, was the recently promoted Captain Pat Campbell. On the morning of 11 November 1918 he was awaiting orders to advance with his guns from his position near Mauberge when his senior officer, Major Cecil, rode up at speed with a letter. He invited Pat to read it.

> *It was only orders for the day, but when I opened the envelope I saw there was only a single sheet inside, instead of the usual sheaf of papers. I opened it and read:*

'Hostilities will cease from 11.00 hours today November 11th.'

'What does it mean?' I asked him.

'The War's over,' he said ...

I looked at my watch. It was ten o'clock already; there was no possibility now of any of us being killed ...

At a few minutes before eleven o'clock we all went to where the guns were, drawn up in a line behind a hedge ... Major Cecil was standing on the left of the line, by Number One gun; he was holding the big battery watch in his left hand and a whistle in the other. He's trying to make it seem like Zero Hour, I said to myself, but he can't, it's not real.

I heard him blow the whistle and all the guns fired. This was the first time I had heard our guns firing blank ammunition. It was not the proper sound, there was no report, as there would have been with live shells. The noise was no more than a bang, and puffs of white smoke hung over the muzzles of the guns and drifted slowly away. Some of the men started to cheer, but their voices sounded as unnatural as the noise of the guns, and they soon stopped. There was Silence. It had come to stay.[14]

Silence there may have been, and great relief too. However, that evening, as Pat began to weigh matters up, he found little to celebrate and much to concern him.

I'm not complaining. God knows – I don't want the war to go on. I don't want to die, and death would probably have been my lot if the war had gone on for another year. But I'm not so happy as I ought to be feeling. It's fine to think that there will be no need for them at home to worry about me any more now. By Jove! There'll be some happy people in England tonight. And yet it's only now that I'm beginning to realise what death has done. In the next few weeks, or months, we, the survivors, will go home leaving the others, and the better ones, behind us. Then we shall realise their loss. For four years now, death has not seemed real; these years have been like a nightmare, but now there's a difference: we're waking up and we find that part of the dream was true. There are some fathers and mothers who have lost all, to whom no-one will be coming back. My God! I'm sorry for them and I'm sorry for those who have been killed in these last few weeks.

Pat's mind turned to the future and the realisation that it too had its challenges.

And though the War is over that very fact brings us another anxiety, just as it takes the old one away. What are we going to do in the future? To me, at any rate, every career seems distasteful. For four years I've refused to think about the future. What was the use of worrying about it, when I never expected there would be any future?

And then how happy I have been in the brigade! I remember how frightened I was when I left school. I thought I should never make even a tolerably efficient officer. But I did learn in time, from both the other officers and the men: they were a fine lot of people to work with. I can think of nearly every one of them with feelings of real friendship.

And perhaps it is one's friends that matter more than anything else. In a few months we shall be scattered over the world.

Before going to bed I went outside for a few minutes. There was a great stillness over the land. The moon was a little beyond the first quarter and it was a bright, starry night – a perfect night for bombing. I shall never be frightened of a full moon again. I shall never listen to the three short blasts of a whistle, a warning that aeroplanes are passing overhead.

The silence of the night was uncanny.

We knew where we stood while the war lasted; now we have been uprooted.[15]

MEMORY
AND
MASTERS
OF-THE
SCHOOL
THEIR-LIVES
COUNTRY
IN-THE
GREAT-WAR

Chapter 16

'Too Many Empty Chairs'

The Armistice

In Oxford, news of the Armistice was received on the morning of 11 November with great enthusiasm. Flags were flown; crowds of residents, students, soldiers (wounded, as well as fit) and children gathered. The bells rang, including 'Great Tom' in Wren's Tom Tower at Christ Church (which had been silenced for the duration). Those who had followed George V's example of giving up alcohol till the war ended took their first drink since 1915. At 6 p.m. the mayor read out the terms of the Armistice in the city centre. The day concluded with fireworks and an effigy of the Kaiser being consumed on a bonfire outside St John's College on St Giles, a stone's throw from where the O.P.S. had opened in 1877.

All this, but no celebrations at the O.P.S. for the simple reason that it was, to all extents and purposes, closed. Influenza, the worldwide killer of considerably more people than died in the war, had been particularly virulent in Oxford in the autumn of 1918. The *Daily Telegraph* of 7 November reported that Oxford had sustained 118 deaths from influenza in the two weeks leading up to 2 November. The elementary schools closed and, for the first time in the history of the O.P.S., the boarders were sent home so that they might avoid infection. There were a dozen pupils who, for a variety of reasons, could not go home; they stayed and 'had some jolly expeditions and did a little work'. Some day children who were fit enough continued to come in, but the school at this time numbered 36, rather than the 167 on its roll.

It was not until rather later in the month that the school reassembled, and the Skipper organised some celebratory fireworks.

> *Many boys had never let off fireworks before, and there were moments when it seemed likely they would never let off any more! But there were no serious casualties. It has been suggested that we should abolish Guy Fawkes' Day and institute Nov. 11th instead, and burn a far less respectable and much more cowardly villain in effigy.*

German Naval Surrender

As part of the Armistice agreement, arrangements were quickly made for the Germans to hand over their naval forces. Reggie Tyrwhitt, now Rear Admiral Sir Reginald Tyrwhitt, was one of the most senior of Old Dragons. He had enjoyed a

Left: O.P.S. War Memorial, designed by the Skipper's father, Mr Charles Lynam F.R.I.B.A.

very successful war and on 20 November 1918 took the surrender of German U-boats. Reggie felt the need to inform Skipper personally of the day's momentous events, for the benefit of the young Dragons.

> *It was a most impressive sight to me, this long line of over five miles of German submarines steaming peacefully along and one could scarcely realise that a short week ago, the slightest rumour of one such craft being in the neighbourhood was enough to bring our destroyers tearing up from all sides to hunt him to death.*

It must have been a coincidence, but Old Dragon Francis Studdy – a Sub-Lieutenant in the Royal Navy, serving on H.M.S. *Danae* – reported that it was, rather appropriately, the light cruiser H.M.S. *Dragon* that was detailed to lead the first batch of German submarines into captivity.

Studdy was suspicious.

Francis Studdy

> *No-one ever dreamed that the Germans were going to throw up the sponge in the way they did, and we were all wondering what their game was.*

The German navy had been in a state of mutiny. In one submarine the crew had taken a dislike to their captain, so they just ditched him and put someone else in his uniform.

> *They were quite candid about the whole thing, because the officer taking over the boat commented on the youthful appearance of the captain and asked him how long he had been in command. He replied a few hours and then volunteered the above information.*

The next day Commander Geoffrey Freyberg, a veteran of Jutland (see pp. 163–64), was on board H.M.S. *Valiant*. He witnessed the surrender of the German High Seas Fleet, which they escorted up the Forth.

> *There was no cheering, we spoke almost in whispers, for I think the hearts of most of us were sad.*

H.M.S. *Queen Elizabeth* (Admiral Beatty on board) overseeing the surrender of German König-class battleships (in the background), 21 November 1918

This was not a time for jubilation; those present at the surrender of the German fleet were under orders not to humiliate the enemy. Percival Chapman, an Assistant Paymaster in the Royal Navy, was the younger brother of Philip, who had died on Malta as the result of wounds received at Gallipoli (see pp. 132–33). In 1918 Percival was serving on board H.M.S. *Royal Sovereign*, from where he witnessed the hauling down of the German ensigns, marking the moment of surrender.

> *Everybody became a trifle excited as sunset approached, some people having an idea that the Boches might attempt something dramatic when the critical moment arrived, such as a little diversion in the way of explosions etc. Nothing, however, happened except that the Hun battle-cruiser* Derfflinger *and one of their battleships were rather late on it ... whatever the cause, their slackness evoked derisive cheers from the crew of the* Royal Oak. *This was the only sign of jubilation anyone gave, cheers being against orders.*

At Jutland *Derfflinger*, Percival may have recalled, had been one of the ships responsible for the sinking of H.M.S. *Invincible*, with fellow Old Dragon Charles Fisher on board.

Return of the P.O.W.s

The end of the war saw the release of those Old Boys incarcerated in P.O.W. camps and the emergence of their stories. Most of the British prisoners of war were those involved in the two major retreats of the war: from Mons in August 1914 and those caught up in the German offensive of March 1918. Adrian Raleigh, 2nd Lieutenant in the Royal Leicester Regiment, fell into the latter category. The days following his capture (see p. 255) had been testing.

Adrian Raleigh

> *We were kept at Douai about a week; here our daily rations consisted of two bowls of soup, one bowl of coffee and a small portion of black bread. Here I learnt what hunger was for the first time.*

There followed a five-day train journey to Rastatt and a couple of months later Raleigh was moved to Mainz. Here life improved: rather than sitting around waiting for the next meal, concerts, lectures, games and even some study were possible. The best entertainment, however, was when there was an air raid. 'On these occasions we would gather round the windows and cheer and sing *Rule Britannia*.'

The end of the war, when it came, was somewhat unexpected. German officers appeared in mufti, warning them that they had better pack up and be prepared to move. Following the signing of the Armistice, the guards vanished so that these former prisoners were able to walk the streets of Mainz and enter cafés, theatres, etc. as if they were at home. They spent several enjoyable days among the inhabitants, who appeared to be quite friendly and never tired of expressing their satisfaction at the downfall of the Kaiser. Eventually, wearied of waiting for 'immediate repatriation', 200 of them chartered a river steamer, at 20 marks per head, and started down the Rhine.

Two nights were spent in Cologne 'which was strewn with flags and placards bearing the inscription: "Welcome to our brave troops, beaten by no foe"'. Then followed the voyage home. Crossing the Dutch border at Nijmegen took some six days; from there to Rotterdam by train, and finally home 'after a rather varied tour of Germany'.

* * * * * *

Another imprisoned Old Dragon was Aubrey de Sélincourt. He had been shot down by the German ace Werner Voss over Douai on 28 May 1917 (see pp. 219–20) and was subsequently imprisoned at Holzminden, a German military establishment converted to house some 700 prisoners of war (mainly officers), in 1917. Aubrey became an author after the war, but the only time he wrote about his time as a prisoner was for the August 1919 edition of *The Draconian*.

Inmates of the Holzminden P.O.W. camp; de Sélincourt is seated on the right

I will not tell of the slow-footed weary months behind barbed wire fences, where torn nerves and unnatural conditions, forced companionship, and long division from the persons and the things one loves, infuse their insidious poison into the bodies and minds of all but the strongest; nor describe the heterogeneous crowds of men with whom I came into contact. Let it suffice that there were, within those narrow spaces, kind men, morose men, stupid men, cruel men, English, German, French or Russian, an indiscriminate cosmopolitan herd – and most of them unhappy, either because they were prevented from doing what they wished, or because they were doing what they hated.

Aubrey spent 18 months in captivity. Other men were there for four years, starved of proper food, awaiting the Armistice and 'a new and better world'.

* * * * * *

The second of the two Dragon V.C.s and Royal Air Force hero Captain William Leefe Robinson met with considerable hostility from prison camp guards. Robbie's many attempts at escape led to him being transferred to Holzminden (nicknamed 'Hellminden' by its inmates), which he reached on 18 July 1918.

Holzminden P.O.W. camp in Lower Saxony, late 1918

Robbie discovered on arrival that a major escape attempt was already under way. The tunnel had taken some eight months to dig and, if all had gone to plan, they hoped that around a hundred men could have got away. Robbie was too recent an arrival to be included. In the event only 29 prisoners of war made it out of the camp before the tunnel became blocked; ten of them subsequently made it to Holland and safety. This attempt is reputed to have inspired the 1944 escape from Stalag Luft III, made famous by the film *The Great Escape* (1963), starring Steve McQueen.

If Karl Niemeyer, the camp commandant, was not already rather annoyed – he had declared his camp to be escape-proof – he was even more so when Robbie tried to escape. Determined to revenge the death of the airship commander shot down by Robbie, he subjected him to numerous spells of solitary confinement and on one occasion a whipping that left Robbie on the point of collapse.

Niemeyer was, according to F.W. Harvey, the Gloucestershire poet and writer and fellow prisoner of war, 'a cad, boaster, and a bully of the worst type'.[1] Having spent some time in the United States he had acquired some English – or rather American. Some recompense for all the suffering he caused was that he was relatively easy to mimic. One British officer became so good at imitating his roar that he could fool the German soldiers as well as his own colleagues.

> *Officers would hastily hide the maps they were copying, and sentries would spring to attention ... One day after an escape Niemeyer, passionate with rage, was striding through the camp flourishing a pistol, and shouting, 'I guess you think dat I do not know nothing, but I know damn all', when his impersonator, shouting equally loudly, came suddenly round the corner, and they met face to face. But before the astonished Hun could recover himself to do anything unpleasant, the officer had vanished.*[2]

An anonymous 'Captain in the R.A.F.', since identified as Captain David Tidmarsh M.C., recalled spending some more pleasant times in captivity with Robbie.

> *At Karlsruhe we both learnt French from a M. Schorestine and tried to drown our sorrows in work, but we were separated in about two weeks. I went to Stroken and he to Freiburg from where he made a successful escape, but was retaken near the frontier.*
>
> *We met again on Aug. 17th at Bad Colburg, he having come from Holzminden. He was looking quite well and many a hard set of tennis we had together. He was with us until Nov. 6th, when he left for a camp near Berlin.*
>
> *I was most awfully sorry when he left – we did quite a lot of work together, chiefly aeroplane construction and maths, and among other things he taught me the Calculus. We frequently went for walks and discussed our plans for the future; he was really keen on his job and was determined to master it thoroughly, both theoretically and practically. In Bad Colburg the Huns made him report about eight times a day, which was horribly annoying, but he was far too sensible to worry over their petty strafes.*

William Leefe Robinson (Captain, R.A.F.)

Robbie was repatriated on 14 December in a very poor state of health. Many blamed Niemeyer for that, and it left him too weak to resist the influenza epidemic. He saw only 17 days of freedom, dying on 31 December 1918.

> *During the delirium which preceded his last moments, Captain Robinson was haunted by the vision of the arch brute. He imagined that Niemeyer and sentries with fixed bayonets were standing by his deathbed. Several times he called out to be protected from the fiend.*[3]

At his bedside were his sister Kitty and Joan, his fiancée.

'With Love and Gratitude'

The war had also taken its toll on the Skipper; as with the surrender of the German High Seas Fleet described by Geoffrey Freyburg, he was in no mood to celebrate either. As the year drew to a close, he sent this letter of appreciation to all his Old Boys who had fought in the war.

> *To you and all my dear Old Boys who have lived through the Great War, and have served our country on sea or land or in the air, abroad, or in home defence, or in other work of national importance.*
>
> *I am proud of you all and thank you for the noble work you have done, the great example you have set us all, the sacrifices you have made, the discipline and self-control to which you have so willingly submitted, the wounds maybe, and the hardships you have borne.*
>
> *I glory with you in the victory you have won – you have fought in a just cause and you have triumphed.*
>
> *But the cost has been heavy: out of four hundred and eight of you who have served, seventy-three – eighteen per cent – will come back to us here no more. They have given their lives. All honour to them, and we thank God for them. Their memory will not fade and their example will be a possession for ever.*

> *But their loss is a bitter grief to us – At one time I looked forward to a great Gathering of the Old Boys when the war was over; but now there would be too many empty chairs, too many 'faces of old ghosts' looking in upon our feast; and I do not feel that I could face it at present. Later on, when time has to some extent softened the sense of loss, I hope this promised Gathering will take place; and meanwhile let me say how gladly we shall welcome any of you individually who can come and pay your old school a visit.*
>
> *Yours, with love and gratitude,*
>
> *SKIPPER.*
> *December 1918*

Noone seems to have been in any mood to celebrate, although over 40 Old Dragons did take up Skipper's invitation to visit the following term. Skipper noted how the conflict had changed them.

> *Few of them bear the marks of what they have been through. The war seems to have given many of them a broader, more tolerant view of life, and wider sympathies. Many have told me that their deepest impression is the revelation of the supreme worth of a British Tommy. This seems to have formed a bond between classes which must in the end wipe out many class distinctions.*

One distinguished visitor was Sir Reginald Tyrwhitt, invited to receive the Freedom of City of Oxford on 3 February 1919. Reggie arrived at O.P.S. the day before – straight from spending a few days with the royal family at Sandringham, where there had been a moment of embarrassment.

G.C. Vassall (with John Betjeman vying for his attention), the Skipper, Admiral Tyrwhitt, F.C. Ford, B.E.Tyrwhitt, Hum Lynam and sundry Dragons, 4 February 1919

I found brekker rather a trying meal, as the King's parrot took a violent fancy to me and insisted on sitting on my shoulder and making violent love.[4]

This, unsurprisingly, was not the subject of the address he gave at the school's Sunday service. He wished to impress on young Dragons that they should be making their own minds up, rather than rely on the advice of others.

I remember I was generally somewhere near the bottom of my form, but I did learn how to make up my own mind ... The advice of others is very useful occasionally, but when one gets too used to outside advice one cannot help oneself, and when the emergency comes one cannot get on alone.

The following day many Old Dragons and staff were present at Oxford Town Hall to see him receive the Freedom of the City, while the children at the O.P.S. had the inevitable 'extra half'. The next day Reggie returned to the school with his brother and another Old Dragon of his era to satisfy Dragon autograph-hunters and appear in the school photo. He then went on to the Sheldonian Theatre to receive an honorary doctorate.

The Final Casualties

Charles Pittar (2nd Lieutenant, Coldstream Guards)

For many who had served, the end of the war was not the end of the suffering. Under the terms of the Commonwealth Graves Commission charter, those who died of their wounds – or as a consequence of illness or accident on active service – up to the date of 31 August 1921 were eligible to be commemorated. Nine Old Dragons died from what were accepted as war-related causes after 11 November 1918: three of influenza, two of tuberculosis, two from accidents and one of a heart attack.

The final resting place of the last Old Dragon to qualify (by only three days) for a Commonwealth war grave is in the Wolvercote Cemetery, a mere 2 miles (c.3 km) from his old school. Charles Pittar had won a scholarship to Eton in 1912 and was still only 17 when the war broke out. Thus he saw action in only the final two years of the war – but that was time enough to win the M.C. for scouting in broad daylight 'right up through the enemy outpost line, a distance of some 700 yards'.[5] After the war Charles came back to Oxford to study at Queen's College for the Indian Civil Service exams. During this period he worked part-time at the O.P.S., teaching classics to the top form.

In its account of his death *The Draconian* recorded only what *The War Office Gazette* published, namely that 'nervous trouble owing to the effects of gassing and shell-shock were the cause of his death on August 28th, 1921'. But the painful reality was that his parents found Charles dead in bed, along with a note addressed to his mother. A verdict of gas poisoning during a fit of temporary insanity was returned. The note movingly revealed his mental anguish.

> *I don't think you will ever realise my general state of mind. There seems to be a sort of cloud which oppresses me. Today I've been in a most extraordinary state – a mixture between deep depression and wild excitement, and always this cloud.*[6]

These words were echoed by Tyrrell Brooks, who came to talk to the school in 1922. He described his own feelings on returning from war as a recently promoted Temporary Lieutenant Colonel in the Duke of Cornwall's Light Infantry.

Tyrrell Brooks

> *The war was over, and we who had been living on our nerves for five years were subject to deep fits of depression, alternating with optimism – in other words, the main issue of one's professional life had passed and had left a blank, and the world seemed upside-down, and nothing normal.*

What it is that leads one person to suicide and another to turn a corner and live a long and fruitful life we can (perhaps) never know.

* * * * * *

In the final analysis, 425 Old Dragons served in the First World War. Including the war-related deaths between 1919 and 1921, the eventual number of those who lost their lives rose to 87 Old Boys and staff. This was from a school that did not come into existence until 1877 and did not reach 100 pupils until 1905. The number of pupils who would have been of the right age to serve amounted to around 600. On that basis, 70 per cent of them served and of those who served nearly 20 per cent died 'for King and country and the Dragon School'.[7]

Their bravery is reflected in the medal tally. Old Dragons won two Victoria Crosses and 22 were awarded the D.S.O. Two more won the D.F.C. and 50 the M.C., while 125 were 'Mentioned in Dispatches'. Thus, 199 received recognition for their valour: nearly half of those who served.

The Draconian also registered 70 Old Dragons as having been wounded. Taken together with the 87 killed, 37 per cent of the Old Dragons who served were casualties of the conflict. Bob Bourne, a Captain in the Herefordshire Regiment, had lost the sight of one eye in a game of rounders as a child at school. Now, with one hand crippled and a lung seriously injured at Suvla Bay in August 1915, this Olympian oarsman would never row again. Another, Hugh Channer, a Major in the Royal Marine Light Infantry, had lost a leg in Gallipoli.

In Memoriam

The war over, the authorities soon turned their attention to the war graves scattered over the various battlefields, especially in northern France. Those in isolated graves were moved to the graveyards to be managed by the Imperial War Graves Commission, formed in 1917. None were to be repatriated – officers and men who died together would lie together.

How the O.P.S. might best mark the lives of those who had given theirs (some of whom had no known grave) had long been the subject of correspondence in *The Draconian*. Fluff Taylor had first raised the subject in the April 1917 edition, and it sparked considerable discussion.

Skipper himself had been in favour of a War Memorial building, but he refused to commit himself until everyone had had the chance to contribute their ideas. Claude Burton ('Touchstone'), whose son Paddy had been killed on the Somme, had proposed a different scheme.

> *It seems to me that since the Old Boys have fought and died for those who are to follow them, the memorial most fitting them would be one which would benefit directly the future boys of the School, and I would therefore suggest that the bulk of the money subscribed should be employed in founding Scholarships which should give a better chance in life to those who need it.*

Geoffrey Carpenter, who had been a Captain in the Uganda Medical Services, had another important point to make.

Geoffrey Carpenter

> *But why only for those 'who have given their lives for their country in this great war'? Surely this war is not the first occasion on which Dragons have died for their country or for others? Nor will it be the last … Would not this occasion, when we are all trying to do our bit, be a most suitable one for collecting funds for a memorial for all time, past, present and future, of our friends who have died, are dying and will die for others long after we have gone?*

The Skipper then set up a committee of Old Boys and parents, past and present, to come to a final decision. The committee included Fluff Taylor, Frank Sidgwick (Hugh's brother), C.R.L. Fletcher and E.B. Poulton (fathers respectively of George and Regie Fletcher and Ronnie Poulton), Captain W.W. Fisher R.N. (brother of Charles and Edmund Fisher) and Treffry Thompson. A meeting of this committee was held on 7 March 1918 at which it was decided that above all the War Memorial 'should be to *inform* and *inspire* present and future Dragons'.

The idea of a substantial building, either chapel or hall, was deemed to be beyond their means, 'remembering that our boys are not drawn from the wealthy classes'. Instead the committee unanimously approved of the proposal to erect a sculptured Cross in a prominent place in the school grounds, with a pedestal on which the names of Old Boys and Masters who had given their lives would be inscribed. It also determined that books and albums should be provided, giving further information about those who had died and their deeds.

It was added that Skipper's 89-year-old father, Mr. C. Lynam F.R.I.B.A., F.S.A., an expert on old crosses, had agreed to submit a design for the committee's consideration. The August edition of *The Draconian* featured three designs and suggested various possible sites.

O.P.S. Memorial Cross, designed by the Skipper's father

The discussion started by Fluff Taylor as to how to honour those who had died finally culminated in a decision to build a Memorial Cross on the bank of the River Cherwell, at the bottom of the school's playing field.

Over £1,650 was raised, but the difficulty in getting the skilled labour immediately after the war necessitated a delay in its completion. The service of dedication was finally held on 8 November 1920. The new Bishop of Oxford, Dr Burge, former Headmaster of Winchester College (1901–11), performed the dedication. He recalled the sacrifice made by these Old Dragons in powerful and moving terms.

All their gifts, all their promise – light-hearted and happy they were, on the threshold of the Golden Age of early manhood – they put on one side in the choice they made at their country's call. The truest comradeship, undaunted, unflinching courage, and loyal service and self-sacrifice for their country and her cause in the hour of her deep need marked that choice.

Nine of the 83 names on the Cross were Old Boys of Winchester. A number were known personally to Dr Burge, who challenged those present to live up to the standards of those who had died.

> *Those whose names are inscribed on the Cross differed in their lives and in their temperaments; some had surely been cut out for great things, and some for the quieter life of the student. Yet at the time of great emergency all took their stand for the right. May you also be given the same power to take up the challenge when it comes, to accept the high, and maybe, the seemingly impossible line.*

Per Mallalieu reciting Dr Alington's poem 'Trust' at the Oxford Town Hall, 1921

As part of the service, Per Mallalieu was allotted the task of reciting Dr Alington's poem 'Trust'. He did this to such good effect that he was deputed to open the World Service Exhibition with it in the Oxford Town Hall early in 1921. The *Daily Mirror* published a photograph of him performing this, under the heading 'The Spirit of the New Age Speaks'. Per later commented that this 'assured and happy spirit really knew very little about the New Age'.[8]

The End of an Era

In January 1920 Frank Sidgwick returned to the O.P.S. to review the annual Shakespeare production – this time *Henry V*. A certain John Betjeman caught his eye.

> *Having beheld him manufacture, out of two small parts, the Earl of Cambridge and the King of France, two separate, distinct and perfect gems of character-acting, I am not prepared to say that he could not have played, with equal insight and brilliance, Henry the Fifth, Fourth, Sixth or Eighth, or Othello, Falstaff, Imogen, Caliban, Hamlet, Juliet's Nurse, Ariel, or Lance and his dog Crab. I can't give him higher praise than by saying that he ought to play Bottom; but if next year he is cast for the part of Biondello in the* Taming of the Shrew, *who I believe has little to do except eat an apple, I will again break all engagements to come and see him do it.*

In his final year at the O.P.S. John Betjeman's talent – and eccentricity – became more apparent. Per Mallalieu recalled his friend in bandages; he had been intoning some chant while pulling in time the rope that opened a skylight. The glass duly shattered, leaving John deluged with fragments.

In another initiative, John and his friend Ronald Wright drew up 'plans for taking over the state of San Marino and keeping it as a pet'.[9] The two of them were also often found at the piano, abusing music hall songs of the day.

> *They also went in for elaborate hoaxes. Once I received a letter on expensive notepaper with a letterhead gravely printed 'The West London Lunatic Asylum' and signed by a physician. The perfectly typed text told me, with regret, that two school friends of mine, Ronald Wright and John Betjeman, had just been admitted to the asylum babbling about someone called 'P.M.M.P.'.*
>
> *'Having,' wrote the doctor, 'discovered that the correct name is Mallalieu, I thought it best to let you know the nature of their illness which is that they imagine themselves to be tea cups and we have had to provide large saucers for them to sit in.'*[10]

* * * * * *

The Prizegiving audience, 21 July 1920

The Prizegiving of July 1920 was the fourth, and last, attended by John Betjeman as a Dragon. He attempted a scholarship to Marlborough and, while not getting one, did well enough to be excused taking the normal entrance examination.

Unlike John's first Prizegiving, held in the School Hall in 1917, this took place on the fields in the presence of the O.P.S.'s most famous living Old Boy.

Jack Churchill receives his prize from Jack Smyth

Both John Betjeman and his friend Ronald Wright received awards from Jack Smyth V.C., fresh from being himself presented with the M.C. the previous day; it was also the day before his own wedding. Ronald won the Skipper Prize for Piano and John the Mr Fitch Prize for Speeches.

Another prize winner that day was a young Jack Churchill – whose exploits in the Second World War were to win him both a D.S.O. and bar and the M.C. and bar. He became known by the nickname of 'Mad Jack' and was said to have gone into battle armed with a longbow, broad sword and bagpipes. And so, on a peaceful summer day in Oxford, a Dragon hero of the First World War met a future hero of the Second.

However, for those present, this was not to be the most memorable moment of the day. Even Jack Smyth was upstaged by the Skipper, who announced his retirement. *The Draconian* recorded this startling event.

> *The most dramatic moment of the Prize-giving was at its outset, when the Skipper flung off his academic robes and retired to his well-earned rest, the background and a pipe.*

Skipper explained the thinking behind his decision in that term's edition of *The Draconian*.

> *At the age of 62 and after 40 years schoolmastering in Oxford, I feel that the School should be run by younger men, so I have got Hum to be Joint Headmaster and am leaving the greater part of the management of the School to him.*

In short, in the future the Skipper would still be around – but no longer about.

* * * * * *

Jack Smyth congratulates the Skipper on his retirement

With both John Betjeman and the Skipper leaving the main stage, it is fitting to end this story here, on a summer's day in 1920. The war was over and the peace restored. It was the end of the Skipper's era – the good ship Dragon was well and truly launched and its future secured. Now it was the turn of his brother to take the helm. This Hum did, subsequently announcing in *The Draconian* that the O.P.S. was changing its name.

> *We have decided to revert to the old name of the School, viz, the Dragon School, Oxford, instead of the Oxford Preparatory School. The boys have always been 'Dragons', but the School has come to be known as 'Lynam's' or 'the O.P.S.' and we prefer 'the Dragons'.*

Frank Sidgwick put it better in verse – and it seems right that a Sidgwick, and another 'particular favourite' at that, should have the last word.

> *Authority at length lays down the rule –*
> *No more the 'Oxford Preparatory School';*
> *'THE DRAGON SCHOOL' cancels the O.P.S. –*
> *And 'Dragons' is our Cable Code Address.*

Epilogue

There were headmasters broken by the losses their schools had sustained, but the Skipper was not one of them. The fragility he exposed in his letter of 1918 soon wore off, and no doubt the enthusiasm of the young about him reinvigorated him. He wished to continue being involved in school life, 'to spend some happy years in the position of (shall I say) warden of the School – and do some teaching and supervision and to keep up intimate connections with Old Boys and Girls'. He also wanted to devote time to his *War Memorials* of all those Old Boys killed in the war, which was duly published in 1922.

The Skipper was to have 20 years of very happy 'retirement'. He always remained on hand to preside over Old Dragon dinners and attend Armistice Day services at the Cross, where he would personally read out the names of all those killed – no doubt in that 'gruff old voice' that John Betjeman remembered.

There were, of course, many summer holidays spent with family and Old Dragon friends on his boat, the third *Blue Dragon*. Skipper even undertook trips to South Africa and Australia (partly paid for by Old Dragons) to visit family.

In 1936 the Skipper was elected an Honorary Fellow of his old Oxford college, Hertford. This award was welcomed by the *Oxford Magazine*:

> *The Dragon School holds a unique place among English educational institutions. It has exercised, and will exercise, a deep influence on preparatory school life: and the mammoth proportions to which it has grown have not, as some feared might happen, diluted its flavour … to have achieved this may, without exaggeration, be called greatness.*
>
> *The Skipper has achieved it by force of character, sincerity, simplicity, an unlimited capacity for friendship and a personal magnetism of which no-one who meets him can be unaware … in all he has done he has shown an originality equally remote from convention and eccentricity.*[1]

On Thursday 20 October 1938 the Skipper came to the School Hall to say goodbye to the boys before setting off, now aged 80, on another trip to Australia. With him he took the boys' holiday diaries to read and mark on the journey. Asking his brother Hum to grant them an 'extra half … and no prep!', he exited the hall through a crowd of cheering boys. After a few words with Hum and members of staff, he said goodbye and left.

A week later news came from the ship *Alcinous* that the Skipper had been taken ill and had died at sea (of angina, it was said). The following day, as he had wished, he was committed to the deep, 'ten miles north of Cape Bon, at four o'clock on a calm afternoon with a bright sun and a light following wind – just the wind for a yachtsman'.[2]

Position: latitude 37.13 degrees north, longitude 11.07 degrees east.

Author's Acknowledgements

First, grateful thanks are due to the late Jon Stallworthy for giving me the encouragement to start on this project in the first place. Thanks also go to the archivists of numerous schools and Oxford colleges for information and images: Gina Worboys (Bedford), Catherine Smith (Charterhouse), Dr C.S. Knighton (Clifton), Lesley Edwards (Lancing), Ian Quickfall (Malvern), Clare Russell and Grainne Lenehan (Marlborough), Elspeth Langsdale (Oundle), Clare Sargent (Radley), Paul Stevens (Repton), Daniel McLean (Rugby), Chris Nathan (St. Edward's, Oxford), Robin Brooke-Smith (Shrewsbury), Elizabeth Wells (Westminster), Suzanne Foster (Winchester); Anna Sander and Bethany Hamblen (Balliol), Judith Curthoys (Christ Church), Julian Reid (Corpus Christi), Ben Taylor (Magdalen), Jennifer Thorp (New College), Kate O'Donnell (Somerville), and Robin Darwall-Smith (University and Jesus); also to those who helped with detailed proof reading and chasing of permissions and to Edward Hudson and Richard Hancock for general encouragement with all matters First World War over the decades. This book (and the blog) would not have been possible without the help of all these people, but in particular the research of Eric and Gill McVey and the work done in the Dragon archives by Gay Sturt have been crucial.

Without Catherine Bradley and the team at Scala Publishers, this would certainly not have been 'a splendid volume' worthy of the Skipper's vision. That Rory Stewart (who suffered my early attempts to teach history many years ago) has been prepared to provide a foreword was a tremendous bonus. Many thanks to all of them. However, without the lifetime's work of G.C. Vassall, editor of *The Draconian* from 1908 until his death in 1941, none of this would have been possible.

This book is dedicated to the Skipper and the Oxford Preparatory School (1877–1920).

Endnotes

Preface

1. J. Betjeman, *Summoned By Bells*, 1960. London: John Murray, pp. 44–45.
2. *The Draconian*. The majority of quotes are from the many editions of *The Draconian* and are not credited individually in this book. Any unattributed quote is from either this source or in some cases the *War Memorials* for the fallen, a work compiled by the Skipper after the First World War and published by the school in 1922.

Chapter 1 Summer Term 1917

1. J. Betjeman, *Summoned By Bells*, 1960. London: John Murray, p. 45.
2. John Betjeman's name was in fact spelled 'Betjemann' throughout his time at Highgate Junior School and the O.P.S.
3. F. Sidgwick, *The Skipper*, 1940. Oxford: The Dragon School, p. 41.
4. J.P.W. Mallalieu, *On Larkhill*, 1983. London: Allison & Busby, p. 30.
5. J.P.W. Mallalieu, *On Larkhill*, p. 31.
6. J. Betjeman, *Summoned by Bells*, p. 46.
7. J.P.W. Mallalieu, *On Larkhill*, p. 29.
8. J. Betjeman, *Summoned by Bells*, p. 45.
9. J. Betjeman, *Summoned by Bells*, p. 44.
10. E.B. Poulton, *Ronald Poulton*, 1919. London: Sidgwick & Jackson, p. 50.
11. E.B. Poulton, *Ronald Poulton*, p. 51.
12. E.B. Poulton, *Ronald Poulton*, p. 53.
13. L.K. Haldane, *Friends and Kindred*, 1961. London: Faber, p. 215.
14. Ronald Clark, *J.B.S. The Life and Work of J.B.S. Haldane*, 1968. London: Hodder & Stoughton, pp. 27–28.
15. L.K. Haldane, *Friends and Kindred*, p. 216.
16. Sir John Smyth, *The Only Enemy*, 1959. London: Hutchinson, p. 24.
17. Sir John Smyth, *The Only Enemy*, p. 23.
18. Sir John Smyth, *The Only Enemy*, p. 27.
19. Sir John Smyth, *The Only Enemy*, p. 27.
20. Sir John Smyth, *The Only Enemy*, p. 28.
21. Sir John Smyth, *The Only Enemy*, p. 32.
22. J.P.W. Mallalieu, *On Larkhill*, p. 30.

Chapter 2 The Oxford Preparatory School

1. C.H. Jaques, *A Dragon Century*, 1977. Oxford: The Dragon School, pp. 2–3.
2. C.H. Jaques, *A Dragon Century*, p. 6.
3. C.H. Jaques, *A Dragon Century*, pp. 6–7.
4. F. Sidgwick, *The Skipper*, 1940. Oxford: The Dragon School, p. 13.
5. C.H. Jaques, *A Dragon Century*, p.7.
6. C.H. Jaques, *A Dragon Century*, pp. 8–9.
7. C.H. Jaques, *A Dragon Century*, p. 9.

8. C.H. Jaques, *A Dragon Century*, p. 9.
9. C.H. Jaques, *A Dragon Century*, p. 9.
10. F. Sidgwick, *The Skipper*, p. 124.
11. C.H. Jaques, *A Dragon Century*, p. 262.
12. C.C. Lynam, *Norway and the North Cape in Blue Dragon II, 1911–12*, 1913. London: Sidgwick & Jackson, p. xix.
13. C.C. Lynam, *Norway and the North Cape in Blue Dragon II, 1911–12*, p. xx.
14. Sir John Smyth, *The Only Enemy*, 1959. London: Hutchinson, p. 32.
15. Sir John Smyth, *The Only Enemy*, p. 32.
16. Sir John Smyth, *The Only Enemy*, pp. 32–33.
17. Nevil Shute, *Slide Rule*, 1954. London: William Heinemann, p. 11.
18. *The Royal Cruising Club Journal, 1912*, p. 6.
19. Arthur Ransome, 'The Art of Telling What Happened', *The Eyewitness*, 4 April 1912, pp. 502–3.
20. F. Sidgwick, *The Skipper*, p. 36.
21. F. Sidgwick, *The Skipper*, p. 36.
22. F. Sidgwick, *The Skipper*, p. 32.
23. F. Sidgwick, *The Skipper*, p. 32
24. F. Sidgwick, *The Skipper*, p. 32.
25. F. Sidgwick, *The Skipper*, pp. 40–41.
26. C.S. Lewis, *Surprised by Joy: The Shape of My Early Life*, 1959. London: Collins (Fontana Books), pp. 85–86.
27. F. Sidgwick, *The Skipper*, p. 23.
28. C.H. Jaques, *A Dragon Century*, p. 59.
29. C.C. Lynam, *Norway and the North Cape in Blue Dragon II, 1911–12*, pp. 98–99.
30. J. Betjeman, *Summoned By Bells*, 1960. London: John Murray, pp. 48–49.
31. J. Betjeman, *Summoned By Bells*, p. 49.

Chapter 3 Growth and Development

1. C.H. Jaques, *A Dragon Century*, 1977. Oxford: The Dragon School, pp. 27–28.
2. J. Betjeman, *Summoned By Bells*, 1960. London: John Murray, p. 48.
3. J.P.W. Mallalieu, *On Larkhill*, 1983. London: Allison & Busby, p. 37.
4. J. Betjeman, *Summoned By Bells*, p. 49.
5. Gerald Carr-White, known as 'Flea', Billy Smyth and Geoffrey Buck were the boys involved.
6. Ronald Clark, *J.B.S., The Life and Work of J.B.S. Haldane*, 1968. London: Hodder & Stoughton, p. 23.
7. L.K. Haldane, *Friends and Kindred*, 1961. London: Faber, p. 222.
8. D.L. Crane (ed.), *Letters between a Victorian Schoolboy and his Family (1892–1895)*, 1999. Durham: New Century Press, pp. 1–2.
9. D.L. Crane (ed.), *Letters between a Victorian Schoolboy and his Family (1892–1895)*, pp. 41–42.
10. D.L. Crane (ed.), *Letters between a Victorian Schoolboy and his Family (1892–1895)*, p. 228.
11. *Letters from Rupert Brooke to his Publisher*, 1975. New York: Octagon Books, n.p.
12. E.B. Poulton, *Ronald Poulton*, 1919. London: Sidgwick & Jackson, p. 80.
13. Ronald Clark, *J.B.S., The Life and Work of J.B.S. Haldane*, p. 25.
14. E.B. Poulton, *Ronald Poulton*, p. 178.

15. Naomi Mitchison, *All Change Here*, 1975. London: The Bodley Head, p. 70.
16. C.H. Jaques, *A Dragon Century*, p. 22.

Chapter 4 1914: The Clouds Descend

1. All asterisks are references to members of O.P.S. staff: 'Cheese' Vassall, 'Tortoise' Haynes, 'Pug' Wallace and 'Hum' Lynam.
2. *The Royal Cruising Club Journal 1914*, published February 1915, pp. 71–72.
3. *The Royal Cruising Club Journal 1914*, p. 91.
4. D.L. Crane (ed.), *Letters between a Victorian Schoolboy and his Family (1892–1895)*, 1999. Durham: New Century Press, p. 83.
5. A.R. Haig-Brown, *The O.T.C. and the Great War*, 1915. London: *Country Life*, p. 19.
6. A.R. Haig-Brown, *The O.T.C and the Great War*, p. 21.
7. A.R. Haig-Brown, *The O.T.C and the Great War*, p. 21.
8. James Corsan, *For Poulton and England: Life and Times of an Edwardian Rugby Hero*, 2009. Leicester: Troubador Publishing (Matador), p. 104.
9. E.B. Poulton, *Ronald Poulton*, 1919. London: Sidgwick & Jackson, p. 85.
10. J.P.W. Mallalieu, *On Larkhill*, 1983. London: Allison & Busby, p. 26.
11. Francis Wylie, unpublished reminiscences.
12. J.P.W. Mallalieu, *On Larkhill*, p. 35.

Chapter 5 'Over by Christmas'?

1. H.S. Souttar, *A Surgeon in Belgium*, 1915. London: Edward Arnold, p. 91.
2. H.S. Souttar, *A Surgeon in Belgium*, p. 126.
3. H.S. Souttar, *A Surgeon in Belgium*, pp. 161–62.
4. Captain J.C. Dunn, *The War the Infantry Knew 1914–1919*, 1989. London: Cardinal, p. 87.
5. E.L. Francis, interview with Humphrey Carpenter, 1974.
6. E.L. Francis, interview with Humphrey Carpenter, 1974.

Chapter 6 The Western Front

1. Sir John Smyth, *The Only Enemy*, 1959. London: Hutchinson, p. 40.
2. *London Gazette*, issue 29240, 24 July 1915.
3. This flag was sent to George Fletcher's parents after his death. It was hung for a few days in the O.P.S. Hall and is now in the Eton College Ante-chapel.
4. Frank Richards, *Old Soldiers Never Die*, 1933. London: Faber, p. 98.
5. Frank Richards, *Old Soldiers Never Die*, p. 98.
6. Frank Richards, *Old Soldiers Never Die*, p. 98.
7. Frank Richards, *Old Soldiers Never Die*, p. 227.
8. E.B. Poulton, *Ronald Poulton*, 1919. London: Sidgwick & Jackson, pp. 322–23.
9. Ronald Clark, *J.B.S. The Life & Work of J.B.S. Haldane*, 1968. London: Hodder & Stoughton, p. 38.
10. Martin Goodman, *Suffer & Survive*, 2007. London: Simon & Schuster, pp. 270–71.
11. Martin Goodman, *Suffer & Survive*, p. 271.
12. Ronald Clark, *J.B.S. The Life & Work of J.B.S. Haldane*, p. 37.
13. Ronald Clark, *J.B.S. The Life & Work of J.B.S. Haldane*, p. 37.
14. Ronald Clark, *J.B.S. The Life & Work of J.B.S. Haldane*, p. 40.

15. Ronald Clark, *J.B.S. The Life & Work of J.B.S. Haldane*, p. 40.
16. Ronald Clark, *J.B.S. The Life & Work of J.B.S. Haldane*, p. 42.

Chapter 7 Summer 1915

1. Cherwell House was Jack Haldane's family home, on the site of what is now Wolfson College.

Chapter 8 The Gallipoli Campaign

1. Captain Wedgwood Benn, *In the Side Shows*, 1919. London: Hodder & Stoughton, p. 29.
2. Certain words or lines published in *The Draconian* were censored – it is not clear whether the original authors or G.C. Vassall, the editor, did this.

Chapter 10 The War at Sea

1. A. Temple Patterson, *Tyrwhitt of the Harwich Force*, 1973. London: Macdonald, p. 5.
2. Sir William James, *Admiral Sir William Fisher*, 1943. London: Macmillan, p. 4.
3. Sir William James, *Admiral Sir William Fisher*, p. 22.
4. Michael Partridge, *The Royal Naval College Osborne*, 1999. Stroud: Royal Naval Museum Publications/Sutton Publishing, p. 46.
5. Michael Partridge, *The Royal Naval College Osborne,* p. 44.
6. Sir William James, *Admiral Sir William Fisher,* pp. 44–45.
7. A. Temple Patterson, *Tyrwhitt of the Harwich Force*, p. 62.
8. A. Temple Patterson, *Tyrwhitt of the Harwich Force*, p. 62.
9. A. Temple Patterson, *Tyrwhitt of the Harwich Force,* p. 63.
10. Sir William James, *Admiral Sir William Fisher*, p. 66.
11. Sir Henry Newbolt, *Naval History of the War*, 1920. London: Hodder & Stoughton.

Chapter 12 'The School-house afar ...'

1. H.A.L. Fisher's Preface to *Petrarch*, ed. C.D. Fisher, 1917. Oxford: Clarendon Press.
2. J.P.W. Mallalieu, *On Larkhill*, 1983. London: Allison & Busby, 1983, p. 28.
3. Francis Wylie, unpublished reminiscences.
4. J. Betjeman, *Summoned By Bells*, 1960. London: John Murray, p. 43.

Chapter 13 War in the Air

1. Nevil Shute, *Slide Rule*, 1954. London: William Heinemann, p. 18.
2. Nevil Shute, *Slide Rule*, p. 21.
3. Nevil Shute, *Slide Rule*, pp. 21–22
4. Naomi Mitchison, *Small Talk*, 1973. London: The Bodley Head, p. 81.
5. Sir John Slessor, *The Central Blue*, 1956. London: Cassell, p. 7.
6. Sir John Slessor, *The Central Blue*, p. 7.
7. Sir John Slessor, *The Central Blue*, p. 6.
8. J.D.I. Hardman, *Recollections (1914–1918)*, Leeds University Library, Liddle Collection, LIDDLE/WW1/DF/GA/HAB/14.

9. J.D.I. Hardman in interview with Peter Liddle (1976), Leeds University Library, Liddle Collection, LIDDLE/WW1/AIR/148.
10. Sir John Slessor, *The Central Blue*, p. 14.
11. Sir John Slessor, *The Central Blue*, p. 11.
12. Leslie Wm Bills, *A Medal For Life*, 1990. Tunbridge Wells: Spellmount, p. 84.
13. John Masters, *Fourteen Eighteen*. 1970. London: Corgi, p. 72.
14. Jonathan Black, *War in the Sunshine: The British Army in Italy 1917–18*, 2017. London: Estorick Collection of Modern Italian Art, p. 25.
15. Floyd Gibbons, *The Red Knight of Germany*, 1930. London: Cassell, p. 179.
16. Floyd Gibbons, *The Red Knight of Germany*, p. 180.
17. Floyd Gibbons, *The Red Knight of Germany*, p. 181.
18. Floyd Gibbons, *The Red Knight of Germany*, p. 177.
19. The National Archives ADM 273/13/171 (C.W. Emmett).
20. The National Archives ADM 273/13/171 (C.W. Emmett).
21. *London Gazette*, issue 30780, p. 30780, 5 July 1918.
22. *London Gazette*, issue 31170, p. 2040, 8 February 1919.

Chapter 14 1917/18 The Losses Mount

1. P.J. Campbell, *In the Cannon's Mouth*, 1979. London: Hamish Hamilton, p. 20.
2. P.J. Campbell, *In the Cannon's Mouth*, pp. 64–65.
3. P.J. Campbell, *In the Cannon's Mouth,* p. 67.
4. P.J. Campbell, *In the Cannon's Mouth,* p. 68.
5. *London Gazette*, issue 30561, 7 March 1918.
6. The National Archives WO 374/70011 (H.G. Turrell).
7. *London Gazette*, issue 30561, 7 March 1918.
8. G. Crile (ed.): *George Crile, an Autobiography*. Vol. 1, 1947. Philadelphia: Lippincott.
9. Tom Patterson, *Arthur Hugh Sidgwick*, 2017, Oxford, privately published, p. 329.
10. Undated letter from Hugh Sidgwick to his brother Frank (Balliol College Historic Collections, Sidgwick Papers 20.04a).
11. Letter (15 September 1916) from Hugh Sidgwick to his sister Ethel (Balliol College Historic Collections, Sidgwick Papers, 20.018).
12. Letter (19 November 1917) from Skipper Lyman to Hugh Sidgwick's mother (Balliol College Historic Collections, Sidgwick Papers 3.09a and 3.09b).
13. Capt. G.K. Rose, *The Story of the 2/4th Oxfordshire and Buckinghamshire Light Infantry*, 1920. Oxford: B.H. Blackwell, pp. 150–51.
14. *The Times*, 3 May 1918.

Chapter 15 The Road to Victory

1. Capt. G.K. Rose, *The Story of the 2/4th Oxfordshire and Buckinghamshire Light Infantry*, 1920. Oxford: B.H. Blackwell, p. 158.
2. P.J. Campbell, *The Ebb & Flow of Battle*, 1977. London: Hamish Hamilton, p. 10.
3. P.J. Campbell, *The Ebb & Flow of Battle*, p. 15.
4. P.J. Campbell, *The Ebb & Flow of Battle*, p. 20.
5. *London Gazette*, issue 30813, 26 July 1918.
6. *London Gazette*, issue 30813, 26 July 1918.
7. An experience of discomfort or pain to the eyes. It is caused by light exposure or the presence of actual physical sensitivity of eyes.

8. *London Gazette*, issue 30813, 26 July 1918.
9. The National Archives WO 339/60341 (W.E. Dyson).
10. The National Archives WO 339/60341 (W.E. Dyson).
11. T.E. Lawrence, *Seven Pillars of Wisdom*, 1935. London: Jonathan Cape, p. 574.
12. P.J. Campbell, *The Ebb & Flow of Battle*, p. 111.
13. P.J. Campbell, *The Ebb & Flow of Battle*, p. 111.
14. P.J. Campbell, *The Ebb & Flow of Battle*, pp. 160–61.
15. P.J. Campbell, Diary (unpublished).

Chapter 16 'Too Many Empty Chairs'

1. F.W. Harvey, *Comrades in Captivity*, 1920. London: Sidgwick & Jackson, p. 225.
2. F.W. Harvey, *Comrades in Captivity*, pp. 225–26.
3. R.L. Rimell, *The Airship VC*, 1989. Bourne End, Bucks: Aston Publications, p. 96.
4. A. Temple Patterson, *Tyrwhitt of the Harwich Force*, 1973. London: Macdonald, p. 212.
5. *London Gazette*, issue 30997, 7 November 1918.
6. *The Newcastle Sun*, 8 November 1921.
7. J. Betjeman, *Summoned by Bells*, 1960. London: John Murray, p. 44.
8. J.P.W. Mallalieu, *On Larkhill,* 1983. London: Allison & Busby, p. 49.
9. J.P.W. Mallalieu, *On Larkhill,* p. 36.
10. J.P.W. Mallalieu, *On Larkhill*, p. 36.

Epilogue

1. F. Sidgwick, *The Skipper*, 1940. Oxford: The Dragon School, p. 85.
2. F. Sidgwick, *The Skipper*, p. 91.

Index

**Denotes an indivudual not connected to the O.P.S. as pupil, ex pupil, parent or staff.*

Credits

Text Acknowledgments

The author is grateful to the following for granting permission to reproduce excerpts of their texts in this book. The author has made extensive efforts to contact all copyholders, however if there are omissions, this is unintentional and this will be corrected in future editions.

Captain Wedgwood Benn, *In the Side Shows*, 1919. Courtesy Hodder & Stoughton, London.
J. Betjeman, *Summoned By Bells*, 1960. Courtesy of John Murray (Publishers).
Letters from Rupert Brooke to his Publisher. © The Estate of Rupert Brooke.
Jonathan Black, *War in the Sunshine: The British Army in Italy 1917–18*, 2017.
P.J. Campbell, *Diary (unpublished)*. By kind permission of the Campbell family. By kind permission by Jonathan Black.
P.J. Campbell, *The Ebb & Flow of Battle*, 1977. By kind permission of the Campbell family.
P.J. Campbell, *In the Cannon's Mouth*, 1979. By kind permission of the Campbell family.
Ronald Clark, *J.B.S. The Life and Work of J.B.S. Haldane*, 1968. Reprinted by permission of Peters Fraser & Dunlop (www.petersfraserdunlop.com) on behalf of the Estate of Ronald Clark.
D.L. Crane (ed.), *Letters between a Victorian Schoolboy and his Family (1892–1895)*, 1999. Permission courtesy New Century Press, Durham.
Captain J.C. Dunn, *The War the Infantry Knew 1914–1919*, 1989. Courtesy of the Trustees of the Royal Welch Fusiliers Regimental Museum.
E.L. Francis, interview with Humphrey Carpenter, 1974. By kind permission of Ali Crowther and Felicity Roberts (née Sergent).
Floyd Gibbons, *The Red Knight of Germany*, 1930. Reproduced with kind permission of Hodder & Stoughton.
L.K. Haldane, *Friends and Kindred*, 1961. Kind permission of Kennedy & Boyd.
J.D.I. Hardman, *Recollections* (1914–1918). Reproduced with the permission of Special Collections, Leeds University Library.
F.W. Harvey, *Comrades in Captivity*, 1920. By kind permission from Eileen A. Griffiths and Elaine Jackson.
Sir William James, *Admiral Sir William Fisher*, 1943. By kind permission of the James family.
C.S. Lewis, *Surprised by Joy: The Shape of My Early Life*, 1955. © C.S. Lewis Pte Ltd.
J.P.W. Mallalieu, *On Larkhill*, 1983. Reproduced courtesy of Ann and Ben Mallalieu.
John Masters, *Fourteen Eighteen*, 1970. Reprinted by permission of Pollinger Limited (www.pollingerlimited.com) on behalf of The Estate of John Masters.
Naomi Mitchison, *All Change Here,* 1975. Reproduced by kind permission of the Estate of Naomi Mitchison and Kennedy & Boyd.
Naomi Mitchison, *Small Talk*, 1973. Reproduced by kind permission of the Estate of Naomi Mitchison and Kennedy & Boyd.
Michael Partridge, *The Royal Naval College Osborne*, 1999. Courtesy of Royal Naval Museum.
Arthur Ransome, 'The Art of Telling What Happened', *The Eyewitness*, 1912. © Arthur Ransome Literary Estate. R.L. Rimell, *The Airship VC*, 1989. Courtesy of Aston Publications, Bucks, 1989.

Royal Cruising Club Journal (1912, 1914). Reproduced with the permission of the Royal Cruising Club.
Nevil Shute, *Slide Rule*, 1954. © United Agents LLP on behalf of The Estate of Nevil Shute Norway.
Hugh Sidgwick's letters are reproduced by kind permission of the Master and Fellows of Balliol College.
A. Temple Patterson, *Tyrwhitt of the Harwich Force*, 1973. Courtesy Hodder & Stoughton, London.
Sir John Slessor, *The Central Blue*, 1956. By kind permission of Anthony Slessor.

Picture Credits

All images © By kind permission of the headmaster of the Dragon School, unless stated below:
p. 17: from Sir John Smyth, *Milestones*, (Sidgwick & Jackson, London, 1979), from the author's own collection, reproduced by kind permission of Sir Timothy Smyth; p. 22: Bridgeman Images; pp. 58, 220, 258, 272, 273: public domain; pp. 71, 199: courtesy of St. Edward's School, Oxford, archives; pp. 114, 137, 138: courtesy of Ali Crowther, Felicity Roberts (née Sergent) and Lindsay Benoist; pp. 120, 170, 252: with the kind permission of Stephen Johnson of The Surrey Infantry Museum; pp. 150, 183: reproduced by kind permission of the Master and Fellows of Balliol College; pp. 153 (left), 209, 261: by kind permission of the Headmaster & Governors of Shrewsbury School; pp. 154, 197, 237: by kind permission of The Warden and Scholars of Winchester College; pp. 158, 165: by kind permission of the James family; pp. 169, 177, 193, 212, 224 (bottom), 229, 231 (top), 250, 263, 266: by kind permission of the Hardman family; p. 192: The National Archives, ref. WO339/37962; p. 201: by kind permission of Principal and Fellows of Somerville College, Oxford; pp. 233, 241: reproduced from Capt. G.K. Rose, *The Story of the 2/4th Ox & Bucks Light Infantry*, (B.H. Blackwell, Oxford, 1920); pp. 246, 247: by kind permission of Nigel and Michael Thomas; p. 262: IWM (Art. IWM ART 3138). © Imperial War Museum (Art.IWM ART 3138).

Captions

The endpapers show childhood pictures of 72 of the 87 Old Dragons who were killed in First World War (starting from top row, left to right)

Front endpaper

Top row: C.H. Counsell, A.H. Sidgwick, G.S. Buck, F. Benham, E.B. Deane, R. Drew, C.W. Emmett, W. Esson.
Second row: B.S. Bickmore, O.C. Blencowe, W.G. Hardman, D.W. Brown, F.H. Holt, O.J. Dowson, C.D. Fisher, R.M.J. French.
Third row: St. J. Backhouse, R.S. Burch, J.F. Raikes, E.M.P. Fisher, L.P. Freyberg, M.H. Collier.
Fourth Row: H.P.C. Burton, H.W. Arden, W.P. Campbell, E. Gay, R.B. Gibson, A.R. Haig-Brown, G. S. Falkiner.
Fifth Row: P.E. Chapman, C.M. Childe, A.G. Clarke, T.H.L. Addis, R.W. Fletcher, C.R. Haigh.

Back endpaper

Top row: G. Hume-Gore, A.R.A. Leggett, F.G. Ling, E.R. Osler, C. Pittar, G.W. Thomas, G.F. Thuillier, A.R. Venis.
Second row: A.J-B. Percival, W.G. Fletcher, F.E. Spurling, R.W. Poulton Palmer, S.C. Taylor, J.S. Ricketts, F.W. Twigg.
Third row: R.R. Pratt, R. Rawlinson, K.S. Rudd, H.G. Turrell, W.F. Wells-Cole, N. West.
Fourth Row: J.F. Ruttledge, W.D. Scott, W. Sheepshanks, J.S. Pratt, H.S. Way, T. Whittingham, E.G.E. Wright.
Fifth Row: A.R.C. Jenks, C.B. Highmore, L.F.W.A. Kendall, E.H.G. Leggett, F.G. Ling, A.S. Macdonell, G.H. Stack, R. Stonehouse, M.B. Thompson.